CRM Systems in Industrial Companies

CRM Systems in Industrial Companies

Intra- and Inter-Organizational Effects

Andrea Perna and Enrico Baraldi
Uppsala University, Sweden

First published 2014 by
PALGRAVE MACMILLAN

Palgrave Macmillan in the UK is an imprint of Macmillan Publishers Limited, registered in England, company number 785998, of Houndmills, Basingstoke, Hampshire RG21 6XS.

Palgrave Macmillan in the US is a division of St Martin's Press LLC, 175 Fifth Avenue, New York, NY 10010.

Palgrave Macmillan is the global academic imprint of the above companies and has companies and representatives throughout the world.

Palgrave® and Macmillan® are registered trademarks in the United States, the United Kingdom, Europe and other countries.

ISBN 978–1–137–33565–4

This book is printed on paper suitable for recycling and made from fully managed and sustained forest sources. Logging, pulping and manufacturing processes are expected to conform to the environmental regulations of the country of origin.

A catalogue record for this book is available from the British Library.

A catalog record for this book is available from the Library of Congress.

Contents

Figures, Tables and Boxes

Figures

Tables

x

Boxes

Acknowledgments

This book is the result of a research journey that started in 2005. It would not have been possible to carry out this study without the involvement of two key organizations: the Department of Management at the Polytechnic University of Marche, Ancona, Italy and the Loccioni Group, Italy. Throughout the entire research process we received support from a great number of people working within both organizations. First of all, we would like to thank Professor Gian Luca Gregori at the Polytechnic University of Marche, who actively supervised and introduced one of the authors during a visit to the premises of Loccioni while the CRM project which is a focus for this study was being developed. Gian Luca, together with Loccioni's management, organized and planned the entire CRM project. Therefore, his contribution to making our research possible was crucial.

The opportunity to work on the development of a CRM system at Loccioni Group led to a wonderful journey. The welcoming atmosphere at this company greatly contributed in many ways to the book's realization. The helpfulness of the entire Loccioni family – the President, Enrico Loccioni, and his wife, Graziella Rebichini, as well as their son Claudio and daughter Maria Cristina – allowed us to conduct several interviews and spend time at their premises to gather data between 2005 and 2008. The company also made it possible for us to return numerous times to collect additional data. Many thanks for this enduring engagement in our research.

We are also grateful to the many managers of the Loccioni Group. In particular, we would like to thank Renzo Libenzi and Maria Paola Palermi for their strong commitment to the research project. Moreover, all the people who worked at Loccioni in its marketing department between 2005 and 2008 deserve a big thank-you for their active support and for inspiring us. Special thanks go to all the personnel at Loccioni's ICT department: we would in particular like to mention and remember the late Alessandro Olivi, who contributed, with Gloria Rossi and Gabriele Rossetti, to the creation of the CRM software and took care of all the technical aspects of its implementation.

Finally, we would like to thank Dr Antonella La Rocca for her suggestions on how to deal with important research issues and her collaboration in co-authoring an article on a topic closely related to this book.

Andrea Perna and Enrico Baraldi
Uppsala, October 2013

1
Introduction: Research Purpose, Methodology and Contribution

This introductory chapter starts by defining our research context (B2B relationships and CRM) and our research purpose (Section 1.1). Then, we briefly introduce our theoretical frame and more specific research questions (Section 1.2). We also provide details of the methodology behind our study (Section 1.3) and position it by specifying our contribution (Section 1.4). We conclude the chapter by presenting the outline of the rest of the book (Section 1.5).

1.1 Research context and purpose

For companies operating in business-to-business (B2B) markets, customers represent the most important asset (Corey, 1976; Ford et al., 2006). However, there are many aspects that make these relationships hard to forecast and manage. Since the 1970s Industrial Marketing and Purchasing (IMP) scholars have investigated interactions and relationships between sellers and buyers in industrial market settings, stressing the possibilities and challenges in managing customer relationships. Since the 1990s there has been a parallel upsurge in the practice and theory of Customer Relationship Management (CRM), which encompasses a philosophy, strategies, processes, methods and Information Technology (IT) tools for managing customer relationships. However, CRM entails so many dimensions that its conceptualization is still rather vague and appears today as a buzzword applied to designate quite disparate things, still objects of extensive debate (Payne and Frow, 2005; Zablah et al., 2004). There is also an ongoing debate in the literature about the challenges (Bull, 2003) and the benefits for companies implementing CRM (Landry et al., 2005; Campbell, 2003). This book aims to contribute new knowledge at the intersection between the two phenomena and research fields above, namely knowledge about CRM as applied in the context of industrial marketing and buyer–seller relationships.

The actual effects and value of CRM in helping companies to better manage customer relationships are widely discussed by both academicians and practitioners. Some intriguing questions concerning CRM are: should we consider CRM as a misleading or a successful approach? If the core ideas are valuable in principle, does it mean that all problems reside in the way CRM is concretely implemented? Evidence of failed CRM projects abounds, which triggers the question of why so many companies still struggle with it. Not surprisingly, many books and articles label CRM as a fascinating but challenging phenomenon. Indeed, starting in the 1990s, the academic literature has assumed two distinct positions about CRM and its value: either as an opportunity or as a source of problems.

The positive voices about CRM stress that it can improve customer-service reliability and service monitoring (Berkley and Gupta, 1994), that it helps companies to manage valuable information (Mithas et al., 2005) and that it can provide customized products to the market (Rigby et al., 2002). Critics stress that employee resistance is a risk associated with CRM implementation (Xu et al., 2005) and that CRM negatively impacts on the freedom of employees in carrying out their daily activities. Another type of critique is that CRM often is merely utilized to categorize customers into segments, thereby failing to be the useful tool that companies wish to have (Fournier and Avery, 2011). Many problems in CRM implementation and adoption are not of a technical nature but are closely linked to organizational changes (Schwartz et al., 2002). Lack of capabilities and commitment of firms when managing CRM projects has been pinpointed as one of the main reasons for the failure of many CRM projects.

Against this background, we aim to contribute to the academic debate on CRM by assuming a balanced position when investigating CRM, in the sense that we aim to highlight both the opportunities and the limitations of CRM as a tool for managing customer relationships. In other words, our study recognizes CRM as a potentially valuable tool for companies even though its value will depend on how it interacts with other resources surrounding it. Being balanced also means recognizing that CRM might produce both positive and negative effects which are not defined unilaterally by it: the effects of CRM will depend on a blurred and complex set of technical and social mechanisms of interaction.

We also aim to contribute to the debate on CRM systems by investigating the actual process behind their development, implementation, embedding and use (cf. Van de Ven et al., 1999). Our standpoint is that it is inappropriate to investigate CRM by assuming that organizations will gain advantages by simply following a trustworthy recipe for implementation. The implementation of CRM systems and their broad consequences have to be investigated by considering the complexity of this process. Introducing CRM into an organization will lead to effects that are closely dependent on how CRM interacts with other relevant resources. Therefore, the purpose of this book is to investigate, on the one hand, the intra-organizational effects derived from embedding a CRM system inside a B2B firm, and, on the other hand, the inter-organizational effects on the firm's customer relationships.

More precisely, this study is concerned with understanding how a focal CRM system is constructed and embedded in a using company operating on an industrial market and what contribution it makes to managing customer relationships, viewed from the perspective of the supplier. Thereafter, this book analyzes the effects of CRM at two levels: (1) the intra-organizational effects derived from embedding a CRM system inside the organization that installed and uses it; and (2) the inter-organizational effects on the firm's customer relationships, including how CRM impacts the process of managing these relationships.

1.2 Theoretical frame and research questions

Our theoretical frame is based on the IMP perspective, because it allows us to deal with the two pillars of this research: customer relationship and IT systems (namely CRM) in a B2B setting. As our research purpose is to analyze the use and effects of a CRM system, that is, an IT tool applied for CRM, we need to understand both the embedding of CRM in the using company and the effects it produces on the company's customer relationships. Therefore, we adopt as a main part of our theoretical framework (see Chapter 2) the IMP perspective on buyer–seller relationships (Håkansson, 1982; Ford, 1990; Håkansson and Snehota, 1995; Håkansson et al., 2009; Ford et al., 2011).

Moreover, the IMP perspective is suitable also for building our alternative view about CRM. We need an alternative definition of CRM for at least one important reason: CRM is not a monolithic and deterministic IT tool that can automatically produce its effects, but needs to be connected with other resources before it can produce any effect (Baraldi and Waluszewski, 2005). In this vein, CRM is simply a resource to be combined with others, such as other IT tools, individuals and organizational units. Most importantly, the value and contribution of CRM will depend on those resource combinations (Baraldi, 2003). In order to investigate how companies develop and embed CRM, we need accordingly to analyze the patterns of resource interactions around CRM, which requires in turn an analytical tool capable of capturing how resources are combined and interfaced. The analytical tool that we will employ for this purpose is the so-called 4Rs model (Håkansson and Waluszewski, 2002), which categorizes resources into four basic types and analyzes their interactions as well as their interfaces (see Chapter 5).

Relying on the 4Rs model, CRM can be viewed as a facility that interacts with users who insert data inside it to receive back processed information which they can use for managing customer relationships (Baraldi et al., 2013). This conceptualization of CRM highlights the process of resource interaction behind CRM. Based on this theoretical background, the two questions that will drive our analysis are:

1) How does CRM become embedded within the using organization?
2) What are the effects of CRM embedding at both intra- and inter-organizational level?

1.3 Methodology

This study features the main data collected and the key results obtained over a period of three years within a PhD project by means of direct participation by one of the authors in the implementation as well as utilization of a CRM system in an Italian industrial company, the Loccioni Group. Therefore, the bulk of this study has been carried out by performing action research, which is characterized by active participation of the researchers in the organizations being observed, as well as by the use of multiple data gathering sources (Coughlan and Coghlan, 2002).

The book is based on a single longitudinal case study approach (Yin, 1994), which fits the exploratory nature of this research and allows examination of the complex nature of the phenomenon under investigation, that is, how CRM affects companies during its development, implementation, embedding and using. Case studies are useful tools when investigating a complex and context-specific phenomenon (Easton, 2010) and are a means to better understand change processes, as they allow for the examination of heterogeneous factors (Halinen and Törnroos, 2005). We selected our case study due to its rich variety of factors intervening in the phenomenon at hand, and accordingly for the learning potential it offers (Dubois and Gadde, 2002).

This complexity prompts a qualitative in-depth case methodology, which is a fruitful strategy when the focus is on a contemporary phenomenon (Eisenhardt, 1989) related to a real-life context. This method also allows following changes over time so as to examine problems and challenges surrounding the implementation of CRM. In fact, this case study was conducted both in real time and as a "follow up" study (Halinen and Törnroos, 2005): this means that we followed the events as they unfolded and collected data both during the course of these events and "a posteriori", conducting an indirect way of capturing data (Dubè and Parè, 2003).

We collected data with the explicit aim of identifying first the original conditions and goals of Loccioni and then the key aspects of the emerging CRM system. Our data accordingly covers early events in the process of implementation of CRM and enabled us to better understand the unexpected impact of CRM on Loccioni's overall organization. The data were collected in Italy between 2005 and 2008 by means of various different techniques and in different phases of our research. Data collection was based upon internal surveys, face-to-face interviews and direct participant observation in the CRM implementation project.

Two different surveys were arranged and administered via a questionnaire addressed to the users of the CRM system. The specific topics of the first survey dealt with the following: (1) understanding employees' propensity to use IT tools for managing sales and marketing information; and (2) defining employees' specific needs when using IT to manage business relationships. The second survey was aimed at measuring the effects of the CRM system for its users and also on a sample of relevant customer relationships.

Semi-structured interviews were also conducted, ranging from one to several hours. The respondents included personnel from several levels of Loccioni's organization: these include Loccioni's CEO, sales managers, Key Account Managers (KAMs), the marketing and communication manager and after-sales manager, who were all informed of the research purpose prior to the interview. In order to capture the dynamic aspects of CRM embedding, these interviews focused on a few central themes: the need for and the development of CRM, as well as the characteristics of the specific CRM system being introduced; the development and management of some key customer relationships, which we deemed as useful for understanding the inter-organizational impact of CRM; the assessment of CRM in terms of benefits for the users, and even more concretely the problems that were afflicting the CRM system at Loccioni a few months after it had been installed.

As for the direct observations, one of the authors was allowed to participate personally in the entire CRM project at Loccioni, where he was an active member of the project team as well as an active user of the CRM system, by carrying out marketing activities on it. In this way, this researcher could also participate in basically all key meetings: all these direct participant observations provided us with a thorough insight into the case.

Turning to the analysis, the empirical data was first transformed into a description of the case story, which allowed us to identify the timeline of the phenomenon under investigation as well as important events in this process. When we realized that the case study was an interesting example of the implementation, use and effects of a specific type of CRM tool, we decided to focus on the resource layer of the business network concerned and accordingly chose to apply the 4Rs model for further analysis of the empirical material (Wedin, 2001; Baraldi and Bocconcelli, 2001; Håkansson and Waluszewski, 2002). We searched in our data in order to address two main issues: (1) the features of the technical and organizational resources involved in the embedding of the CRM system at hand (e.g., software, organizational units); and (2) the connections and the interfaces between the resources involved (at both technical and organizational level). Then, we mapped out the resource network around the focal resource, that is, the CRM system. After having also defined the structural details of the network, we returned to our timeline and were able to divide the case story into different periods by referring to critical episodes that were now also considered the key resources involved: for instance, project team building, CRM testing and CRM launch. To sum up, thanks to our method that combines participant observation and action research (Levin and Greenwood, 2001), this book can provide a vivid illustration of the process of CRM implementation and use.

1.4 Contributions and positioning

The embedding and the effects of CRM on organizations are important but highly complex phenomena. This book identifies several sources of such complexity. First, when companies implement CRM, they do not deal with a linear and predictable process; rather, CRM implies a set of obstacles that are often hidden or ambiguous, but which need nonetheless to be taken into account. Second, it is still unclear what the actual contribution of CRM to relationship management is, as witnessed by the many failures in CRM implementation. One additional problem here may be the lack of a commonly accepted definition and framework of CRM, which creates confusion among academicians and practitioners alike. Third, CRM involves many different dimensions (resources, we could say), such as IT tools (software, hardware and IT architectures), individual users and organizational structures: implementing and using CRM systems often involves trade-offs between these dimensions, which have to be addressed in order to push the embedding process ahead. It is important to find a balance between all these dimensions of CRM, at least for the sake of reducing the level of conflicts, tensions and problems among them. Finding a balance requires a fine-grained approach that penetrates and reorganizes the resource combinations that embed CRM.

This book provides several contributions, which are tightly connected with each other. The main contribution of this work relies both on the theoretical concepts and on the evidence from the case study, and consists of four dimensions that we propose can frame whether and how CRM affects customer relationships (see Chapter 9). Two of these dimensions are basic characteristics of the customer relationship itself, namely its history/start date and its level of complexity. The third dimension is a characteristic of CRM users, namely the age of the KAM, which indicates the CRM user's willingness to use and attitude toward using IT tools in performing their managerial tasks. The fourth dimension is finally the matching of users' informational needs in performing their managerial tasks: this is a more complex and somehow hidden dimension as it combines several resources simultaneously (the IT tool, the users, their specific needs and managerial tasks). Clearly, these four dimensions can be considered as relevant also from a managerial perspective.

Many valuable books published in recent years about CRM do define CRM, stress its (potential) advantages and contributions, and some even describe the process of introducing and using CRM. However, these books do not provide the reader with a detailed analysis of the challenges, conditions and dimensions affecting CRM implementation, use and effects that we have outlined above. Therefore, our research makes an effort to highlight these issues, including probing into the effects of CRM on customer relationships, supported empirically by an extensive case study. Finally, since the book analyzes both intra- and inter-organizational effects of CRM, it also contributes to research within industrial marketing and network studies. More precisely, this study is an application of the IMP-related "resource interaction" perspective to analyze the implementation of CRM and the effects derived from its utilization.

In comparison to other research on CRM, predominantly made in consumer marketing settings, this book contributes new knowledge on CRM as applied in the field of industrial marketing, and more precisely in a high-tech sector. This study is unique in this respect. Another important distinctive character of this book is that it features a case of implementation and use of an internally developed CRM system, whereas much of the extant literature focuses on off-the-shelf CRM software packages. The very fact the CRM system in focus is an internally developed software brings to salience also the issue of constructing and developing it, which requires penetrating even deeper into the complexities of the implementation and embedding process. To sum up, this book differentiates itself from the others for the following reasons: (1) it is based on a unique case study within a B2B context; (2) it concerns the embedding process of an own-developed CRM system; (3) it conceives CRM as an interactive resource, by highlighting relevant theoretical and managerial implications; and (4) methodologically, one of the authors has been involved in the very process of embedding CRM, including the opportunity of directly interacting with the system for over three years.

1.5   The structure of this book

After this introduction, this book includes nine chapters. Based on literature reviews, the first four chapters (2–5) provide relevant theoretical and analytical concepts to prepare the reader's general understanding of customer relationships in industrial networks, IT systems and organizations, CRM and the "resource interaction" perspective. Then, chapters 6, 7 and 8 present the case study of CRM at the Loccioni Group. This is followed by our analysis of the case, which also provides answers to our research questions (Chapter 9), before reaching our conclusions in Chapter 10. We now take a more detailed look at the contents of the various chapters.

Chapter 2 presents the key dimensions of customer relationships such as their complexity and intensity, which are fundamental to understanding the objects on which CRM systems are applied in industrial markets by organizations aiming to improve these relationships. The nature of customer relationships and the patterns of interactions they include are discussed with the help of literature on industrial marketing, and especially the IMP tradition. Chapter 2 concludes by providing a network view of Key Account Management, that is, the practice of managing key customer relationships.

Both the academic literature and practitioners widely recognize the role of Information Technology (IT) systems in supporting several organizational processes, but also the presence of numerous barriers and challenges when implementing and adopting IT. Therefore, Chapter 3 prepares the ground for our theoretical discussion of the intra- and inter-organizational effects of CRM systems by reviewing IT systems in general, looking at the different categories of IT tools, their application areas and the rationale behind their use. We stress in Chapter 3 that understanding the effects of IT requires analysis of the organizational context where IT tools are utilized. For instance, how IT impacts on users (e.g., their routines and habits) deserves attention, because these individuals represent a key linkage between IT and its effective utilization at all organizational levels.

After having broadly reviewed the theme of IT in Chapter 3, Chapter 4 digs deeper into a particular kind of IT tool, namely CRM systems. This chapter reviews the CRM literature and presents the most common conceptualizations of CRM. The idea is to provide a comprehensive overview of the various perspectives and disciplinary domains that have dealt with CRM over the last 20 years. CRM implementation stands out as a key topic in the literature, but there is a tendency to explain and investigate CRM implementation by considering only one or just a few dimensions. Moreover, the academic literature mostly treats CRM implementation as a linear process which is expected to turn into positive outcomes by simply following certain checklists and phases.

Chapter 5 instead makes clear that this book takes an interactive perspective on CRM and its implementation issues. This chapter further develops our view of CRM as a sociotechnical resource, by presenting the "resource interaction" perspective and the 4Rs model, which also belongs to the IMP approach. More precisely, Chapter 5 presents an alternative view of CRM by conceptualizing it as a device interacting with individuals who input data into it to obtain processed information applicable to handle customer relationships. The aim of this chapter is to show how a "resource interaction" perspective on CRM enables a new understanding of the role, effects, challenges and possibilities of CRM systems when they are embedded in complex industrial networks.

Chapter 6 is the first of the three chapters featuring the case of CRM in the Loccioni Group: the chapter starts with an overview of Loccioni's history, organization and customer base, and then presents the conditions and the context that prompted the company to initiate the CRM project. Chapter 6 also describes the origins, development and implementation of the CRM system at Loccioni. Chapter 7 continues by showing how CRM was adopted by its expected users and how it became embedded in Loccioni's internal organization, pointing at which new routines, interactions and usage patterns emerged around the CRM system, as well as between various groups of users. The empirical case concludes with Chapter 8, which introduces six main customer relationships of Loccioni's and prepares for the discussion, in the following Chapter 9, of the inter-organizational effects of CRM. Chapter 8 first provides an overview of all six customer relationships, including the pattern of interactions between Loccioni and the specific customer, and then presents how CRM is utilized, or not, in each of these six relationships.

Chapter 9 conducts a comprehensive analysis of the empirical materials presented in chapters 6–8, focusing on some key dimensions identified found to be relevant when investigating how CRM affects the host company and its way of handling relationships with customers. Chapter 9 applies the "resource interaction" perspective (introduced in Chapter 5) in order to analyze the embedding of the CRM system, that is, the emergence of interfaces between the system itself and the other technical and organizational resources at both the intra- and inter-organizational level. Chapter 10 concludes our journey by summing up our findings and the lessons learned from the case and its analysis. In addition to managerial implications the final chapter also proposes a research agenda concerning a comparison between CRM in a consumer as opposed to an industrial market context.

2
Customer Relationships in Industrial Networks

This chapter provides a review of the literature and key theoretical concepts about business-to-business (B2B) customer relationships and how they can be managed. After introducing the Industrial Marketing and Purchasing (IMP) perspective on relationships (Section 2.1), we discuss their complex (Section 2.2) and dynamic nature (Section 2.3). Based on this understanding of the characteristics of B2B customer relationships, Section 2.4 addresses the issue of managing relationships, both one by one and as part of a customer portfolio. Section 2.5 concludes the chapter by proposing an alternative, network-based view of Key Account Management (KAM), that is, the practice of managing key customer relationships.

2.1 The IMP perspective on business relationships

Buyer–seller relationships or "business relationships" within industrial markets[1] are an important research topic in the areas of marketing, purchasing, supply chain management and strategy. As our research goal is to analyze the use and effects of a CRM system, that is, an IT solution for customer relationship management, we need to understand not only the way CRM becomes embedded at intra-organizational level in the using company, but also which effects it produces on the company's business relationships. Therefore, business relationships are a key component to be analyzed in our research, and in particular customer relationships. For this purpose, we adopt as a main part of our analytical framework the IMP perspective of buyer–seller relationships (Håkansson, 1982; Ford, 1990; Håkansson and Snehota, 1995; Håkansson et al., 2009; Ford et al., 2011).

The IMP Group is also a research community, which was born in the mid-1970s in Europe and includes nearly 1000 scholars involved in the

11

study of B2B contexts. IMP researchers have contributed a number of important theoretical tools to investigate dynamic business contexts by observing empirically and analyzing how companies interact with each other in complex industrial contexts: "A common experience from these early investigations of about 900 business relationships was that business exchange cannot be understood as a series of disembedded and independent transactions of given resources – but rather as complex relationships between buying and selling organisations" (from the IMP Group website, www.impgroup.org).

We chose to rely on the IMP approach for three main reasons. The first is the fact that IMP provides a view of markets as networks, which emerged because the dominant market paradigm of the 1970s (i.e., markets as based only on the price mechanism) did not explain certain features of business markets, such as the continuous interactions between buyers and sellers in B2B contexts (Håkansson, 1982). A convincing explanation of the origins of IMP as an alternative paradigm for understanding business markets is offered by Snehota (2004). Secondly, IMP researchers have been analyzing since the 1970s how industrial markets work and how companies behave in a complex network setting. One of the conceptual foundations of IMP, which has been largely demonstrated empirically, is that the business landscape is shaped by interactions between firms. This observation has a relevant implication: business relationships are built from interaction processes and are embedded in "their counterparts' context", which takes the shape of a network (Håkansson and Snehota, 2000). Interactions, business relationship and network are three related conceptual cornerstones which allow IMP researchers to shed new light on traditional areas of management such as marketing, purchasing, strategy development, innovation, internationalization and technological development. In other words, by means of contributions based on the IMP view over the years it has been possible to understand how the forces of firm-to-firm interactions shape the business landscape. The third reason deals with the obvious fact that the IMP perspective is leading research aimed at investigating the nature and performance of relationships between firms in business markets and channel systems. The work of IMP researchers has in fact resulted in several hundred publications over the last 30 years. An overview of the group's historical and intellectual development is offered by Turnbull, Ford and Cunningham (1996).

We now delve into the aforementioned conceptual tools of the IMP perspective in order to prepare a discussion of how customer relationships develop and are managed by companies. A large share of business transactions within industrial markets takes place within long-term business relationships. The long-term performance of the company is dependent on its ability to manage properly relationships with customers, suppliers and other counterparts. Business relationships are so relevant that such ability would reasonably represent a pivotal asset for a company (Ford and Håkansson, 2006). In fact, an essential point worth considering is that business exchanges and other complex processes (e.g., product and technology development) between firms are possible because of the existence of business relationships: "it is in relationships that companies access, provide and exchange resources from, to and with others" (Håkansson and Snehota, 1995: 38).

IMP studies produced ample evidence that business relationships constitute the basis of business (Ford et al., 2011). From an IMP perspective, industrial markets are conceived as networks, formed by business units (e.g., producers and consumers) which are related to each other by threads that represent the relationships between the various counterparts (Ford et al., 2011: 182). That is why the IMP view is often termed also the "industrial network approach" (Håkansson and Johansson, 1992), which suggests that companies and their relationships can be viewed as part of a complex network of interconnected relationships. Therefore, firms do not exist and act in isolation; they are connected with other firms by means of direct or indirect business relationships that are embedded in a network of other relationships. The complexity of the industrial market's structure pointed out by IMP researchers cannot be easily handled by companies: firms are embedded in a network context which is always changing and where business relationships shape the network and the network is shaped by relationships. In other words, firms are interdependent with each other as they interact with each other. Therefore, the interaction going on in a business relationship is an important process for development of relationships and for the dynamics of a business network (Håkansson et al., 2009).

Håkansson and Snehota (1995) identify a set of key features of business relationships:

- Relationships are based on the problems and needs of the parties involved in them.
- Relationships are mutually dependent within the business network and heavily interconnected.
- Adaptations appear as both parties involved in relationships change their resources and activities in order to better fit each other: adaptations can be for instance of a technical, administrative, or logistical

character. The notion of adaptations is a key aspect since it refers to the necessary changes in routines and technologies, including investments, made by both parties for the sake of the relationship.

- Another important dimension is the content or substance of relationships. The substance of a relationship changes with the volume exchanged between the parties.
- The functions of relationships, since relationships are embedded in a broader network context, are naturally multiple as they can be utilized by and might affect different actors in different ways.
- Continuity is another key feature of relationships: this means that the current state of a relationship is connected to past events and at the same time it will influence the evolution of future events. Therefore, managing business relationships requires adopting a long-term vision.

Starting from business relationships as a central element for understanding business networks, IMP scholars (Håkansson and Snehota, 1995) have developed a conceptual framework known as the ARA (activities, resources and actors) model, which allows analysis of business relationships and their consequences. The ARA model is suitable for describing the content and the function of business relationships. According to the ARA model, business relationships can be broken down into three layers of content: activities, resources and actors. When companies interact and the relationship develops certain activity links, resource ties and actor bonds arise between such companies (Ibid.). In order to understand complex phenomena, ranging from the development of new product to how strategies evolve, one can look at each of the three layers and at how they are connected.

Activity links refer to the connections between the activities performed by the supplier and the customer, often jointly. Activities can be identified in numerous ways. Dubois (1994) distinguishes between transformation and transaction activities. Individual firms perform transformation activities (e.g., activities related to the production), whereas transaction activities are performed between actors. It is important to stress that activities are coordinated between organizations in particular ways and that they are interdependent across organizational boundaries.

Resource ties, which will be further explored in Chapter 5 in our theoretical review, refer to how the resources of the two firms are connected. Resource ties arise when there are specific mutual adaptations in the resources of the two organizations: the benefit of resource ties can be more efficient exploitation of certain resources and, especially, technical development achieved thanks to new combinations of resources. Within the IMP tradition, several researchers show that new resource combinations are behind the creation of innovations (see for instance Baraldi, Gressetvold and Harrison, 2012). Chapter 5 will explore the resource layer of industrial networks by using the so called "4Rs model" proposed by Håkansson and Waluszewski (2002).

Finally, actor bonds refer to the contacts between various individuals or groups involved in a business relationship connecting two companies. Actors play the key role of performing activities and controlling, directly or indirectly, resources. Over time the actors inside the supplier and the customer organizations tend to become mutually oriented and committed to each other, in such a way that they develop social, cultural and intellectual bonds. The creation of actor bonds can be viewed as a learning process during which each part deepens its perception of the counterpart.

A relationship between two companies is shaped by the evolution of the three layers of activities, resources and actors. Therefore, in order to analyze a particular relationship one needs to explore the existing links, ties and bonds. Moreover, the three layers are dependent on each other: actors control resources and perform activities, which in turn activate and link resources to each other (Håkansson, 1987). These interdependencies between the three layers can help identify the other relevant dimension of a business relationship, namely its function. Typically one and the same business relationship can perform several functions. Starting from the individual firm involved in a relationship, the functions of a business relationship arise both from within the relationship itself (for instance, its impact on a supplier's sales) and from the way that relationship is connected to other relationships in a business network, such as the possibility of reaching a third party (Håkansson and Snehota, 1993; 1995). According to the IMP literature, there are three distinct functions of each relationship: for the relationship itself (its volumes and future development), for the single parties directly involved and for the other parties, indirectly influenced and spread across the whole network.

The development of a relationship will largely depend on how the three aforementioned layers are connected, due to the interaction processes of exchange and joint actions by the two companies. Secondly, the relationship has a function for the single party that is involved: being involved in a relationship will create certain specific consequences for the single company or even individual actors, in terms for instance of learning, costs and sales. Finally, other parties that are indirectly connected to the "focal" business relationship (for example the customer's customers) will also experience consequences. The concept of business network refers in fact to the interdependence between several business relationships: what happens in one business relationship affects what happens in another, and predicting the patterns of effects among these relationships is almost impossible.

2.2   The complexity of customer relationships

Håkansson and Snehota (1995) stress the complexity of relationships, due to the simultaneous presence of many types of exchanges, connections and dependencies between the parties, at social, economic and technical level. For instance, companies exchange artifacts, money, information and knowledge. We turn now more specifically to the complexity of the customer relationship from the supplier point of view. Our aim is twofold; firstly, we highlight why customer relationships within an industrial market setting can be challenging to manage for the supplier; secondly, we aim to categorize complexity theoretically by defining its dimensions. The idea is to prepare the ground for further discussions about how suppliers approach the management of customer relationships.

When dealing with customers, suppliers need the ability to understand complex customer issues ranging from the customer's technology and needs to its organization and internal processes (Ford et al., 2006), which is not an easy task. According to Ford et al. (2011), the complexity of customer relationships is not just related to the quality of the product or service delivered or the price levels to apply to a specific customer. Complexity also involves interactions during which the supplier provides an offering to address the specific problems and uncertainties of a customer (Ford et al., 2011). There are many factors that influence this complexity. One aspect is that often customers' requirements may be very specific and the supplier has to adapt its offering to be able to maintain the relationship. The complexity of customer relationships can also be observed when customers are enabled to access new technologies thanks to the relationship with a particular supplier. As shown by Perna et al. (2012) in a specific case study within the automotive sector, the impulse to create technical innovation might come from a key customer; then the supplier, in a short term, is required to interact with and adapt to other actors within the business network in order to be capable of embedding the innovation within the customer's using context. Another factor that contributes to enhancing the complexity of customer relationships is related to the customer changing the volume of products required from a supplier. Also in this situation, the capacity of adapting to customers is vital for suppliers. Another element that deserves attention is the organization of logistics activities, as witnessed by the growing importance of just-in-time (JIT) delivery arrangements connecting suppliers and customers. Further, especially when a supplier deals with global customers with locations in many countries, logistical problems may arise in delivering products on time to far-away locations.

Generally speaking, the complexity of customer relationships derives from the wide range of resources, activities and actors involved as well as the continuous adaptations that took place over time within the specific relationship. Closely related to the pattern of adaptations is also the level of mutual dependence between the supplier and the customer, which varies from one relationship to another and, while creating both advantages and disadvantages (Ford et al., 2006), typically always affects the complexity of a relationship. One supplier may become very dependent, for instance in terms of sales, on a particular customer due to the specificity of the products or services provided, which in many cases are totally tailored to a unique customer's needs.

The complexity of customer relationships can be analyzed by looking at certain dimensions such as the intensity of contacts (Ford and Rosson, 1982; Cunningham and Turnbull, 1982), the type of offering and the sales volume. The intensity of contact patterns gives a clear idea about the complexity of a customer relationship: as argued by Cunningham and Turnbull (1982), among companies there might be a complex set of interlocking contacts between people from different departments (marketing, sales, administration, purchasing, R&D, public relations, communication etc.) at different hierarchical levels (i.e., top, middle and low management). These contacts tend to expand and deepen especially when different kinds of adaptations, both technical and social, stem from the relationship. Focusing on the actors' layer, the number of bonds usually indicates how complex the relationship is. Moreover, the people directly involved in the relationships may change, as may their attitudes toward counterparts (Ford et al., 2011), which further affects and can complicate the pattern of contacts.

Turning to the type of offering, in industrial markets the offering often consists of a combination of a physical product and other elements such as service, advice, logistics, price and other indirectly related costs (Ford et al., 2011). Complexity increases when new adaptations are made to elements of the offering, which can happen during the continuous evolution of the customer relationship. Moreover, customers are typically required by their own customers to solve specific problems, which will in turn require their suppliers to react and adapt quickly. The last dimension of the complexity that we introduced above is the sales volume occurring in a customer relationship. Most companies are strongly connected to a small number of important customers, when measuring the volume of exchanges. Relationships become even more complex and intense especially when dealing with customers that account for a large proportion of a supplier's total turnover. The reason for this increase in complexity in large-volume relationships is that these relationships tend to include more adaptations and mutual dependencies, because as much as suppliers can obtain large revenue streams, which can cover the necessary investments to make adaptations, customers are equally likely to gain large benefits from the relationship (e.g., cost reductions) and are motivated to ask for such adaptations.

2.3   Dynamics in customer relationships

Relationships are not only complex, but also characterized by intense dynamics. Relationships dynamics refer to changes taking places during the life of a relationship, from its beginning, through its development and until its termination. Researchers even propose a life cycle for business relationships (Ford, 1980). Moreover, the establishment, development and termination of a business relationship require efforts from both actors involved in it. These efforts entail investing and using in the relationship several material and immaterial resources (Ford et al., 1998). The following sections are dedicated to the beginning (Section 2.3.1) and the development (Section 2.3.2) of relationships, while Section 2.3.3 deals with the issue of discontinuity during the life of business relationships.

2.3.1   The beginning of customer relationships

Studying the beginning of a relationship is relevant, even if this issue does not seem to have been thoroughly investigated, either in the broader marketing literature (Edvardsson, Holmlund and Strandvik, 2008) or within the IMP approach (Holmen and Pedersen, 2001; Aarikka-Stenroos, 2008). One reason is that it is more difficult to observe a relationship during its nascent phase, as for instance its economic benefits are not really yet there: they will arise when a substance (activity links, resource ties and actor bonds) is created a certain time after the take-off of the relationship. Another reason is that the initiation is usually a blurred phase of a relationship (Aarikka-Stenroos, 2008), during which it is even hard to tell if any real relationship will be developed in the following stages.

In line with Holmen et al. (2005), we argue that the origin of a relationship, during which the two counterparts are assessing the potential of the relationship, have important consequences for its development. The beginning of a relationship can even create important conditions for its development. In fact, both the supplier and the customer typically have an idea of what they expect from a relationship[2]: these ideas will form the basis of the emerging relationships (Ford et al., 2003). But the beginning of a relationship in B2B markets may be interpreted according to at least two main perspectives, each assuming different standpoints on the possibility of planning the potential value of a relationship by one of the two counterparts.

On the one hand, the beginning of customer relationships has been considered a routine or a process unfolding in a planned manner. In fact, some studies (Cunningham, 1982; Campbell and Cunningham, 1983; Fiocca, 1982; Salle, Cova and Pardo, 2000) argue that is possible to identify lists of factors by means of which it is possible to categorize existing and potential customers. According to these studies, customer portfolio analysis has been developed as a tool to analyze whether a customer relationship should be started or developed by the firm in order to obtain some specific kind of advantages. In these studies, "the purpose of the analysis is to improve the allocation of scarce technical and marketing resources" between different customers or suppliers in order to achieve the supplier's or the customer's strategic objectives (Campbell and Cunningham, 1983: 369). The beginning of a relationship is interpreted here in terms of a planned behavior by a single counterpart to reach their *ex ante* goals.

On the other hand, other studies assuming a less instrumental perspective point out that the activation of resources among actors in a relationship may be the result of serendipitous events. In this case, it is not possible to decide or plan *ex ante* the potential value of a customer or supplier relationship. As the relationship outcomes derive from the interaction between two actors, and considering that this interaction is embedded in time and space and has to be considered by looking at the network surrounding the two counterparts, it is extremely difficult for a single actor to plan and program the potential development of a business relationship. In this sense, the beginning of relationships and their value is very difficult to forecast.

2.3.2 The development of customer relationships

When the interaction process between buyer and seller intensifies and the first adaptations starts appearing, a business relationship can be said to start its development in proper terms, which opens the way for its further evolution over time. Business relationships develop from a sequence of interactions that take place between two counterparts (Holmlund, 2004: 280), which stresses the role played by interaction in shaping the relationship itself. Not only is interaction a prerequisite for the critical phase of relationship beginning, as described in the previous section, but interaction also characterizes the following development of a business relationship.

This interaction, especially during the earlier development period, allows both customer and supplier to build reciprocal trust and commitment as each party can evaluate the counterpart's behavior and find ways of handling uncertainties and problems (Ford et al., 2011). Afterwards, the major concern for both the parties will be the mutual coordination on a more practical level: "the development of a customer relationship requires coordination of the interactions between a customer and a supplier. This coordination entails costs and problems for both companies and it limits their freedom to coordinate with others" (Ford et al., 2011: 53). Therefore, developing a relationship also entails creating closer activity links and deeper resource ties, which in turn increases the mutual dependence between the parties and tends to provide more fuel to reinforce the business relationship. But at any time a relationship can revert to a previous state characterized by less intensive interactions and weaker activity links or resource ties, with much depending also on the impact of other surrounding business relationships (e.g., with competing suppliers or other customers). Clearly, developing a customer relationship is not a linear process and it would be difficult to plan whether it will grow or not, and especially how it will develop. "The network relationship development processes is not an orderly progression of phases over time, but is essentially an evolution of unpredictable states" (Batonda and Parry, 2003: 1477).

Over the last 30 years several models have been developed in order to shed light on the relationship development process. Some models can be defined as structural, because they describe the stages or phases in the development of a relationship. For instance, Ford (1980) builds a framework for identifying characteristics and phases by highlighting the role of interaction in shaping the development of customer relationships. Dwyer, Schurr and Oh (1987) discuss instead the interaction processes as the driver of different phases in relationship development. In both these models it is pointed out that certain particular episodes affect this development: an episode can be a delivery of a product, the formulation of technical specifications for a product, a price negotiation and all other interaction events needed to conduct business between industrial actors. These models stress interaction between the two parties, because customer relationships do not develop out of the predefined and clear objects of a single party, but are the outcome of complex interactions.

Ford's model (1980) points out that customer–supplier relationships evolve over time under the influence of the following variables: experience, uncertainty, distance (expressed as social, geographical, cultural, technical and time distance), commitment and adaptations. Each of these variables can, alone or combined with the others, influence the development of the customer relationship. More precisely, Ford (1980) identifies five stages in the development of customer relationships: pre-relationship, early stage, development stage, long-term stage and final stage. He reaches the conclusion that the development of the relationship is an evolutionary process where: (1) the level of commitment and experience between the parties increases; (2) uncertainties decrease; and (3) adaptations are jointly managed.

However, the stage-based model presented by Ford (1980) is not deterministic as it admits that a relationship's development can be interrupted depending on the actions of either party or of competing suppliers (Ibid.: 340). This is an important aspect which indicates that both companies are embedded within a network context that can hinder or favor the dynamics of the relationship. This model was revised in 1998, in the book *Managing Business Relationships* by Ford and other senior IMP researchers (Ford et al., 1998). In the new version of the 1980 model, Ford and colleagues illustrate four stages, instead of five: (1) the pre-relationship stage; (2) the exploratory stage; (3) the developing stage; (4) the stable stage (Ford et al., 1998). The stable stage includes the last two stages (long-term and final stage) presented in the model from 1980. The new version also stresses that this life cycle is non-linear and how difficult it is to find predetermined patterns of supplier–customer interactions.

The following Figure 2.1 shows that the involvement of the two parties in a business relationship, which is the basis for the relationship's development, is shaped by a combination of several factors, which are not under the control of one single party.

When a customer relationship develops over time (assuming the shape for instance of the dotted arrow in Figure 2.1), the interaction between individual actors, the coordination of activities of the two actors and the adaptation of resources of the two companies influence the level of involvement of each party (Håkansson and Snehota, 1995). Therefore actor bonds, activity links and resource ties (as described in

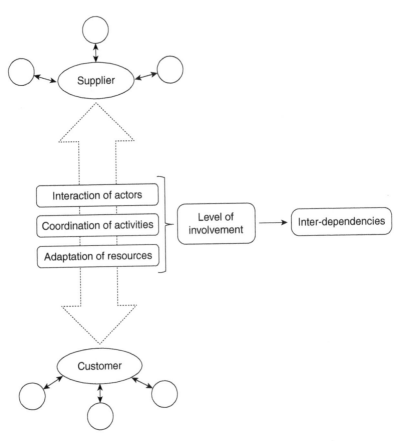

Figure 2.1   Factors influencing the level of involvement in a supplier–customer relationship

Source: Our own elaboration.

the ARA model presented in Section 2.1) define the involvement of the two companies: these three dimensions have to be assessed to define the value and importance of the relationship for the two counterparts (Ford et al., 2011). In particular, the coordination of activities and the adaptation of resources are essential for promoting a customer relationship's development, given their consequences in terms of increased efficiency and development potential for both parties.

The level of involvement has a dual effect on the parties because it can both constrain and increase the possibilities for both the customer and the supplier of reaching their goals. High involvement relationship can at the same time have benefits (e.g., good flow of information) and lead to problems, such as a reduced possibility of switching to other relationships. Dependencies between the parties also always reflect the specific level of involvement between the counterparts. For instance, high customer involvement in a relationship may indicate that the supplier has unique capabilities, for example in terms of technology, which are essential for the customer, who thereby becomes highly dependent on that supplier.

2.3.3 Discontinuity in business relationships

Håkansson and Johansson (1992) suggest that in industrial networks discontinuities may occur because the network structure is not an overarching framework that constrains each single actor in the same way: network participants act in different, unpredictable ways and their different positions in the network make them more or less constrained by the network structure. The consequence is that there are actors in industrial networks capable of promoting change, but due to the heaviness of existing structures changes are incremental, with periods of stability punctuated by discontinuities.

Interaction in business relationships concerns, as previously stated, resources, people and activities (Håkansson et al., 2009); and the interaction process consists of a multitude of exchanges and adaptations between the two firms (Holmlund and Törnroos, 1997). Two important dimensions of interaction processes are space and time. Space represents the context in which the focal interactions take place. It is not necessarily a physical place, but may also be a social and cultural place, where positions are modified, becoming closer to or more distant from other actors depending on what happens in the interaction between the companies. Time relates the two interacting actors by linking their current interactions to their experience of previous interactions and of the adaptations made within the business relationship. Interaction is not constant over time: there are periods when interactions are more frequent and more intense, and there are others characterized by less involvement between the parties (La Rocca, 2011).

The time dimension of the interaction process is essential for understanding both the development and the discontinuity of customer relationships. Business relationships involve long-term interactions (Håkansson and Johanson, 1988; Håkansson and Snehota, 1995) and one of their main structural characteristic is the continuity which derives from the repetition of business transactions over time (Håkansson and Snehota, 1995). However, the continuity of business relationships does not stretch to making them deterministic and never-ending phenomena: discontinuity in business relationships is an equally recurrent feature (Easton and Araujo, 1994). Discontinuities represent a break with the past history of a business relationship and the beginning of new cycles: some relationships may be disrupted, past investments may have to be written off and new cycles of activities may involve new actors and exclude others (Ibid: 5). The concept of discontinuity is also related to the unpredictable and non-linear nature of the interaction process within a single relationship, which in turn is linked to the stability and change in the whole business network (Håkansson and Snehota, 1995: 321). During their life cycle relationships undergo changes propelled by critical incidents in interactions (Halinen and Törnroos, 1998).

According to Skaates (2000), discontinuous relationships entail changes in their actor bonds. In fact, the antecedents of continuity of relationships are strong and stable actor bonds sustained by trust, commitment and adaptive behaviors of the parties involved in the process of interaction (Håkansson and Snehota, 1992; 1995). Trust and commitment belong to the social dimension of the personal interactions in business relationships and characterize the perceptions of the people involved in the relationship. As Morgan and Hunt (1994) state, trust and commitment are pivotal for the longevity (Coughlan, Coghlan and Lombard, 2003) and the continuity of business relationships: if actors trust each other and remain committed to each other, they are likely to continue interacting in the long run. On the other hand, trust seems to be a key element also when relationships are discontinuous, as shown by Hadjikhani, Lindh and Thilenius (2012). In fact, considering the project-based nature of much inter-firm interaction, Hadjikhani (1996) identifies a period of discontinuity in business relationships which he defines as a "sleeping relationship": after a project is ended, typically with the delivery of a tailor-made solution, the relationship becomes sleeping, that is, without many connected activities being performed and reduced resource ties. However, trust at the actor level remains present also during the discontinuous or "sleeping" period and provides the connecting element that enables "waking up" the relationship in the future. In fact, Cova, Mazet and Salle (1996) show that companies which sell project-to-order must cope with great discontinuity in the business relationship with their clients (Cova and Ghauri, 1996; Tikkanen, 1998), when compared to companies which deliver continuously to their customers (e.g., component or raw material suppliers).

As well as the particular type of delivered solutions, the discontinuity of a relationship can derive from internal changes in one of the two counterparts: Gersick (1991) shows that an organization typically experiences many irregular changes that can lead to inter-organizational effects, that is, effects on its relationships with such counterparts as suppliers and customers. When looking at the specific inter-organizational patterns causing discontinuity, Rytkönen and Strandvik, (2005) point out unexpected and deviating incidents, that is, critical incidents, which incrementally create stress in a business relationship. Such stress does not necessarily lead to relationship termination or dissolution (Ibid.: 19), but can be at the origin of discontinuity: "a hidden risk factor in a business relationship can be revealed by the stress concept, which builds on accumulative effects of negative experiences" (Ibid.: 20). To sum up, against a basic tendency of business relationships to be continuous it is important to consider also the possible sources of discontinuity. Runfola et al. (2013) propose in this regard a relevant conceptualization of discontinuity as deriving from two sources: (1) a first type of discontinuity derives from the inner nature of the relationship under analysis, which holds elements that generate discontinuities, as in the case of relationships based on projects to order; (2) another type of discontinuity derives from critical (negative) incidents or stress factors, occurring in otherwise continuous and long-term relationships, because of the behaviors and (lack of) skills of the two interacting organizations (internal stress factors) or because of interdependencies in the resources and activities with other actors in the network (external stress factors).

2.4 Managing customer relationships

Our theoretical review has so far stressed the complex, dynamic, undetermined nature of business relationships. These features suggest that relationships are not easily managed objects. Therefore, a number of questions arise: what are the factors to cope with when managing customer relationships? How does the management of customer relationships by the selling company impact both the intra- and interorganizational level (that is, which effects emerge inside and between the two organizations)? Are there any specific requirements for managing customer relationships? These are common and still open questions that both academics and managers regularly face when dealing with the management of customer relationships.

Before addressing the specific challenges in managing customer relationships it is useful to present a few issues related to the task of managing in business networks in general. In other words, we will shed light on what happens if management is approached from an interactive perspective, instead of a company-focused one (Håkansson et al., 2009). Assuming such a perspective, managerial activities, such as managing customer relationships, should be viewed as the outcome of interaction processes, not of unilateral decisions made by a single firm. Therefore, relationships and network structures influence managing activities. The presence of strong interdependencies over companies' boundaries constitutes an important aspect that managers have to cope with: it means that managers must cope with networks. Therefore, according to the IMP view, managing by looking only inside the company might turn out to be counterproductive because of the company's embedding in the network context.

Returning to how companies can or should deal with customer relationships, an important starting point is that customer relationships are not homogeneous; each one is truly unique. These differences between relationships derive primarily from the fact that there is a large variation in their substance (Håkansson and Snehota, 1995). Moreover, relationships change over time and consequently their management has to adapt to changes. Another important issue when coping with the management of the customer relationship is that each relationship cannot be managed in isolation but must be viewed as a part of an interrelated portfolio of customer relationships (Ford et al., 1998).

Therefore, the IMP literature concerned with managing customer relationships has two main, although connected focuses: (1) managing a single relationship with a customer; and (2) managing a portfolio of several connected customer relationships (Ford et al., 1998; Ford et al., 2003; 2006; 2011). What characterizes both focuses is that the central unit of analysis is the interaction between the parties, either within a single relationship or across several relationships. The analytical priority assigned to supplier–customer interactions by IMP distinguishes IMP from other research perspectives that analyze the same topic of customer relationship management. For instance, the "Relationship Marketing"[3] perspective, so widespread among marketers, focuses on the supplier's side in the process of customer relationship management, while downplaying the importance of mutual influence and double-oriented interactions between supplier and customer.

Table 2.1 proposes a summary of the key points companies need to consider when coping with customer relationships, both taken one by one and at portfolio level. We have grouped and compared the contributions by Ford et al. (1998) and Ford et al. (2006). The first work proposes three main factors that influence how single customer relationships are managed: (1) how broad and important they are in terms

Table 2.1   Managing single customer relationships and relationship portfolios

Authors	Managing individual relationships	Managing a portfolio of relationships
Ford et al. (1998)	Key influencing factors: 1. *Scope of exchange*: extent (volumes and importance) and content of offerings 2. *Posture* in the customer relationship: adaptations, personal selling, actor bonds 3. The *customer's supply strategy*: purchasing scope, posture toward suppliers, supply network structure	Categorizations: By *relationship contribution*: • Today's profit • The "cash cows" • Yesterday's profits • The "old men" • Tomorrow's profits • New technical/commercial requirements • Minor relationships • The "fall guys" By *extent of integration* (ARA model): • Transactional relationships • Facilitative relationships • Integrative relationships *Three-dimensional analysis*: • Relationship handling costs • Net achieved value • Long-term value
Ford et al. (2006)	Key tasks: • Learning and teaching • Investing • Adapting • Committing and trusting • Managing distance • Managing interdependencies • Managing power and conflicts • Managing communication and interaction Evaluation/audit: • Relationship history and current status • Relationship atmosphere • Potential and investment • Network position • Current operations	Categorizations: • By *relationship contribution* (see Ford et al., 1998) Objectives of portfolio management: • Making choices between relationships in portfolio for maximizing the return on relationship investment • Investing resources in relationships that make different contributions to the firm

Source: Our own elaboration.

of scope of exchange; (2) how close they are in terms of posture; and (3) the customer's strategy in handling suppliers, stressing the interactive nature of managing customer relationship; and three different ways of categorizing relationships in a portfolio: (1) their contribution to the selling company; (2) their level of integration across the activity, resource and actor dimensions of the ARA model; and (3) their costs and values according to a tridimensional grid.

The second work (Ford et al., 2006), while proposing similar portfolio categorization tools, focuses instead on the key tasks the selling company need to handle in relation to customers (from learning and teaching to investing and managing power and conflicts) and introduces the importance of evaluations and audits of such characteristics of customer relationships as history, atmosphere, investments and potential. These evaluations are in turn an important input in order to categorize any given relationship according to the schemes proposed for instance by Ford et al. (1998) in terms of contribution, level of integration, and costs and values. In fact, even if Table 2.1 distinguishes between managing single relationships and portfolios, these two levels of management of customer relationships need to go hand in hand: after categorizing its customer relationships, the selling company can realize whether its portfolio is balanced, in the sense of including various types of relationships that can differently contribute to its overall strategy, or whether some key types of relationships are missing. A good overview of a company's customer relationship portfolio can therefore provide guidance as to how intervene at the level of single relationships, by changing the scope and posture in selected relationships. The objectives of portfolio management (see Ford et al., 2006 in the lower part of Table 2.1) are allocating resources to customer relationships in a way that maximizes the return on such investments and exploiting each single relationship according to their varying contributions to the selling company.

We now focus on Table 2.1 in discussing three key questions concerning the management of customer relationships: (1) factors and tasks influencing single relationship management; (2) the evaluation of customer relationships; and (3) the categorization of relationship portfolios.

1) *What are the key factors and the key tasks that influence the management of a customer relationship?* In addition to factors and tasks having their origins in choices made by the selling company, Ford et al. (1998) also show how suppliers have to take into account how changes in

the supply strategies of customers affect their management of the customer relationship: customers may change their level of outsourcing, which would impact the scope of the customer relationship. The consequences may be tensions and conflicts that jeopardize the relationship's stability (see the discussion on the discontinuity of relationships in Section 2.3.3).

2) *How can the evaluation of customer relationships be conducted?* Ford et al. (2006) suggest recognizing and evaluating which customer relationships (both taken individually and at portfolio level) are key is vital for the sake of the relationship. For instance, an evaluation of the previous experiences with that customer (history and current status) will also facilitate current key tasks such as the management of interdependencies. Evaluating the relationship's atmosphere correlates with success in terms of high commitment and trust levels in customer relationships. Ford et al. (2011) even stress the importance of organizing the process of relationship management, especially by maintaining intense interpersonal interactions with customers and by keeping enough flexibility to make adaptations to the seller's offering when required by customers.

3) *How can the relationships in a customer portfolio be categorized?* IMP researchers have on several occasions elaborated concepts and tools to analyze relationship portfolios (Fiocca, 1982; Turnbull and Zolkiewski, 1997). One of the important ideas behind relationship portfolios is that suppliers should constantly analyze their customer base by identifying certain dimensions of customer relationships that can help them optimize the allocation of resources. Portfolio-based studies shift from the analysis of single dyadic relationships to the whole network of customer relationships managed by the supplier. Before considering how IMP researchers have categorized customer relationships, we shall examine which dimensions of customer relationships are relevant for such an analysis. Ford et al. (2011) propose a classification which considers that customer relationships differ on the following dimensions:

- "Age of the relationship": distinguishing between established and new customer relationships.
- Proportion of the supplier's total sale: this can also vary from customer to customer, from a minimal fraction to well over 50%.
- The importance of the customer in terms of the supplier's operations can also vary greatly, as different customers impact differently production and delivery processes.

- "Share of supplies": different suppliers are usually awarded different proportions of the total or category purchases of a customer (share of wallet).
- The level of involvement (as explained in Section 2.3.2) may also vary: some customers are highly involved, while with others the involvement may be much lower.
- Outcome or effect of the customer relationship: some customer relationships provide an opportunity to develop innovation, while others may connect the supplier with final users. Relationships can also be more or less profitable. Some may develop, while others may decline.
- Social aspects: some customer relationships provide a pleasant context to work in, while others are frown with conflicts and misunderstandings.

Even though in industrial markets the number of customer relationships that a supplier entertains is relatively limited, each and every one is in many ways unique. Their variety can also present itself in different forms. To be able to cope with such a variety requires an evaluation of each relationship (see above). This evaluation helps a company understand how resources should be allocated among the various customer relationships in a portfolio. To exemplify this issue, we can consider the categorization by relationship contribution proposed by Ford et al. (1998; 2006) and further developed by Ford et al. (2011). As shown in Table 2.2, this categorization identifies eight categories, which derive from considering two key dimensions of customer relationships, namely the level of profit obtained in a relationship and the point in time when

Table 2.2   A categorization of portfolio relationships

Level of profits	Medium–high	1		2		3	
			• Yesterday's profits	• Today's profits • Fall guys		• Tomorrow's profits	
	Low	4		5		6	
			• Old men	• Cash Cows • Minor relationships		• New technical requirements	
			Past (or no current profit)	Current		Future	
				Profit's occurrence over time			

Source: Modified from Ford et al. (2011).

these profits emerge (or emerged). This second dimension indicates the historical and expected trend of profits over time.

The ideal, but also challenging situation for a supplier is having customer relationships that cover simultaneously the top-middle area (square 2) and the top-right corner (square 3), meaning customers that generate currently high profits and will do so also in the future. However, most customer relationships are usually distributed in the other quadrants of Table 2.2 or reside just in square 2 but not in square 3 (customer providing high profits now but not in the future). There are customer relationships that currently contribute to a supplier's growth, but with a different level of profits (squares 2 and 5); but also customer relationships that do not do so any longer, even if they did so in high volume in the past (square 4) or that never really did so at satisfactorily levels (the "old men" of square 4). There are also customer relationships that are currently not profitable but are forecasted to start providing some profit in the future, such as those where new technical requirements from the customer postponed expected profits (square 6, even if such relationships may even be put in square 4 if they were profitable in the past).

Managing a customer relationships portfolio however does not stop at the categorization of such relationship over a matrix, but entails actively influencing customer relationships so that they provide the right contribution to the supplier, including especially moving them to the "right" quadrant in Table 2.2. Managing different types of relationships requires moreover different levels of resources and entails different costs. For instance, "tomorrow's profits" relationships (square 3) may have the potential for future growth, but typically require high management costs. It is also costly and resource-demanding to promote movements of relationships across Table 2.2. For instance, in order to move "cash cows" and "minor" relationships (square 5) toward square 3, the supplier will probably have to concede considerable adaptations that would impact negatively on its costs. One of the tricky types of customer relationships to manage is the "old men": these are typically long established relationships that have become not profitable at all. Probably, they are still in the portfolio because of the presence of tight social interactions among people from both parties.

As managing customer relationships, taken one by one or within and across a portfolio, is a matter of how the supplier organizes this task and which managers are engaged, the next section discusses the practice of KAM. This practice constitutes a way of managing relevant customers (and the associated relationship) by means of one or more designated managers, usually belonging to the sales department, who become the most representative and often unique interface with the customer within the supplier's organization.

2.5   A different perspective on KAM: The network view

The idea behind KAM is to commit specific human resources, in the form of one or more managers, to the development of a key customer relationship. Which customers will have such an account manager allocated to them is based on a portfolio analysis and evaluation similar to the ones we saw in the previous section, aiming to identify who are the most important or special customers among the others. KAM programs also employ specific tools (such as IT systems) applied in performing customer portfolio analysis. As stated by Ojasalo (2001: 201), "KAM refers to the selling company's activities including identifying and analyzing their key accounts, and selecting suitable strategies and developing operational level capabilities to build, grow and maintain profitable and long-lasting relationships with them."

The literature about KAM is mostly focused on how to organize and implement a specific approach for managing major customers (Spencer, 1999). For instance, the often quoted definition by Barrett (1986) states that KAM consists of steering the most important customers by providing them with special management concerning activities in marketing, sales, administration and service. The supplier, by relying on the engagement of dedicated managers, can thereby improve the quality of these selected business relationships. According to Shapiro and Moriarty (1984: 4), these efforts are motivated by the notion of a "major account", that is, an account that because of its size in terms of present or potential purchasing volume requires and can justify special treatment: thus the supplier has to organize itself for serving those major accounts. According to Diller (1992), KAM is a managerial concept, including selling strategies, aimed at achieving long-lasting customer relationships.

A key issue in the literature about KAM is how to select those customers who are of strategic importance for the future of the supplier. For instance, Millman and Wilson (1996) propose to focus on both hard (sales, profitability) and soft (trust, commitment) criteria in defining what is meant by a key account. However, the traditional KAM literature does not provide an integrated framework connecting the practice of KAM with its intra- and inter-organizational context (see for instance Shapiro and Posner, 1976; Shapiro and Moriarty, 1984). According to Pardo, Salle and Spencer (1995) what is missing in this literature is the complexity of the network context in which supplier–customer relationships develop and evolve. In order to be effective in a network-like context, "KAM strategy needs to integrate the very complexity of the supplier organization itself, in terms of strategy, characteristics, and relationships between units and functions, certain dimensions of which may be beyond its direct or immediate control" (Spencer, 1999: 307).

From an IMP perspective there are reasons to downplay the impact of KAM programs, mostly because KAM (similarly to "Relationship Marketing") applies a one-sided approach to managing a network-embedded phenomenon such as a customer relationship, while neglecting the role of the counterpart in the interaction and its influence on the supplier's customer management strategy. But what is then the IMP's way of conceiving the role of KAM in an industrial network setting?

As discussed previously, two key general traits of business relationships are their duration and continuity (Håkansson and Snehota, 1995), even if relationships can vary from being well established relationships with numerous daily contacts to being characterized by spot interactions. The volume of business among the parties is another important dimension, with some relationships representing a large proportion of the supplier's total sales while others cover lower volumes. Successful management of a customer relationship involves both an analysis of customer behavior and the awareness by the supplier of the customer's attempts to manage the very same relationship, but as a "supplier relationship" (Ford et al., 2003: 67). Another aspect that reduces the impact of KAM is the fact that a customer relationship is highly complex and evolves over time, for instance due to changing customer needs triggered by technology dynamics (Selnes and Johnson, 2004), which might not be possible for KAM to handle. One of the basic IMP standpoints when dealing with customer relationships is that they emerge from a process that unfolds over time, without following a distinct plan, thereby defying the possibility of control by a single organization (Ford et al., 2011). In other words, IMP researchers stress how difficult it is to succeed in managing customer relationships unilaterally by adopting KAM programs.

2.6 Summary

This chapter has introduced the key concepts about B2B customer relationships, which are the very object on which IT systems such as CRM systems are applied. Bearing these concepts in mind will help the reader better grasp the possibilities and limitations of CRM systems as emerging from the case of Loccioni in chapters 6–9. This chapter has also discussed how business relationships can be analyzed, for instance via the ARA model, and managed. However, while taking the IMP perspective on relationships certainly enabled us to penetrate their complex and dynamic nature, it also highlighted the implicit difficulties in managing unilaterally a relationship which involves two independent (or, better, interdependent) parties. Further, this chapter has stressed that, especially from an industrial network perspective, it is important to handle not only single relationships, but also the connections among them. A simplified form of customer network analysis is defining a company's customer portfolio, composed of customer relationships with different values and roles for the selling company. Finally, we addressed the issue of KAM, which will be salient in the Loccioni case, as KAMs are the primary expected users of CRM software. Our purpose with this theoretical review on KAM was to show how complex and challenging this task is if one assumes an interactive perspective on B2B marketing.

3
Connecting IT Systems, Users and Organizations

This chapter reviews the broad theme of Information Technology (IT). IT provides many applications for businesses and since the 1960s it has experienced an almost capillary diffusion into society, with investments in IT by organizations almost constantly growing over the years. From a managerial perspective, IT has gained a lot of interest from researchers due to its critical role inside companies. Our review first sums up the recent history of IT business applications and theories concerning how IT can support organizational operations and decision-making processes (Section 3.1). Our review also touches upon central themes such as the relation between IT and the performance of daily work by users. Then, Section 3.2 provides definitions and categorizations of information and IT systems (IS/IT). We then explore (Section 3.3) the factors that sustain the embedding of IT, including the contributions it can make to an organization installing a new IT system, as well as the critical issues that arise when IT is installed. Section 3.4 concludes the chapter by investigating the impact of IT on organizations, stressing both the positive and negative effects. For instance, how IT impacts on users deserves attention, since these individuals represent a key linkage between IT and its effective utilization at all organizational levels.

In order to provide the reader with an idea of the economic importance of the IT sector, Box 3.1 shows some features of the USA IT market, which is one of the largest and most competitive ones; this is also due to the presence of intensive R&D of IT technologies in the USA.

3.1 The evolution of IT

Very much has been written over the last 60 years concerning what IT represents and how it can be investigated within the domain of Information Systems (IS) studies. IS has contributed to the understanding of

---

Box 3.1   An overview of the IT market in the USA

The largest IT market in the world is the USA, where in 2012 IT spending reached US$ 560 billion. US spending on IT is forecast to reach US$ 674 billion by 2016. A major advantage for the American market is the presence of the world's largest and most important IT companies such as Microsoft Corporation, IBM, Hewlett-Packard and Dell. In this country there are moreover many large corporations and SMEs providing a strong demand for IT hardware, services and software. Due to the ongoing world-wide crisis, the largest growth opportunities now come from new technologies such as cloud computing, which is a new technology likely to change entirely the way IT products will be sold. Other promising applications with high forecasted demand are customer relationship management (CRM), business intelligence, enterprise resource planning (ERP) and other financial management systems (Table 3.1).

The hardware market is predicted to decrease from 25.8% of the total sales in 2013 to 24.3% in 2016. In contrast, services spending is expected to grow in the same period from 44.8% to 45.5%, as well as IT software from 29.4% to 30.2%.

Source: Modified from Business Monitor, Q4 2012

---

several IT-related phenomena (Avgerou, 2000), such as (1) how to develop and then use IT, (2) social and economic changes associated with IT, (3) how to exploit IT for supporting the functioning of organizations and (4) the impact of IT on organizational processes.

Before providing an historical perspective on IT, we briefly present two different but related views about IT. Firstly, Hedman and Kalling (2002) propose viewing IT as composed of two different but complementary technologies, namely information technology in proper terms (computers, software and information-handling systems) and communication technology (radio, TV, cellular phones). As a result of the recent convergence between information and communication technologies, often incorporated in one and the same product (e.g., smartphones), several authors suggest talking about ICT, that is, Information and Communication Technology. We choose however, to make use of the more traditional term IT, as we are not directly concerned with the

Table 3.1 The US IT industry – historical data and forecasts, 2009–2016

	2009	2010	2011	2012	2013(f)	2014(f)	2015(f)	2016(f)
IT market (total sales in billion US$)	487,053	508,97	529,39	559,108	586,591	616,022	644,504	673,608
IT market as % GDP	3.50	3.50	3.50	3.50	3.50	3.50	3.50	3.50
% Incidence of hardware on total sales	27	27.4	26.7	26.2	25.8	25.3	24.8	24.3
% Incidence of services on total sales	44.2	44.2	44.4	44.6	44.8	45	45.3	45.5
% Incidence of software on total sales	28.8	28.6	28.9	29.2	29.4	29.7	30	30.2

Source: Own elaborations on BMI, 2012.

telecommunication-related facets of these technologies. Still, computers and telecommunications constitute the central part of IT, in the sense that these technologies enable businesses to redefine their markets and increase their efficiency by supporting various types of processes: this can be an initial motivation of the interest of companies in investing so much in IT. Secondly, next to this focus on technical aspects, Ryssel, Ritter and Gemunde (2004) stress that computer hardware, software and telecommunications systems may be the core of IT, but they suggest that studies of IT need to include also other dimensions, such as personnel and other non IT-related resources.

Our historical review of IT considers academic contributions from the area of management studies that have appeared in recent decades (see Table 3.2). A central concern of this review is the use and adoption of IT systems, a theme closely related with the overall research purpose of this book. Moreover, investigating "IT in use", rather than its mere technical features and its expected results, allows us to understand the true significance and role of IT for management (Haigh, 2011). Therefore, our review also attempts to provide a picture of the historical evolution of the use of this technology within actual organizations.

During the 1950s management studies started to show interest in issues concerning the relation between computers and the use of IT in certain research and applied fields such as Operations Research (i.e., Diebold, 1953). At the same time, researchers were exploring the possible applications of computing in actual managerial settings such as production. It is in this period that the terms "information systems" and "information technology", as well as "information engineers", were coined. From a technology point of view, large and centralized computers known as mainframes were adopted to perform standardized data processing tasks, for instance in insurance companies.

By the early 1960s Management Information Systems (MISs) had become the most frequently invoked concept in managerially oriented discussion of the proper function of the computer in corporate administration. During the 1960s one clear research interest was the possibilities offered by computers for doing business, as well as how to properly employ computers for processing data. Most contributions dealt with the opportunities and possibilities that IT offered in supporting managers for carrying out their activities by means of tools such as computers and databases (Wagner, 1969). For instance Beged-Dov, Ehrenfeld and Summer (1967) stated that thanks to IT tools it would possible to conduct more effective market evaluation or production control. At the same time, Decision Support Systems (DSSs) research

Table 3.2 Historical review of IT technologies and selected research in management studies

Period	Overarching goal of IT	Type of technologies	Academic contributions
1950s	– Data processing	– Electronic data processing – Mainframes	– Diebold (1953)
1960s	– Data processing – Management Information Systems (MISs)	– Electronic data processing – Transaction processing – First databases	– Beged-Dov, Ehrenfeld and Summer (1967) – Wagner (1969)
1970s	– MISs	– Database Management Systems – Reporting systems – Decision support systems	– Mintzberg (1972) – Gorry and Scott Morton (1971) – Simon (1977) – Hedberg and Jönsson (1978)
1980s	– Information and innovation support	– Personal computers – Mini and micro computers – Client-server	– Davis (1989)
1990s	– Business integration and restructuring	– Enterprise Resources Planning (ERP) – Data warehouse – Intranet	– Leidner and Elam (1993) – Nord and Nord (1995) – Nonaka and Takeuchi (1995) (also knowledge era) – Keen (1991)
2000s	– Knowledge era	– Internet – Telecommunications	– Evans and Wurster (2000) – Orlikowski and Barley (2001) – Orlikosky and Iacono (2001)

arose as a domain within managerial IS/IT studies. In the 1970s the focus came to be on adopting computers for "reporting" management information (Keen, 1991). However, the idea that computers would allow monitoring of every contingency of a firm, which constituted the basis of MISs, led many to overstate the concrete possibilities of MISs. From a technical point of view, a new generation of software tools was commercialized under the name of DataBase Management Systems (DBMS); it also became easier to share data between applications and to maintain data files on disk rather than tape. Toward the end of the 1970s several researchers showed that MISs could also cause negative effects on companies: for instance Hedberg and Jönsson (1978) argued that IT systems increased the rigidity of organizations by constraining them to adopt certain working models, which may not fit a specific organization. On the other hand, based on an empirical study, Mintzberg (1972) also found that managers ignored IT-based reports and relied on "gossip" as a key source of the information they used for making decision. This and other ways of bypassing structured IT systems would be a recurrent theme in several empirical studies on the use of IT within actual organizations.

The early 1980s witnessed an interest in how IT interplays with other tools and individuals. Researchers from areas such as sociology and organizational studies focused primarily on the organizational and social impact both at an individual and group level of IT implementation (Orlikowski and Robey, 1991; Suchman, 1987). The well known and extensively adopted theory of Technology Acceptance User, or TAM (Davis, 1989) is an attempt to explain individuals' intentions to use IT systems. This theory assumes that the perception an individual has of the proposed system influences the intention of using it. The theory underlines how social norms matter when individuals are approaching an IT system. It is important to stress how this new research focus on the interface between individuals and computers is linked to the appearance of the first personal computers, which brought IT much closer to individual users compared to mainframe computers, which were usually located at central computation laboratories. The 1980s were also the decade during which technology development allowed linking together of computers of different kinds, including so-called microcomputers, as a way to allow client–server connections as well as more interactive interfaces between people and computers.

During the 1990s, an important innovation in the IT field was ERP software packages, which were rapidly adopted by companies. They would integrate financial data, operations, human resource management, sales and logistics functions under a single umbrella. At the same time, also as a way to support the functioning and complex data requirements of ERP systems, IT providers proposed the concept of "data warehouse", reminiscent of the single centralized databases of the 1970s. With all due improvements such as greater flexibility, upgradability and transferability compared to their ancestors in the 1970s, the data warehouses of the 1990s constituted a comprehensive data repository which allowed quick data retrieving operations. Moreover, information would be uploaded periodically from disparate databases avoiding overloading the information flow. Another "hot topic" appearing in the 1990s was Knowledge Management, which rapidly spread and was converted into new internally oriented ICT applications known as Knowledge Management (KM) systems (Davenport, De Long and Beers, 1998). In parallel, IT-based project management tools became another important set of available IT tools, also thanks to the new communication possibilities offered by company-wide Intranets. KM turned soon into the subject of many scientific articles and books, accompanied by changes in managerial practice including even the creation of a specific managerial position within companies known as Chief Knowledge Officer (CKO).

From the 1990s onwards, IT has been applied by companies, and accordingly researched by management scholars, within electronic exchanges and markets that allow rapid communication between suppliers and customers (Gadde and Håkansson, 2001). In fact, in 1994 the Internet became a publicly available technology and by the late 1990s its effects had spread all over the world and to several areas of business. Influential and best-selling books were also written about how the Internet would change the very way companies made their strategy, such as "Blown to Bits: How the New Economics of Information Transforms Strategy" by Evans and Wurster (2000). In spite of the swarm of favorable expectations accompanying every new wave of IT, such as the Internet, there is a deeper issue that is indeed essential for IT to eventually fulfill its expectations: a key driver for IT to produce any effects at all is that it gets adopted by users, both individually and in groups. And studies show clearly that the intention to use IT depends on how users perceive it as useful in their daily tasks (Bhattacherjee and Premkumar, 2004). In short, users are willing to adopt an IT system only when its benefits are clearly and ideally immediately visible, which stands in contrast with the fact that the advantages of adopting IT often emerge over time and often are not predictable. Therefore, the following section examines how IT relates to how users perform their work.

3.1.1 IT, work performance and users' reactions

The use of IT and work performance were the subject of several studies such as DeLone and McLean (1992). Their challenging aim was to evaluate whether more frequent use of IT improves job performance or not. However, the authors encountered several issues, mainly due to the difficulty in measuring either the use of an information system (Straub, Limayem and Krahanna-Evaristo, 1995) or the performance of work itself. Another theory developed by Goodhue (1995) stresses how work performance will be enhanced when individuals perceive a "fit" between IT and the task to be performed. A limitation of this approach is however the assumption that a task is predetermined, without considering the possibility that the very task can change along with the individual's perceptions or learning.

There are moreover reasons to investigate how users' reactions to IT implementation and adoption frame the impact of IT on work performance. The key question is therefore what influences a user's reaction to IT. Clegg et al. (1997) summarize empirical contributions aimed at answering this question and find first of all that timing is an important element that influences users, including how the IT system's immediate and emerging functionalities impact in the present and the future a user's job content and skills. These authors also find that the commitment of the user to her work organization and its processes is another important element in forming users' reaction to IT: therefore managers are advised to invest time and effort in discussing with users what type of IT solutions they need to cope with their job. Finally, the reaction of users to IT is also dependent on training activities, whose lack typically results in a limited use of IT, which impedes gaining benefits from computers in organizations.

Both these theories, focusing respectively on the "fit" between IT and tasks and on timing, commitment and training, consider these elements within a static framework. However, there are a number of unpredictable and changeable elements that emerge only when individuals and technologies start interacting, and these elements do have an impact on IT implementation and use. The relation between individuals and IT systems is in fact complex and partly ambiguous, calling for more extensive reflections. Often research on IS/IT has been carried out from a deterministic perspective (Hedman and Kalling, 2002), looking at IT as a device that somehow creates improvements in economy, without considering how the effects of IT are instead highly dependent on how a specific IT tool is combined and related to other material and immaterial resources (Baraldi, 2003), activities and institutions, both inside and outside the organization where it is installed.

Indeed, two relevant questions for the purpose of this book are: how are IT systems embedded within organizations, their resources and activities? And how are IT systems adopted by users when the using context is changing? Our research concerns moreover the study of inter- and intra-organizational effects of a specific IT system, whereby the interplay between individuals and the IT system being adopted play a key role for the emergence of such effects. In line with Orlikowski (1993), we state that in order to understand the adoption and use of IT systems we cannot disregard the social context of systems development, but must consider the intentions and actions of individuals as well as the implementation process.

Since we posit that the intra- and inter-organizational effects deriving from the embedding of IT systems are intertwined, we analyze CRM, as a particular example of IT tool, by means of an analytical framework that can capture embedding not only within one single organization but also among organizations, indeed at network level (Håkansson and Snehota, 1995). Chapter 5 presents this framework and accordingly provides an innovative conceptualization of CRM, with the purpose of gaining new insights in the role, effects, challenges and possibilities of CRM systems when they are embedded in complex industrial networks.

3.2 Conceptualizing information and IT systems: Classification and taxonomy

This section reviews the key concepts and typologies related to information and IT systems (IS/IT). In general terms, IT systems transform input-information into output-information for certain managerial purposes. More precisely, an IT (or information) system, as defined by Boddy, Boonstra and Kennedy (2002: 6), is a set of people, procedures and resources that collects and transforms data into information and disseminates this information. While IS is a concept focusing on the *information* being processed and exchanged, without necessarily relying on computer technology, IT is a concept highlighting also *technical* dimensions and elements. Hence, IT in proper terms includes ICT, the Internet, as well as the related infrastructure, such as computer hardware and software, and those modern technologies that process or transmit information to enhance the effectiveness of individuals and organizations.

In the present study IT is viewed as an artifact, that is, a system composed of materials and logical elements from the technical domain of IT. IT systems have a particular feature: they handle information automatically by performing computations in order to create new information (Kallinikos, 2001) by following certain software instructions. The word "artifact" derives from the Latin *arte* (which means "by skill") and *factum* (which means "thing made"). The term "artifact" allows researchers from different disciplines and with different perspectives to conceptualize IT as a mixture of tangible and non-tangible elements. Therefore, an IT artifact includes machines, tools, software, languages and, if viewed from a system perspective, also the very users and organizations where they are installed. Even if users are part of a system only insofar as they use, input and extract data and interact with it, central dimensions of IT systems are people, technology and organizations (Hevner et al., 2004). This conceptualization of IT allows us to study such implications of IT as how IT relates to mechanisms of organizational coordination or how IT interplays with, but also impacts on, organizations (see Section 4).

3.2.1 Classifying IT systems

Piccoli and Ives (2005) refer to IT in terms of "assets", including hardware components, platforms, software applications and data repositories. They also distinguish IT *infrastructure*, which brings together technical and human assets, from *information repositories*. This latter is a collection of data accessible and usable for certain decision-making purposes. If we focus on the internal composition of IT artifacts, the following key elements are typically present in all IT systems and tools (Baraldi, 2003):

1) **Hardware solutions**: these are the elements that constitute the "physical" and touchable part of IT systems, such as processors, microchips, video terminals and routers.
2) **Software programs**: these represent the instructions that guide hardware and allow it to process data. Software includes, for example, applications that allow users to search for data or perform calculations.
3) **Databases**: these are virtual repositories where data are collected, acting as electronic libraries.
4) **Graphic User Interface (GUI)**: this is the visible part of the IT system that allows the user to interact with the software and databases, including entering and viewing information in the system. GUIs include control panels and other tools that allow users to display data and images that the IT system creates.
5) **Embedded models**: these are simplified representations of concrete activities (for instance a delivery process), resources (for instance a product) and actors (for instance a customer), and of the connections between these elements. A model can for instance cover the activity whereby a customer receives a product, by setting various parameters

such as product price and construction, delivery time and customer location.

6) **Logical structures**: these allow the connections between databases, models and programs, thereby keeping the whole IT system together.

Those six elements taken together constitute the core internal features of IT systems. The combination of these elements allows users to perform various operations on the data: input, collect and receive data, and then store, analyze and display data, or send it to (or share it with) other users who need it. The six elements can be combined in various ways to create actual IT systems addressed to particular applications. Hence there is a very broad variation of IT tools, which authors have classified according to different categories.

For instance, the categorization by Hedman and Kalling (2002) divides IT systems by business areas where their benefits are expected to emerge from their adoption: for instance, CRM systems help marketing departments to handle customer knowledge and relationships; Computer-Aided Design (CAD) systems support technical departments in the product design phase of the product development process; Supply Chain Management (SCM) systems are applied in logistics; ERP systems are employed to integrate information from different functional divisions in order to facilitate the coordination of different processes across the whole firm. An important aspect of ERPs is that their standard core includes not only software applications and databases, but is also heavily influenced by embedded models and methods (the so-called "best practices") that prescribe how to perform managerial tasks (Baraldi, 2003).

Gorry and Scott Morton (1971) provide instead a categorization that separates IT systems supporting *operational* tasks from those supporting *strategic* tasks. They separate the so-called Operational Systems (OSs) from MISs. OSs systems include a wide range of solutions:

- *Transaction processing systems*: systems that allow users to record transactions such as orders claims and dispatches.
- *Office Automation Systems*: systems that allow users to organize activities in coordinated workflows or to manage the documentation produced (Workflow Management Systems). The most noticeable application of office automation systems is certainly Microsoft (MS) Office suite. It includes word processing software (i.e., MS Word), spreadsheets software (i.e., MS Excel), presentation software (i.e., MS

PowerPoint), desktop publishing (i.e., MS Publisher) and e-mail messaging software (i.e., MS Outlook).

- *KM Systems*: these systems allow generating, preserving and sharing of tacit and explicit knowledge both inside and outside organizations. In order to distribute and share knowledge, most KM systems use the Internet as a tool. A typical example of a knowledge management system is database software such as Microsoft SQL Server and Access.
- *Process Control Systems*: these include logistics-material flow and production scheduling systems used to administer transportation, inventories and manufacturing.

MISs aggregate data from Operational Systems into information relevant to carrying out more strategic tasks. Falling into this group, Executive Information Systems navigate, find and process operational data into such information as "sales per country" or "monthly delivery precision" (Kallinikos, 2001: 43). Another category that belongs to MISs is DSSs, which are composed of complex software algorithms and models that aggregate, process variables and provide guidelines to assist in strategic decisions (e.g., whether to withdraw from the market a given product or service). For example, DSSs might help companies that want to expand their business to check if they have the ability and potential to do so.

A third classification (Ryssel, Ritter and Gemunde, 2004) distinguishes between IT systems from an internal perspective (systems that carry out activities within the corporate boundaries) as opposed to an inter-organizational perspective (i.e., systems shared between companies). Following this categorization, Electronic Data Interchange (EDI) is a shared inter-organizational IT tool, while ERPs are internal tools for information processing.

3.2.2   Information significance and classification

Next to the technical core of the IT artifact, the other main element of IT systems is the information that they collect, process and deliver to users. Information has been defined and conceived over time in different ways, often depending on the specific disciplinary field. Just to give a few examples, in physics information is viewed as signals across a channel (Shannon and Weaver, 1949) while in semiotics it is viewed as the meaning of signs.

In management studies it is widely accepted that information represents a critical success factor for companies. Information is recognized as an important resource for companies, which invest in organizational and technical structure to improve their capabilities for collecting, storing, processing and distributing information (Wixom and Watson, 2001). Several researchers from business studies (e.g., Ackoff, 1996) have defined the connection between three related, although different concepts, namely "information", "data" and "knowledge". Data are symbols that represent objects; information is conveyed by answers to such questions as "who, what, where, when and how many?"; finally, knowledge is equated with "know-how" (Ibid.: 28). Similarly, Davenport and Prusak (1998) point out how knowledge is originated by information, which in turn arises from data. Therefore, information and knowledge are strongly related with each other, as shown by the "Infological equation" (Langefors, 1995: 144): information results from the interpretation that a subject makes of certain data, based on her previous knowledge. This approach indicates that the same data can have different meanings, hence become different information, for different users of an IT system, depending on their experience and, one may add, their social context. Moreover, information flows produce effects on knowledge. In this respect, the communication between two different organizational units affects their respective level of knowledge.

As we aim to emphasize how and under which conditions companies adopt IT for managing customer relationships in business networks, we need a definition of information that allows us to cope with the intra- and inter-organizational complexity of these contexts. For this purpose, information can be conceived as a "meta-resource", that is, as a representation of other resources, such as organizations, products, equipment or customers (Baraldi, 2003). In practice, information assumes the form either of documents, that is, "information bases" containing descriptions of resources, and of messages that are exchanged between individual users or organizational groups. A document can in turn be transformed into a message as soon as it is transmitted to another user. In this case, the message has three main functions: (1) containing representations of resources; (2) delivering meanings to the recipient; and (3) implying intentions from the sender (Ibid.: 25).

The performance of managerial tasks implies complex arrangements whereby information is created, diffused and applied in making decisions. For instance, organizational departments need information to carry out their tasks and activities, which typically originates flows of messages containing the required information between various actors. Then, these messages contribute more or less to task performance depending on two key features: (1) information quantity (namely, the amount of details in representing resources); and (2) information quality (i.e., the correctness, validity and relevance of the representations for the task at hand).

For our research purpose, we conceive information primarily as an input and output of IT systems which is provided by or made available to individual users. Information then becomes in turn a key element for managers in their decision-making process and for other specific managerial tasks. Such tasks have three main features that affect the amount of information to be processed (Galbraith, 1980): (1) the degree of uncertainty concerning task requirements; (2) the number of elements the manager needs for making decisions; (3) the level of inter-relatedness between these two elements. These features tend together to increase the amount of information necessary for a managerial task. There are moreover three other classifications of information that define how it can be used, and whether it turns out to be useful, in performing a given managerial task:

1) *Format and media*: distinguishing between *well structured* (e.g., computer database) or *unstructured* (e.g., oral discussion) information (Ramström, 1973: 10).
2) *Frequency*: distinguishing between routinized (e.g., daily orders) and non-routinized (e.g., negotiations) information (Ramström, 1973);
3) *Time orientation*: distinguishing between *strategic* and *operative* information (Anthony, 1965). The former usually covers a long-term horizon and can be highly speculative, such as forecasts, while the latter refers to a short-term horizon, and is often precise detailed and formalized information, such as a delivery date.

3.3   The contributions of IT and factors favoring its embedding

At a general level, Huber (1990) views the main contributions of IT as giving to individuals or organizations abilities to: (1) store and retrieve information quickly; (2) access information more selectively; (3) combine and reconfigure information accurately to create new information; (4) storing, combining and using decision models; (5) recording and retrieving reliable information about organizational transactions. These improved IT-based abilities to handle information are then expected to contribute to improved decision-making in the organization. Therefore, several authors have stressed the strategic importance of IT: for instance, Porter (1980) conceives IT as one of the strategic assets of companies and

Rapp (2002) states that applying IT to functions such as marketing and R&D can improve a firm's services and products.

However, determining the actual contributions of IT has turned out to be a complex issue, both for economists and for IS/IT researchers. Next to tangible and direct work efficiency gains at macro-economical level, which have only recently been demonstrated, much of IT's contribution appears to be indirect and intangible. Researchers have also been in disagreement as to how, how much and why IT creates business value, and improves firm performance, productivity and competitive advantage (Hitt and Brynjolfsson, 1996; Melville, Kraemer and Gurbaxani, 2004). Customer agility has also been proposed as one of many IT-based value outcomes (Sambamurthy, Bharadwaj and Grover, 2003). The problem with identifying the effects and contributions of IT to business performance is that such effects are often hidden, require time to emerge and derive from complex combinations between IT and other complementary investments and resources (Brynjolfsson and Hitt, 2000).

Therefore, in order to shed light on what are the contributions and the value of IT, it is necessary not to consider IT systems as isolated artifacts, but to look at their connections with other entities, individuals and resources surrounding them, such as products, machines and users (Baraldi, 2003). In order to allow this type of analysis, which we will perform in Chapter 9, we will introduce in Chapter 5 a model featuring four resource types, known as the 4Rs model (Wedin, 2001; Håkansson and Waluszewski, 2002; Baraldi, 2003).

At this point we can however consider the general factors that, according to the literature, favor the implementation, use and contribution of IT. One of the most widely recognized factors is executive commitment (Henderson and Venkatraman, 1993; Kettinger et al., 1994). Top executives can speed up the process of implementation, integrating it with the company's strategy and ensuring continuity in IT investments. Moreover, IT adoption by CEOs can turn out to be a good practice for spurring the use of it among employees. IT implementation and proper adoption also calls for organizational flexibility. In fact, IT impacts on the flexibility of organizations, but is at the same time affected by it. Flexibility is therefore an important factor in facilitating IT implementation and use: adaptations are required from employees and whole organizational structures, which suggests that the more an organization is able to adapt to IT requirements the less "painful" the introduction of IT will be. As pointed by Orlikowski and Gash (1992), IT requires adaptations in three settings, namely managers, technologists and users. An example of how flexibility can support IT embedding and use comes from the implementation of ERP systems in organizations. ERP implementation increases the level of integration among the various processes and functions of a company; but the whole process of implementing and regularly using these IT systems remains very difficult to accomplish. A reason is the lack of organizational connections, particularly among multinational companies with operations in several countries: such companies lack homogenous data sets and processes, and each subsidiary often has its own IT systems which are not properly connected to the headquarters. These large organizations often lack the flexibility to change processes and systems rapidly. While flexibility is important per se, it is also necessary that managers consider how much adaptation a new IT system will require from the organization.

There are also external factors influencing IT adoption, such as customers and suppliers (Swan, Newell and Robertson, 2000). Focusing on SMEs, De Burca, Fynes and Marshall (2005) show that their commercial counterparts often demand the adoption of specific IT tools. Also Perna, Cardinali and Gregori (2013) point out how companies adopting CRM systems to improve selling activities can be influenced in their implementation of such IT systems by changes in their distribution network, with new partners pushing the company to invest in a new IT system. Another factor influencing the adoption of IT is the choice of IT solution itself. The technological characteristics of IT tools (e.g., compatibility, security) play a relevant role because they have a direct impact on where, when and how to implement IT (Grandon and Pearson, 2004). Of course the costs of a certain IT solution, the payment conditions defined by IT providers and the payback time of the IT investment are other factors that influence IT implementation. However, our discussion has so far stressed that the development and/or selection of a certain IT tool has to be considered in relation to users: the IT system will interact with users, who in turn become the drivers for successful use and implementation of IT.

3.4   The impact of IT on organizations

In General Motors' Environmental Activities Staff the dawning of the personal computing/communicating era has brought major changes. Within eighteen months of its introduction, integrated management information technology quickly spawned increases in organizational efficiency, effectiveness, creativity, and innovativeness. Many of these increases were caused by changes in traditional organizational forms. Many, in fact, would have been impossible without changes in traditional roles and relationships brought about by the new technology.

(Foster and Flynn, 1984, p. 229)

The above quote dates back to the beginning of the 1980s and highlights how one of the leading global automotive companies, General Motors (GM), dealt positively with IT. In order to cope with and extract value from IT, it is clear that GM needed to face a set of changes. Actually, the changes that accompanied IT implementation and its adoption did not only happen inside the organization, but also stretched outside its boundaries. These intra- and inter-organizational effects of IT (which will be discussed theoretically in Chapter 5) affect every internal function and require organizational flexibility (Benjamin and Levinson, 1993) to avoid imbalances within the company.

We turn now to reviewing the growing literature that since the 1980s has analyzed the impact of IT on organizations (Keen, 1991). A shared opinion among researchers is that the implementation and adoption of IT within organizations can easily turn out to be very costly and painful, sometimes well beyond the benefits and advantages that organizations might gain. However, despite the many studies already made on this topic, the advent of new IT tools still deserves continuous investigation.

In a literature review on the impact of IT on organizations McLean (1979) identifies four different levels where such an impact can be manifest: individuals (employees), groups, organizations and society. This study proposes a contingency approach which considers as important factors associated with the effects of IT such contingencies as the organizational culture and climate. Dewett and Jones (2001) rely on an extensive literature of articles published in 1995–1999 in six leading management journals and conclude that IT effects are indirect in nature. The reviewed literature considers IT a "moderator", in the sense that it produces effects only if supported by other factors such as openness of culture and users' commitment for producing performance advantages. In other words, in order to create effects, IT has to fit with processes already present in firms. In this respect, as also observed by Yates, Orlikowski and Okamura (1999), the time dimension plays an important role: in fact, IT has to be continuously adapted to the organization over time, since organizations constantly change dramatically. Consequently instead of simply considering the unilateral impact of IT on organizations, it is more appropriate to consider the mutual interaction between IT and organizations.

The interaction between IT and organization is recognized to be very complex, as it involves so many aspects such as organizational structure, business processes, culture, employees' skills and experience, and managerial decision structure and control. These dimensions mediate the effects of IT, both within a single organization (at intra-organizational level) and between several organizations (at inter-organizational level). Table 3.3 summarizes significant academic

Table 3.3   The impact of IT on organizations at intra- and inter-organizational levels

Impact of IT on organizations			
Level	**Dimension**	**Sub-dimension**	**Authors**
Intra-organizational	Employees/ managers	– Number of employees – Functional roles – Skills – Experience and age	– Hoos (1960) – Whisler (1970) – Wynne and Otway (1983) – Zuboff (1988)
		Decision-making authority – Centralization – Decentralization – Formalization and control	– Emery (1964) – Lado and Zhang (1998) – Lawler, Mohrmann and Ledford (1998) – Zuboff (1988)
		Learning	– Huber (1990)
	Culture	Values and norms	– Dewett and Jones (2001)
	Flexibility		– Lucas and Olson (1994)
Inter-organizational	Business relationships	– Improvements in supplier–customer relationship (quality of the relationship) – Information sharing between counterparts – Communication efficiency – Learning mechanism	– Wilson and Vlosky (1998) – Dewett and Jones (2001) – Leek, Turnbull and Naude (2003) – Ryssel, Ritter and Gemunde (2004) – Baglieri, Secchi and Croom (2007)

contributions about the impact of IT on organizations, distinguishing the inter- and the intra-organizational levels, which are reviewed in the next two sections.

3.4.1 Intra-organizational effects of IT

The "technological imperative" (Markus and Robey, 1988) views IT as capable of producing important changes within organizations, both for individuals and for collectives. Studies from the 1960s onwards argue that IT affects employment volumes (Osterman, 1991). For instance Hoos (1960) shows that IT reduces the number of middle managers, since it permits top managers to bypass middle managers. This finding is also supported by Whisler (1970), who more generally demonstrates that IT negatively impacts the number of employees. However, there are also studies showing opposite results: Wynne and Otway (1983) suggest that IT increases the number of employees, especially those dealing directly with information, since more data and information available require more managers to handle them. These managers also become more important and receive more responsibility due to the availability of specific information provided by IT that enables them to make more complex decisions. Another effect of IT on employees concerns their skills and the (new) tasks they can perform thanks to IT (Foster and Flynn, 1984). As showed by Zuboff (1988), workers interact with computers that generate data representing their working practices and results, which become ready for them to study and analyze. Therefore, IT "informates" work, that is, makes it more transparent by producing reflexive information about work processes. Hart et al. (2004) stress however that the impacts of IT on individual employees are mediated by their working experience, with more experienced (and usually older) managers less likely to be influenced by IT.

IT also has effects on organizational decision-making processes. This effect is coupled with the aforementioned effect of IT on the number and skills of employees. The debate on the effects of IT on decisional centralization dates back to Emery (1964). His argument was that IT is a factor enhancing centralization, as it allows organizations to store, retrieve and use greater quantities of data for the sake of the organization itself. The possibility of controlling employees are also improved by IT, including unpleasant forms of panoptical control (Zuboff, 1988), whereby individuals perceive IT tools as omnipresent "guards". These mechanisms tend to push decision-making authority up in the organizational hierarchy. This effect is further reinforced by the fact that IT facilitates information transmission between managers (and hierarchical levels) and also reduces the distance between center and periphery in organizations with multiple locations. Moreover, fewer managers would be able to supervise many other managers as IT enables them to manage information more quickly and accurately, while also reducing uncertainty in their decisions (Lado and Zhang, 1998). But even if the increased formalization, information flows and control caused by IT make the balance lean toward increased centralization of organization, IT may also promote decentralization. In fact, IT tools made available to all organizational members can empower them by improving middle-to-low-level managers' knowledge concerning events, facts, strategies and other critical decisions in the organization (Lawler, Mohrmann and Ledford, 1998).

IT has also been shown to influence the learning mechanisms present in an organization: IT can provide employees with information which facilitates problem solving and thereby increment their ability to learn (Huber, 1990). Moreover, a variety of new IT applications (Intranet, video conferencing) allows companies to integrate and then spread knowledge more efficiently. Culture is another dimension which is affected by IT: the availability and use of Intranets and email provide fast mechanisms for spreading the norms and values belonging to an organization's culture. News about important results achieved by the organization, such as new products or services successfully launched, can be more easily communicated to members via IT, so as to enhance a common social identity and sense of belonging.

Finally, Lucas and Olson (1994) show how IT can influence organizational flexibility. According to the authors, flexibility is the company's attitude to and capability of adapting quickly to changes. They report the case study of American Airlines, which needed to cope with an increasing number of reservations in 1990s. In order to provide a better response to market demand, this company took on the new challenge of enhancing the possibilities for customers to make quick reservations via a new IT reservation system. While the IT system was opening American Airlines core business to external influence, it also contributed greatly to making it more flexible as each new reservation had to be quickly processed.

3.4.2 Inter-organizational effects of IT

The impact of IT on organizations is likely not to be homogeneous on all organizations, but as Robey (1977) suggests, computing affects organizations in different ways depending on the level of complexity of the environments they face, which stresses the relevance of the inter-organizational setting. Moreover, the IT installed inside one company can have effects on surrounding organizations. Studies on the impact of IT systems at inter-organizational level mostly concern how IT influences the development and management of business relationships. Many of these studies focus on supply chain management in the manufacturing and retail sectors (Mulligan and Gordon, 2002). For instance, Baglieri, Secchi and Croom (2007) use the case of Ferrari Auto to analyze the impact of IT on industrial purchasing and supplier relationships. Ferrari implemented a platform called "Partner", aimed at strengthening relationships with suppliers by creating a greater sense of belonging within the Ferrari brand. Ferrari's suppliers recognized a positive impact of the IT platform on the quality of their relationship with the customer. However, Leek, Turnbull and Naude (2003: 125) reach opposite results as to the impact of IT on business relationships:

> The developments in IT are not slowing down and will continue to impact on business to business interactions. At the moment, companies are not making full use of IT's capabilities, which suggests that in the near future relationships will still require considerable face to face interaction, be informal and close, trusting and cooperative. However, in the future, they may become increasingly impersonal and formal and more difficult to manage as technological developments continue and filter through to companies.

Wilson and Vlosky (1998) analyze the implementation of inter-organizational information systems (IOSs) within a stable relationship. IOSs are automated information systems that are shared by two or more companies (Johnston and Vitale, 1988) to facilitate information flows and management. Wilson and Vlosky (1998) find that the implementation of IOSs can actively contribute to strengthening the relationship between customer and supplier, by enhancing the level of trust and commitment between parties as manifested during a complex project requiring high mutual engagement. In a similar vein, Ryssel, Ritter and Gemunde (2004) show that IT does influence B2B relationships. In particular, these authors show that there are several factors that foster the use and effects of IT in relationships, such as the customer's trust and commitment, the supplier's and the customer's internal IT infrastructure, the IT system's reliability and user-friendliness and the nature of transactions in the relationship. As for the latter factor, IT tends to facilitate especially exchanges and deliveries of standardized products.

When implemented and exploited by organizations that share a common platform, IT may further facilitate ongoing communication between them (Dewett and Jones, 2001). By creating shared data repositories it is possible to share documentation that speeds up such processes as common marketing campaigns.

3.5 Summary

This chapter has reviewed the field of IS/IT, starting from a description of the historical evolution of IT business applications. We have also encountered a set of key theoretical concepts necessary in order to make sense of IT and its effects on organizations and businesses. For instance, IT systems were defined as artifacts capable of automatically processing information and making it available to users. Information is another key concept, which we defined as a representation of other resources, and which takes the shape of either a static document or a message traveling between a sender and a recipient. The chapter has also proposed various categorizations both of information and of IT systems. Further, we stressed that understanding the effects of IT requires analyzing how IT tools are connected, or embedded, within an organizational context composed of several other resources. Factors such as executive commitment and organizational flexibility were pointed out as facilitators of IT implementation and use, together with requests of key external partners and the very choice of IT system. Finally, we reviewed the impact of IT on organizations, both at intra- and inter-organizational level. This impact includes not only such positive effects as increased employees' skills and learning or trust in relationships, but also negative effects such as reduced number of employees, increased control on individual users and centralization of decision-making.

4
CRM, Its Roots in Management Studies and Recent Research Trends

This chapter provides an in-depth literature review of CRM, viewed both as a general marketing philosophy and as a set of IT solutions applied to marketing actions. The aim of this literature review is threefold. First we discuss the origins of CRM (Section 4.2). Then we review the main research areas covering the topic of CRM (Section 4.3), leading to a review of the most adopted definitions of CRM. Afterwards, we focus on key issues concerning both the technology and organizational dimensions of CRM implementation (Section 4.4). Implementation of CRM systems in fact deserves close attention due to its critical importance in enabling companies to eventually effectively employ CRM tools. This chapter concludes with an overview of CRM when applied in a business-to-business (B2B) context (Section 4.5). Having a clear idea of what is meant by CRM helps us frame the key object of our empirical investigation of chapters 6–8, as well as how CRM can be conceptualized and analyzed, as shown in chapters 5 and 9.

4.1 Introduction

CRM represents a broad phenomenon whose boundaries are however often blurred. In fact, there is massive literature dedicated to the topic of CRM, which analyzes it from several perspectives. In literature as well as in practice, it is rather difficult to find a dominant or a common view concerning CRM. From a technological point of view, CRM systems belong to the large family of Information Technology (IT) tools supporting a number of managerial activities. It becomes instead more difficult to generalize what CRM embraces when talking about its relation with people, organizations and processes.

As explained by Keen (1991), in general IT allows companies to manage organizational complexity. Such a complexity derives from external and internal conditions to the organization and it can lead to confusion as well as to organizational dysfunctions. IT can be accordingly viewed as a tool to solve or manage these dysfunctions. If we apply this metaphor to CRM, when an organization encounters problems in managing its customer relationships, the technology side of CRM can assist the company in improving its customer relationships.

4.2   Setting the ground: The origins of CRM

There is an ongoing debate in the literature about what CRM represents (Payne and Frow, 2005; Zablah, Bellenger and Johnston, 2004), and the term CRM itself has been applied by various research disciplines to designate different phenomena and in relation to different concepts. The academic literature on CRM originates in the 1990s. Some of these earlier contributions, such as Stone, Woodcock and Wilson (1996), focus explicitly on the use of IT in managing customer relationships. These authors refer to the use of IT tools, such as databases, in order to maintain the relationship with customers as long as possible. A particular emphasis in their work rests on looking at empirical examples where IT has been applied to managing customer relationships in a business to consumer (B2C) context.

In earlier research contributions, one of the conceptual building blocks for CRM is the concept of "relationship marketing" (Grönroos, 1994), coupled with the way IT can support the management of customer relationships, viewed as one of several managerial tasks (see Chapter 3 for a review of the use of IT in organizations). This matching of CRM and relationship marketing is not surprising, since the 1990s witnessed both the appearance of new IT tools and an increased attention to the relationship marketing approach, belonging to Service Marketing and more precisely to the "Nordic school of services" (Gummesson, Lehtinen and Grönroos, 1997). The very essence of relationship marketing provides the conditions for connecting to relevant IT tools: "Relationship marketing is attracting, maintaining and in multi-service organizations enhancing customer relationships. Servicing and selling existing customers is viewed to be just as important to long-term marketing success as acquiring new customers" (Berry, 1983: 25).

Especially in the context of B2C, service is considered a means of improving the quality of the relationship, stimulating customer loyalty and extending the customer life cycle (Grönroos, 1990). One aspect common to service marketing researchers focusing on B2C relations is that customer relationships are unilaterally managed by the provider, or at least that the latter is the active party and has much more influence in managing customers, typically consumers, than envisaged by the IMP approach to B2B relationships (Håkansson and Snehota, 1995). Consequently, within the relationship marketing domain the tools applied by the dominant and more active party in the relationship, such as IT, can assume a strong role in managing customer relationships. For instance, in line with Vavra (1994), who points out that databases consisting of customer information files have to be established for managing customer relationships properly, a leading figure within relationship marketing such as Grönroos (1996: 11) states that "a well-prepared, updated, easily retrievable and easy-to-read customer information file is needed in such cases to make it possible for the employee to pursue a relationship-oriented customer contact".

Paralleling the improvement of IT solutions as a support of marketing activities in companies, a stream of research belonging to relationship marketing emerged under the name of "database" or "interactive" marketing (Blattberg and Deighton, 1991). By means of databases containing customer information it would be possible to retrieve information for identifying patterns of customer behaviors in order to organize offerings in a customized way. According to Coviello, Brodie and Munro (1997) database marketing could allow marketers to keep and retain customers over time simply by heavily investing in tools and techniques able to manage huge amounts of data in a logical manner. Another similar conceptualization concerning the adoption of databases for developing marketing strategies belongs to the domain of one-to-one marketing, as proposed in the popular book "The One to One Future: Building Relationships" (Peppers and Rogers, 1993). Addressing marketing action so to focus on one customer at a time was considered a relevant recipe, especially among practitioners, because it suggested how to exploit technologies, namely IT, for making customers more profitable and satisfied. This approach highlights the key role of organizing customer data and information by means of IT tools as a way for companies to successfully manage their relations with customers.

In sum, a first insight derived from the academic literature is that CRM was rooted within a B2C context. As stated by Gummesson (2004: 137) "the focus of CRM is most often consumer mass markets, where there is the need to handle millions of customers efficiently and where each customer is small".

4.3   Multiple perspectives on CRM

This section reviews the literature concerning CRM taking two key questions into account: First, which are the most common disciplinary domains, topics and perspectives in academic contributions about CRM? Second, which are the most commonly adopted definitions of CRM? By combining the answers to these two questions, we aim to prepare a better ground to address the purpose of our research by penetrating the nature and the conceptualizations of CRM, the key object of our investigation.

4.3.1   Key disciplinary domains, topics and perspectives in CRM-related research

Ngai (2005) and Kevork and Vrechopoulos (2009) show that CRM represents a blurred concept and a theme investigated by several managerial disciplines. Those authors carry out their respective literature reviews of academic contributions concerning CRM with the specific aim of classifying CRM and finding specific disciplines and frameworks addressing the phenomenon of CRM. Covering publications over a period of ten years (from 1992 to 2002), Ngai (2005) reaches one interesting, although not surprising finding: there seems to be substantial number of articles about CRM published in the field of Information Systems and Information Technology (IS/IT). Specifically, the articles appeared in the 1990s investigate CRM much more from its technological side, rather than considering its "strategic" contribution to companies' processes of managing customer relationships.

Kevork and Vrechopoulos (2009) conducted basically a follow-up study of Ngai (2005) aiming to provide an exhaustive literature review over the contributions on CRM appeared between 2000 and 2006, selected by means of a keyword analysis. From an analysis of about 400 articles they found that an important domain is e-CRM, namely the electronic support of customer relationships management. Moreover, a key emerging topic, consistent across these articles, is cultural, environmental and ethical issues related to the implementation of CRM, confirming also the findings of Ngai (2005) about the 1992–2002 articles.

Over time academic researchers dealing with CRM have studied this phenomenon from different perspectives, typically associated with certain disciplinary domains within management studies. Ngai (2005) finds that the majority of CRM-related articles published between 1992 and 2002 falls into the following functional perspectives: IT/IS, CRM (as a general category), sales, marketing and "service & support". As already mentioned, the IS/IT perspective dominates, followed by general discussions and managerial aspects of CRM. This "general" category contains all the articles that it was not possible to associate with any other specific functional domain, such as marketing, sales and "service and support". Surprisingly, Ngai (2005) identifies that one of the less investigated functional perspectives is represented by sales management. This is also in line with Landry, Todd and Arndt (2005), who analyzed articles from leading marketing and sales journals and found only 38 articles out of 253 taking a sales management perspective. This result therefore contradicts the apparent strong relevance of CRM for sales management (Landry, Todd and Arndt, 2005).

Representing the research area of marketing, Boulding et al. (2005) view CRM as clearly belonging to research in marketing. Several contributions (e.g., Lindgreen et al., 2006; Wilson, Clarke and Smith, 2007) focus on conceiving CRM as supporting managers in managing critical aspects of customer relationships. The contribution of Langerak and Verhoef (2003) also suggests that CRM should be viewed as the result of three aspects of marketing management, namely customer orientation, relationship marketing and database management. The marketing dimension usually highlighted in CRM is however not so much the acquisition of new customers, but especially the retention and handling of present customers in a profitable way. The technological component of CRM, based on the efficient use of IT systems, allows greater validity and speed in making key decisions concerning customers. For instance, the technology side of CRM facilitates the sales and marketing functions by providing more relevant and complete information about their present and potential customers (Swift, 2001).

A great deal of research analyzes CRM from a "life cycle" point of view, implying that CRM is an innovation being introduced in companies. An attempt to categorize the academic literature in terms of its focus on various phases of this life cycle has been carried out by Paulissen et al. (2007). They allocate more than 500 articles and conference papers about CRM to the following categories: adoption, acquisition, implementation, use, maintenance, evolution and retirement. An important result of that literature review is that a considerably larger number of contributions concern the study of the earlier phases of CRM compared to the latter phases. All in all, how CRM is implemented within companies seems to be one of the most common research topics concerning CRM, and this issue will be covered by section 4.4 and also by our empirical investigation in the case of Loccioni's CRM.

4.3.2   Definitions of CRM: An overview

Defining CRM has occupied researchers for almost two decades, proving it hard to find a solution accepted by all researchers. In fact, there is still no consensus within academia on a widely accepted definition of CRM, even if some definitions are more often cited by other researchers. Still, the problem remains that there is a plethora of such definitions, and some widely diverge from each other. One of the most cited scientific contributions that have reviewed CRM definitions is Zablah, Bellenger and Johnston (2004). These authors identified in the literature no less than 45 distinct definitions of CRM, which they categorized into five perspectives, namely CRM as a process, CRM as a strategy, CRM as a philosophy, CRM as a capability and CRM as a technology. The same authors also aim to clarify the conceptualization of CRM and propose the following definition: "CRM is an ongoing process that involves the development and leveraging of market intelligence for the purpose of building and maintaining a profit-maximizing portfolio of customer relationships" (Zablah, Bellenger and Johnston, 2004: 480).

One year after this definition was coined, Payne and Frow (2005) review and classify 30 definitions and, after having isolated the 12 considered most representative, they create a categorization based on the following perspectives: (1) CRM as a particular tactical technology solution; (2) CRM as a wide-ranging technology; and (3) CRM as a strategic tool. Payne and Frow (2005: 168) also define CRM as follows: "CRM is a strategic approach that is concerned with creating improved shareholder value through the development of appropriate relationships with key customers and customer segments . . . " These authors put an emphasis on positioning the CRM concept in the discipline of marketing, but the following parts of their reasoning on CRM expand the definition to include the importance of CRM implementation (technology) and point out that user-related issues are an area in which further research is advocated.

Next to these two widely cited works on CRM by Zablah, Bellenger and Johnston (2004) and Payne and Frow (2005), the META Group (2001) also provides a widely accepted definition of CRM. META Group (2001: 5) identifies three forms of CRM: operational, collaborative and analytical. Operational CRM involves "the business processes and technologies that can help improve the efficiency and accuracy of day-to-day customer-facing operations" and it refers to sales, marketing and service automation. Historically, operational CRM has been a major area of enterprise expenditure as companies develop call centers or adopt sales force automation systems (Payne and Frow, 2005). Collaborative CRM, instead, highlights the importance of IT support for enabling operational CRM. In other words, it comprises technologies such as e-mail and Web which allow companies to interact with customers. Like collaborative CRM the third form, analytical CRM, is also grounded on technologies, although they are applied for "providing analysis of customer data and behavioral patterns to improve business decisions". Even if the three forms of CRM as summarized by META Group have roots in a consultant company, they have been recognized as relevant also among academicians. For instance, the article by Payne and Frow (2005) takes this tripartite definition of CRM as a basis for their research. Tanner et al. (2005) also adopt the distinction between operational, collaborative and analytical CRM for developing a framework useful to be applied in sales-intensive organizations facing CRM implementation. The above definitions of CRM variably rely on three different dimensions or elements that characterize or compose CRM, namely IT, strategy and processes. These three dimensions can be conceived as the main concepts which researchers have used over the last decade for coping with the confusion in defining CRM still reigning over several academic fields.

One of the IT-inspired definitions of CRM is the one proposed by Bose (2002), who defines CRM as "an enterprise-wide integration of technologies working together, such as data warehouse, Web site, intranet/extranet, phone support system, accounting, sales, marketing and production". In a similar vein, Hedman and Kalling (2002) and Brady, Saren and Tzokas (2002) view CRM as a tool for IT-based marketing that helps companies manage customer relationships. IT has affected the way companies collect, store and share information about customers and competitors (Glazer, 1997), which clearly impacts the manner in which customer relationships can be managed. In addition, by means of IT solutions organizations can exploit large amounts of customer data in order to build useful customer knowledge (Greenberg, 2010). Closely related to the IT dimension is also the definition offered by Xu et al. (2002: 442) who state that "CRM is an information industry term for methodologies, software and usually Internet capabilities that help an enterprise manage customer relationships in an organized way".

Among the definitions of CRM as a strategy the one offered by Parvatiyar and Sheth (2001: 5) stands out. These authors define CRM as "A comprehensive strategy and process of acquiring, retaining and partnering with selective customers to create superior value for the company and customer". The authors also stress that only by integrating the traditional functions close to the customers such as marketing, sales, customer service and supply chain would it be possible for organizations to achieve success in delivering value to customers. Also in Buttle's definition (2004) of CRM strategy represents a central element, next to IT enablers: "the core business strategy that integrates internal processes and functions, and external networks, to create and deliver value to targeted customers at a profit. It is grounded on high-quality customer data and enabled by IT" (Buttle, 2004). In a similar vein, Mendoza et al. (2007) define CRM as "a strategic process, human factor and technology that produces the best relationship with customers to intensify value, satisfaction and customer loyalty".

One of the academic articles which investigates CRM from the process viewpoint is Srivastava, Shervani and Fahey (1999: 169). The authors consider CRM a business process that "addresses all aspects of identifying customers, creating customer knowledge, building customer relationships and shaping their perceptions of the organization and its products". Lambert (2010) also approaches CRM as a process and defines it as one of the sub-processes across the supply chain, which is further divided into two distinct levels: the strategic level, conducted under the responsibility of the management, and the operational level, in which the CRM process itself is implemented on a routine basis.

4.3.3   Summing up

The first part of our literature review helps identify some emergent patterns in the extant research about CRM. Even though the interest in CRM began to grow from the 1990s (Xu et al., 2002), it is between 2000 and 2005 that the researchers' attention to CRM as an attractive academic theme really became widespread. This is witnessed by the increasing number of articles about CRM published in management journals. In this respect, Wahlberg et al. (2009) analyze the distribution of CRM articles over the period from 1998 to 2006 and show that in 2004 alone there were almost 100 articles published having CRM as a "specific topic". There are at the moment no systematic reviews of the academic literature on CRM after 2007, but one can assume that the interest of academic researchers on CRM has remained substantial, and most likely has not decreased in the last 5–6 years. In the absence of detailed information about all the most recent topics and perspectives, we can point out that in the last few years CRM has been investigated for instance from the new perspective of "social media".

4.4   Implementing CRM

We have identified the implementation of CRM as one of the key topics in the literature about CRM. Therefore, this section conducts a literature review focusing on relevant articles concerning CRM implementation that have appeared in the last ten years. This topic is particularly interesting because it has been considered relevant for understanding the main reasons behind the high level of failures in CRM projects. Table 4.1 summarizes the theme, message and setting of selected contributions concerning CRM implementation. We have classified articles based on their main themes and we have identified three such themes: (1) the major problems and issues companies face when implementing CRM; (2) how companies should deal with CRM implementation; and (3) which are the significant factors that impact on CRM implementation? This review combines studies that present successful as well as unsuccessful CRM implementations, balancing the fact that most of the recent studies focus on the failure of CRM in delivering business benefits (Ang and Buttle, 2006).

One of the main issues identified in the literature is the lack of a shared strategy when companies implement CRM (Parvatiyar and Sheth, 2001; Bull, 2003). CRM should be accompanied by a holistic approach over the entire implementation process. Companies should embrace a wider vision when implementing it, instead of considering CRM only from either a technology or a final-user perspective. Boulding et al. (2005) argue that CRM projects fail in their implementation mostly due to an absence of coordination between technology and organizational aspects, including people's willingness to adopt IT. Even though there are only a few contributions covering this topic, the choice between a system built in-house and an outsourced one plays an important role in the implementation of CRM systems, as pointed out by Bull (2003). There is a trade-off when coping with complex decisions between CRM sourcing and in-house development. For instance, sourcing CRM can enhance complexity since companies have to manage relationships with software vendors; but on the other hand, developing a company's own CRM system requires having competences and knowledge enough to devise a sophisticated IT solution, which are not easily found in most organizations. In making a choice between internally developed and externally sourced CRM systems, key elements to take into account are the status of the company's IT capabilities, its commitment toward new investments in IT, and a comparison between the costs of the two implementation options, which can be quite different. Alternatively

Table 4.1 Literature contributions on CRM implementation

Authors and year	Theme	Main message	Setting	Type of research
Parvatiyar and Sheth, 2001	CRM implementation issues	CRM should not be viewed as a software implementation process; it requires strategy and process to make it successful.	Not specified	Conceptual
Bull, 2003	CRM implementation issues	CRM is a holistic and complex strategy that requires business processes and integrated systems. Companies should not underestimate choices of sourcing the system.	B2B	Empirical
Boulding et al., 2005	CRM implementation issues	Effective CRM implementation requires coordination of channels, technologies, customers and employees.	Not specified	Conceptual
Meadows and Dibb, 2012	CRM implementation issues	There are specific implementation issues for CRM in relation to the company's staff, the company itself, the customers and the technology.	B2C	Empirical
Reinartz, Krafft and Hoyer, 2004	How to implement CRM	CRM programs require more than just a technology. The implementation of CRM requires a strong people-related component.	B2C	Empirical
Finnegan and Currie, 2010	How to implement CRM	Companies should implement CRM by applying a multi-dimensional perspective based on people, process, culture and technology.	B2B and B2C	Empirical

Ahearne et al., 2012	How to implement CRM	Implementing CRM entails pursuing a strategy. The complexity of the "selling environment" influences top-down or bottom-up strategy for CRM implementation.	B2B	Conceptual
Hart et al., 2004	Factors influencing CRM implementation	The effect of "experience" and "time" influences the overall CRM implementation process.	B2B	Empirical
Zablah, Bellenger and Johnston, 2004	Factors influencing CRM implementation	End-user acceptance of CRM depends on the firm's ability to align business processes with the technology behind CRM.	Not specified	Conceptual
Finnegan and Willcocks, 2007	Factors influencing CRM implementation	"Micro-level" mechanisms are relevant for CRM implementation such as, non-codified knowledge and psychological contracts.	B2B and B2C	Empirical
Alshawi, Missi and Irani, 2011	Factors influencing CRM implementation	Organizational factors (e.g., ICT skills, organizational size), technical factors (e.g., ICT infrastructure, software selection) and data quality factors (customer data quality, structure and data classification).	B2B and B2C	Empirical
Steel, Dubelaar and Ewing, 2013 (in press)	Factors influencing CRM implementation	The impact of the "context" conceived as culture, organizational structure, industry norms, customer type and relationship expectations of customers.	B2B and B2C	Empirical

companies might prefer to supplement in-house capabilities with external experts; a typical example is hiring consultants to help in-house teams implement CRM.

Another central theme emerging from our literature review is how CRM should be implemented. Researchers have been dealing with this topic for over a decade and there is a vast number of contributions on it. However, our point here is that there is not a common and clearly recognized path in the literature suggesting how companies should successfully implement CRM. We agree with Reinartz, Krafft and Hoyer (2004), who pointed out that how to implement a CRM system largely depends on the firms' characteristics. Therefore, there is no preconceived "recipe" to make the implementation of CRM successful. Still, there appears to be a consensus in the literature that the implementation of CRM depends on a blend of factors such as people, process, culture and technology (Chen and Popovich, 2003; Finnegan and Currie, 2010). The central role played by users is often recognized as a fundamental aspect to deal with: as showed by an empirical-based research by Avlonitis and Panagopoulos (2005), users such as salespeople should take part in the implementation process and managers must focus on spreading within the organization knowledge about the benefits of CRM. Alternatively, CRM implementation can be organized as a series of small CRM projects, as highlighted by Kumar and Reinartz (2012): firms should pay attention to "operational" CRM projects that enable the company to meet technical and functional requirements of CRM strategy, and also to "analytical" projects aimed at obtaining a good understanding of the customers' needs.

Turning to the main factors influencing CRM implementation, we found in the literature a particular attention to the following ones: CRM context (Steel, Dubelaar and Ewing, 2013); the ability of firms and their top management to show to the users a high level of commitment (Zablah, Bellenger and Johnston 2004); time and level of experience with ICT (Hart et al., 2004); and quality of data and type of IT infrastructure (Alshawi, Missi and Irani, 2011), as well as some "hidden" factors at a micro level (Finnegan and Willcocks, 2007). More precisely, these latter authors stress that managers struggling with CRM implementation have to focus much more on understanding the end user's perceptions on CRM, which also entails building reciprocal trust and commitment between proponents of CRM and end users. In particular, Finnegan and Willcocks (2007) show that there are some specific psychological mechanisms that influence CRM implementation.

In a similar way, Homburg, Workman and Jensen (2000) posit that CRM implementation affects the organization in terms of people's ways of working, which could create resistance in the adoption process. For instance, sharing customer information within the organization, which constitutes one of the potentially positive effects of CRM, is not always accepted by salespeople, who often see in CRM systems the risk of losing control of the relationship with a key customer. A reason for this is that superior managers can monitor and control each piece of information in the relationship. Moreover, sales personnel indicate that CRM is a time-consuming tool mainly for data input activities and that the efforts of putting information in the system are not balanced by the output received back. Therefore, employee resistance is a risk associated with CRM implementation (Xu et al., 2002). CRM initiatives will be successful only if employees perceive the system as useful in organizing activities and resources to handle customer relationships, and if they become committed to the system. In this respect, marketing capabilities have been held to play an important facilitating role (Chang, Park and Chaiy, 2010). An empirical study among banks by Shum, Bove and Auh (2008) finds a correlation between employees' commitment to the CRM initiative (in terms of their willingness to the change) and the positive outcomes of a bank's performance. While the users' time and level of experience is important to enable CRM implementation, according to Hart et al. (2004), engaging consultants and suppliers can further enhance the level of experience on the CRM practice making less problematic the process of implementation.

An intriguing question for both academicians and practitioners concerns the benefits of investing in CRM systems. The above literature review shows how companies deal with barriers when implementing CRM, which appears to be a painful and demanding process, with several ramifications from strategy to the entire organization. Therefore, why should company still invest in CRM? In this regard, there are several contributions that illustrate, also from a practical point of view, what companies can gain from CRM projects.

While resistance to new technology is one of the major issues hindering the implementation of CRM (Zablah, Bellenger and Johnston, 2004), research shows that CRM can provide important advantages, such as better firm performance when managers focus on maximizing customer value (Ryals, 2005). According to Berkley and Gupta (1994), CRM can improve customer-service reliability and service monitoring, while Mithas, Krishan and Fornell (2005) state that companies implement

CRM systems in order to use customer information within the organization more efficiently. In this respect, Salojärvi, Sainio and Tarkiainen (2010) state that investments in CRM lead to a more efficient use of customer knowledge. Since CRM software has the potential to facilitate the process of gathering customer data, these IT tools can be useful for companies in providing customized products to the market (Rigby, Reichfeld and Scheffer, 2002). Using a tool such as CRM to assist the management of customer relationships is particularly important when relationships evolve (Lindgreen et al., 2006). According to a study by Ata and Toker (2012) in a B2B context, CRM adoption has a positive effect both on customer satisfaction and organizational performance. Another benefit that companies might receive from CRM implementation concerns the intra-organizational side: CRM can aid in breaking down the barriers between the departments, by playing the "integrator roles" around a customer management strategy (Ingram, LaForge and Leigh, 2002).

4.4.1   A note on the technology side of CRM implementation

Even though technology is just one side of CRM implementation and deployment, in this section we briefly discuss aspects related to the "hardware" side of CRM, in terms of the IT tools that need to be assembled to constitute the backbone of CRM systems. A technology-based view of CRM enables understanding of why technology can help companies conduct their customer relationship management. Darrell, Reicheld and Schefter (2002) point out that new technology allows the carrying out of several combined activities such as: (1) analyzing customer data; (2) conducting marketing communications; (3) keeping track of relevant customers' transactions; (4) providing information to employees in charge of customer contact; (5) distributing customer knowledge to all relevant employees; and (6) tracking customers' service satisfaction levels.

As pointed out by Bose (2002), from an IT point of view CRM revolves around an integration of technologies such as databases, business intelligence systems (e.g., data warehousing and data mining), websites, intranet, extranet and phone support systems. On a similar vein, Payne and Frow (2005) state that CRM is composed of two major IT elements: "data repositories", collecting information on customers, and a set of tools that he defines as "applications" that enable interacting with customers. In particular, databases are electronic repositories for storing data about customers gathered from several sources such as sales forces, customers themselves and ERP systems.

According to Winer (2001), a customer database constitutes a pivotal component of CRM systems and it should ideally contain information concerning the following:

- *Transactions*: referring to purchase history in terms of price paid and delivery date of goods.
- *Customer contacts*: the database should contain information regarding how, when and why the supplier gets in contact with customers. This means mapping all the contact points with customers and reporting them in the system recording the contents and medium of interactions (phone calls, e-mails, sales visits, etc.).
- *Descriptive information*: referring to all the features of the customer (e.g., size, locations, areas of operations) that can be of interest for making decisions and customer analysis.
- *Response to marketing stimuli*: the database should also contain a section where customers' responses to, for instance, an offer or other business propositions are recorded.

Databases should not only be storages of data, but they must also allow users to make analyses. Moreover, in order to be really useful, databases should be kept updated as much as possible. As reported by Peppers and Rogers (2004), customer databases need to be connected with other IT tools, such as websites and call centers' telephony systems, in order to capture real time data from customers. The logic that organizes the different databases depends on elements such as the architecture of the information systems that a company has already installed (Davenport, 2000). Other factors such as investment, corporate culture and firm size also influence how the different databases inside one company are connected to customer databases (see e.g., Baraldi, 2003). In fact, several companies usually have more than one database, and these are not connected to each other: for instance, the various functions such as marketing, sales and administration might have their own databases, each one built for specific purposes. The so called "business intelligence systems" allow the extracting and aggregating of data and information contained in a centralized data warehouse, which is typically created by bringing together the disparate databases and data sources that companies have. Business intelligence systems apply data mining techniques, that is, computer applications capable of tracking and finding relevant data, in order to support certain business processes and decisions (Hill and Scott, 2004). For instance, data contained in databases are usually analyzed to obtain customer profiles or to promote customer satisfaction activities, or to create useful knowledge about the customer that facilitates targeted marketing strategies, such as developing an offering in line with the customer's needs (Xu and Walton, 2005).

4.5 Taking a B2B perspective on CRM

As the overall purpose of this book is investigating the impact of CRM on a company operating on an industrial market, it is useful to examine the role and patterns of use of CRM within the context of industrial or B2B marketing. In Chapter 2, the nature of business relationships has been discussed, examining their substance (Håkansson and Snehota, 1995) and their role of connecting actors, activities and resources within a network context (Ibid). We highlighted the importance of managing customer relationships in an efficient way as a priority for B2B companies. Accompanying the increased importance of IT for such companies, in recent years CRM has gained space also in B2B settings. Recently, CRM has become important also for B2B companies as witnessed by the increasing investments they are making in CRM applications (Zablah, Bellenger and Johnston, 2004). However, due to the particular nature of business (B2B) relationships and of business markets, often defined as network-like structures (Snehota, 1990), CRM needs to be conceived differently compared to typical consumer markets, that is, the usual B2C setting for which CRM was originally conceived. In a B2B context, CRM needs to embrace the complexity of relationships as well as the interdependences between actors. As pointed out also by Venkatesan, Kumar and Ravishanker (2007), adapting CRM models taken from B2C settings might be problematic since the complex and interacted decision processes in B2B relationships need special consideration. Therefore the implementation, adoption and utilization of CRM have to be conceived in relation to the typology of customer relationships that the company aims to handle by means of the CRM system (Lindgreen et al., 2006; Steel, Dubelaar and Ewing, 2013). Also Zablah et al. (2012) show that in a B2B setting, the adoption of CRM depends on its impact on different customers: one important variable for understanding the adoption, use and effects of CRM in this respect is represented by the customer's size. The use of CRM has positive effects on the perceptions of large accounts while smaller customers do not perceive any positive effect.

Academic researchers have also shown a growing interest in investigating CRM as applied within industrial markets. According to LaPlaca and Katrichis (2009), CRM as a research topic in B2B settings has grown considerably. Focusing on the specialized journal *Industrial Marketing Management*, these authors identify Hartley (1976) as one of the earliest CRM articles about industrial customers and then they point that "From this beginning of a single article in 1976, research in industrial CRM has grown to as many as 34 articles published [in *Industrial Marketing Management*] between 2004 and 2006" (LaPlaca and Katrichis, 2009: 13). While the early article by Hartley (1976) investigates the use of customer data by industrial companies in order to enhance customer profitability and market penetration the following research by B2B researchers has expanded the traditional concepts and focus of CRM. For instance, a special issue of *Industrial Marketing Management* in 2004 was dedicated to "Customer Relationship Management" and it challenges the traditional CRM concepts by taking a value-network perspective on it (Ehret, 2004).

4.5.1 Central research issues on CRM in a B2B setting

An important topic that emerges from the literature is related to the contribution of CRM to creating customer knowledge and the consequent use of this knowledge for managing customer relationships. Customer knowledge refers to the creation of new knowledge based on information provided by customers. This knowledge should be subsequently disseminated within the organization and possibly incorporated into products or services (Nonaka, 1991). The sources of customer knowledge can be identified in personal interactions with customers, or daily transactions with them. Customer knowledge can be described in terms of a process that collects knowledge during the interaction with customers. In essence, it is the mutual interaction between supplier and customer that allows the two parties to exchange streams of information and learn from each other: by interacting with the supplier the customer gains knowledge to enhance its decision-making process, while the supplier can improve its knowledge about the customer as a way to increase the level of service offered or to develop a new product.

Stein and Smith (2009) point out that CRM systems can help an organization overview external changes, as visible through the lens of customers' behavior. In fact CRM systems typically combine several information sources into one integrated database or data warehouse: transaction data and account plans, the company's marketing programs (and single customers' reactions to them) and competitive and market information (Ibid). When analyzed from a historical perspective, such data can help obtain an overview of the changes going on in the external environment.

A study by Campbell (2003) sheds light on the importance of having specific competences when dealing with the creation, adoption and use of customer knowledge by means of CRM. Moreover, creating and developing reliable and functional customer knowledge depends on several factors, such as the availability of rich and updated information: this is an important factor that affects the outcome of CRM efforts and often CRM fails because of the sheer complexity of the issues related to the quality of customer data (Kaila and Goldman, 2006). Therefore, it is not surprising that there is a strong connection between data quality and successful use of CRM, since one of the cornerstones of CRM is to deliver to users reliable information for managing customer relationships. A study by Reid and Catterall (2005) points out that in order to avoid problems with data quality it is necessary to implement a "data management strategy" from the beginning of the CRM implementation process. In this respect these authors suggest completing the following steps: (1) categorizing data sources; (2) organizing an assessment of data quality aimed at identifying guidelines for data quality; (3) carrying out data cleaning to give consistency to the data; and (4) establishing organizational processes in order to improve staff skills when they interact with data.

In a recent contribution, Stein, Smith and Lancioni (2013) examine whether companies adopting CRM programs are effectively using data from CRM systems for decision-making. According to their research, even if there is a strong potential for companies to employ CRM data in making key customer-related decisions, only a few companies make a consistent use of it. An interesting result is that a good and profitable utilization of information depends on the education of the people who input/generate data and of the users who apply the resulting customer knowledge to making decisions. The specific technology on which a given CRM is based plays a secondary role in this respect: it is the capability of managers of reading through the data that is much more relevant. Interestingly, the more reliable and "cleaned" the data are, the more users are willing to adopt them for managing their relationships.

Another relevant topic in the literature concerns the effects of CRM on business relationships and, at a more general level, on the organization's performance. Richard, Thirkell and Huff (2007) carry out a qualitative investigation among ten private sector organizations aimed at investigating whether CRM impacts on their customer relationships. Their results shows that, since personal communication represents the most critical element in B2B relationships, CRM can improve customer relationships by centralizing customer-specific information, so that it will be available to several managers involved in that customer relationship, and by prompting timely communications to the customer. The potential positive impact on business relationships of CRM is also recognized by Steel, Dubelaar and Ewing (2013), who state that CRM can be structured as a tool to organize and simplify the typical concerns with managing the large amounts of information needed by B2B companies to support efficiently their highly customized interactions with customers.

As for the impact of CRM on organizational performance, Keramati, Mehrabi and Mojir (2010) provide a summary of the most significant contributions. For instance, Ata and Toker (2012) analyze empirically 113 B2B companies and discover that CRM affected positively their organizational performance. These authors conceive organizational performance in terms of two elements: (1) marketing performance, and namely how well an organization achieves its market goals (e.g., market share); and (2) financial performance, expressed as profitability. Another relevant measure of performance concerns sales performance: the empirical study by Rodriguez and Honeycutt (2011) shows that CRM positively affects sales performance, conceived as performance both in relation to customers (i.e., the ability of a salesman to build long-term customer relationships) and in the effectiveness of the sales process (i.e., the ability of sales departments to reach outcomes in the sales process). At organizational level, another conclusion of the study by Rodriguez and Honeycutt (2011) is that CRM can increase the collaboration between salespersons since it allows customer knowledge to be spread throughout organizations.

4.6 Summary

This chapter reviewed the origins, the various definitions and the current research topics concerning CRM. After its origin in consumer-based relationship marketing, especially in the areas of services, the concept and practice of CRM has been matched with IT tools that enable companies to make more efficient the collection, elaboration and diffusion of customer data. The finding of technical solutions capable of handling massive amounts of complex customer information seemed to have greatly improved the possibilities of concretely applying CRM as a philosophy, a strategy and a process aiming at exploiting customer knowledge to improve customer relationships (according to some of the established definitions of CRM).

However, things do not seem to work so easily, as witnessed by the troubles typically afflicting CRM implementation projects: despite the *ideal* match between IT tools and the CRM philosophy posited by several definition of CRM, it soon became clear that the *actual* combination of IT solutions with CRM principles has to be achieved within specific organizational contexts, where several barriers to CRM adoption can emerge. The very concept of "CRM implementation" therefore became essential, also as a way to handle these barriers. The barriers encountered during the implementation of CRM systems include for instance users' resistance due to loss of control, perceptions of being monitored, low perceived quality of customer data, low perceived benefits of the CRM system in relation to the sacrifices it requires, lack of IT experience or negative experiences with IT. And the list could be made even longer. These organizational aspects are important and need to be considered when addressing the effects of CRM on customer relationships: in fact, a CRM system can produce its effects only if it is not only implemented but also daily utilized, that is, "embedded" in the host organizations, a topic to which we turn in Chapter 5. Finally, as a way to prepare the ground for our empirical investigation of CRM in a company operating on an industrial market, this chapter also discussed CRM in B2B settings, where we can expect that CRM implementation and use is even more complex than in general.

5
Conceptualizing CRM as an Interacting Resource

This chapter reconnects directly to Chapter 3, where we discussed IT from an organizational point of view and identified the factors that favor the embedding of IT systems in organizations. This chapter now applies those concepts to CRM systems, viewed as specific types of IT systems, but also expands the organizational perspective on IT to embrace inter-organizational effects. After introducing a new view of CRM as a socio-technical resource interacting with other resources (Section 5.1), this chapter presents the "resource interaction" perspective, an alternative approach to investigating innovation and strategy, as well as technology and business development (Section 5.2). The main analytical model belonging to this perspective, the 4Rs model, is introduced in Section 5.3, paving the way for understanding the phenomenon of "resource embeddedness" (Section 5.4). The chapter continues by applying the "resource interaction" perspective to CRM (Section 5.5.), which will help us frame the intra- and inter-organizational effects deriving from the embedding of CRM systems (Section 5.6).

5.1 Introduction

In order to address our research purpose, namely understanding the intra- and inter-organizational effects of CRM, we have chosen to treat CRM as a socio-technical resource, which can be analyzed within the frame of the resource interaction perspective and the so-called 4Rs model developed by IMP researchers (Baraldi and Bocconcelli, 2001; Håkansson and Waluszewski, 2002). This perspective has been applied to IT systems by Baraldi and Waluszewski (2005), who analyze one of IKEA's major IT systems for product information administration. Following this approach, CRM systems, like any other IT system, can be viewed as an information-handling facility, which processes data into information made available to users (Baraldi, 2003: 33). However, such a facility cannot operate in a vacuum, but needs to be connected to other resources, both technical and, especially, social ones, in order to produce its effects.

More precisely, we envisage a CRM system as a device interacting with people who put data into it to obtain processed information applicable to handle customer relationships. Thus, a CRM system interplays with other resources involved in managerial tasks, such as information, people, business relationships and other IT systems. The connections between the CRM system and the other technical as well as organizational resources which are necessary for it to produce its effects indicate the "embeddedness" of the IT tool under investigation (Baraldi, 2003). This chapter accordingly provides an alternative conceptualization of CRM, which enables a new understanding of the role, effects, challenges and possibilities of CRM systems as they are embedded in complex industrial networks. The specific way in which the interaction among resources embed a CRM system also defines the effects of the system both at intra- and at inter- organizational level.

5.2   Toward an interactive perspective on resources

The importance and the complexity of resources are broadly recognized within management studies. Researchers and practitioners deal with challenging issues such as the definition of the value of resources, how single resources affect the economic system, how resources can be combined for achieving specific purposes and how resources develop over time. There is accordingly a set of central questions related to resources, such as: what is a resource? How can resources be classified? Why do companies need to control resources? How can we understand resource dynamics?

Management scholars agree on the importance of resources in providing the foundations for businesses and their related processes, although the definitions of what is a resource vary greatly. In the field of strategic management, the Resource-Based View (RBV) (Wernerfelt, 1984; Barney, 1991; Grant, 1991) emerged as a mainstream paradigm at the beginning of the 1990s. The RBV literature considers the firm as a bundle of resources, and defines a resource as "anything which could be thought of as a strength or weakness of a given firm ... examples of resources are brand names, in-house knowledge of technology, employment of skilled personnel, trade contacts, machinery, efficient procedures, capital, etc."

(Wernerfelt, 1984: 172). Barney (1991) divided resources into three main groups: (1) physical capital resources – plants, machineries, geographical location, access to raw materials; (2) human capital resources – training, experience, judgment, intelligence, relationships of workers; and (3) organizational capital resources – the formal reporting structure, planning, controlling and coordinating systems of the firm.

The RBV relies on the assumption that resources are the building blocks of sustained competitive advantage, which according to this view rests on two pillars: resources are heterogeneously distributed across firms and resources' transfer is costly. According to the RBV companies hold all capabilities for managing properly their resources in order to compete on the market. Authors like Barney (1986; 1991) focus on the characteristics of a firm's resources and provide a framework that specifies under which conditions resources provide a competitive advantage to firms. In this respect, Barney (1991) states that, in order to create a competitive advantage, resources must be rare (i.e., they are not widely spread among companies), valuable (i.e., contribute to firm efficiency), not imitable (i.e., competitors cannot replicate them) and not substitutable (i.e., each resource should be specific for reaching a particular purpose).

Despite the extensive use of the RBV in strategic management, this view is less useful for understanding the dynamics of resources, namely their development, especially when a new resource, such as a CRM system, needs to be included in a certain context populated by other resources. Combining old and new resources is in fact a topic which the RBV has not directly addressed, as its focus is on the single firm's control of resources capable of providing competitive advantages on the market. According to the RBV, the value of resources derives from their rarity and uniqueness. In our investigation of the effects of CRM systems we are instead concerned with another type of value of this type of resource, namely the value deriving from its use. Therefore, the "resource interaction" perspective (Håkansson and Waluszewski, 2002; Baraldi, Gressetvold and Harrison, 2012) is a more appropriate research tool for our purpose, because it focuses specifically on combinations of resources and their development and it reckons that the value of a resource derives from its use and combination with other resources. We accordingly apply the resource interaction perspective as our theoretical and analytical frame to discuss the development, implementation, use and effects of CRM.

But in order to understand resource interactions, one needs first to become familiar with the tenets of the IMP approach as far as resources are concerned.[1] In their conceptualizations of resources, IMP researchers rely on the concept of resource heterogeneity (Penrose, 1959), constituting the most important assumption related to the resource layer of business networks (see Chapter 2). That resources are heterogeneous means that their economic value depends not so much on their uniqueness or scarcity, but much more on the interaction process in which they take part: any resource element assumes a value only if it is combined with others, thus obtaining different features depending on the resources they are closely interacting with. The features of resources (technical, social, economical) are activated when resources interact with each other. The interaction process, typically occurring across the boundaries of one or more organizations, allows combination of resources which are typically accompanied by adaptations, that is, modifications, for instance in a component supplied by a company so that it can better fit the manufacturing process of a customer. These adaptations are important because they create imprints on the product or other resources (Håkansson and Waluszewski, 2002: 35), with the consequence that it becomes more difficult to combine again the same product or resources with other ones.

If the usefulness of a resource depends on how and with which resources it is combined (Håkansson and Snehota, 1995), understanding how resource combinations occur represents a central issue. Moreover, resource combinations become central because they can influence firms' performances, more than the single resources they control. However, contrary to the RBV, the IMP approach stresses that these combinations may occur both at intra-organizational level (within a company) and especially at inter-organizational level (between resources belonging to different companies). The resources relevant for any business are dispersed across complex inter-organizational networks, and firms therefore need to rely on counterparts for accessing them: therefore, the mechanisms of resource combination across firms' boundaries assume high relevance. In fact, resources exist simultaneously in different contexts; therefore no company controls all the resources they need (Araujo, Dubois and Gadde, 1999). It is important to stress this "incompleteness" of firms, because it means that only by interacting with other organizations, can companies change, recombine, develop and use resources to achieve their goals and develop (Håkansson, 1982). On the other hand, this context-dependent nature of resources also typically creates tensions between actors because companies have their own, often conflicting, agendas.

5.3   Analyzing resource interaction: The 4Rs model

Within the IMP approach, and more precisely within the ARA model (see Chapter 2), resources are one of the three elements forming the substance of business relationships and networks, the other two being actors and activities (Håkansson and Snehota, 1995). Gressetvold (2001) reviews how IMP scholars have conceived resources over years and identifies an early categorization of resources proposed by Håkansson (1987) into three types: physical, financial and human resources. Another classification is the one presented by Håkansson and Waluszewski (2007), who distinguish between two types of resources, material and intellectual ones. The same authors later provide the classification of resources into four types (Håkansson and Waluszewski, 2002), which came to be known as the 4Rs model. This model matches our overall aim of conceptualizing CRM as a socio-technical resource. In fact, in order to investigate how a company has developed and embedded a CRM system requires analyzing the patterns of resource combinations and interactions around the system itself: such an analysis needs to be performed using a framework that can capture how resources are combined and interfaced, which is precisely what the 4Rs model is for. Further, the 4Rs model rests on the IMP assumption that the single company does not itself possess all the resources it needs to pursue its goals, but is dependent on other counterparts providing them, who in turn also need resources to achieve their own goals.

The 4Rs model is an analytical tool (Baraldi and Bocconcelli, 2001; Wedin, 2001; Håkansson and Waluszewski, 2002) that enables us first to categorize resources and second to analyze their interactions by means of the particular concept of resource interface. The model divides resources into four categories: products and facilities, which are of physical and technical character, and business/organizational units and business relationships, which are of social and organizational character.

> *Products*: these represent any kind of artifact and are the result of producer–user interactions. Products include, for instance, raw materials, components, work in progress or final goods. They can be simple or very complex in terms of their inner construction. Products are developed in relation to other products as well as other resources: "product development takes place through interaction across all four types of resources, as organizational units make use

of inter-organizational relationships as well as facilities throughout such processes" (Baraldi, Gressetvold and Harrison, 2012: 268).

Facilities: these include all types of tools and equipment used for producing or otherwise adding value to goods. Like products, facilities are also artifacts which have the capability of transforming products or information. Facilities include machinery, manufacturing plants, logistic systems, warehouses and of course IT systems and tools. The latter represent facilities that process information. Facilities often operate in close connections with other facilities, inside the same firm or at suppliers or customers, within highly interdependent production systems.

Business (or organizational) units: these are immaterial resources representing restricted organizational groups within firms. The key features of business units are their working routines, identity, reputation, competence, personnel, organizational structure and financials. A firm is typically composed of several business units, such as divisions or functional groups (e.g., marketing or production plant X). Business units are capable of creating, processing, receiving and sending information, both within and outside their "mother organization", that is, both at intra- and inter-organizational level.

Business relationships: as discussed in Chapter 2, relationships emerge out of repeated interactions between suppliers and customers and assume a substance composed of resource ties, activity links and actor bonds (Håkansson and Snehota, 1995). Business relationships are not only the result of interactions between business units, but they also assume a value for the involved companies and can accordingly be viewed as resources on their own. Like all other resources they are in fact utilized for achieving goals and they play a critical role in information exchange. The peculiarity and value of this kind of resource among the others is also stressed by Håkansson and Snehota (1995: 138): "relationships are a peculiar type of resource as they cannot be controlled by any single party in isolation but are controlled jointly by the parties involved". Gadde and Håkansson (2008) explore the role of business relationships in combining resources and stress that relationships connect resources found at several firms and help generate increased value for such resources as time passes.

This 4Rs model is particularly useful for investigating changes at technical and organizational level as well as the economic consequences of those changes. For instance, several studies using this model analyze the embedding of new technology in existing resource structures (see e.g., Baraldi, Gregori and Perna, 2011). This type of research issue is very similar to the one faced in this book, which is concerned with the embedding of a new CRM system in a using organization, as well as with its internal and external effects.

Analyzing resources by means of the 4Rs model is also useful for two more reasons: firstly, the time dimension is taken into consideration as the model views resources not as static elements, but considers how they change over time; secondly, the model delves into how the combinations and recombinations of resources creates and relies on specific resource interfaces. According to Araujo, Dubois and Gadde (1999: 499) resource interfaces are "concerned with the technical and organizational interdependences that arise when the resource bases of buyer and supplier are connected through exchange activities." The concept of resource interfaces is a key element in the 4Rs model and it indicates how and how much two resources affect each other (Håkansson and Waluszewski, 2002: 190–200). Wedin (2001) points out that resource interfaces are an area where different resources met and affect each other. Stated otherwise, resource interfaces are the contact points and interconnections between two or more resources (Dubois and Araujo, 2006). Along such contact points, which can be more or less deeply adapted, two or more resources mutually define each other's features such as costs, weight, durability, speed, usability and environmental friendliness. (Baraldi, 2003: 17–18; Baraldi, Gressetvold and Harrison, 2012).

Resource interfaces can be of technical or social/organizational character, depending on the type of resources being combined. Technical and social resource interfaces can be identified, for example, during the development of an IT system: different products and components (hardware, software and other devices) have to be connected with each other, giving rise to several technical interfaces; but, at the same time, in order to make the IT system functional, valuable and usable individuals or groups of individuals also need to be connected and coordinate their activities (for instance the work of software with that of hardware developers, or training sessions for users), giving rise to social/organizational interfaces between these actors. A third type of interface is proposed by Baraldi and Strömsten (2006), who add mixed interfaces indicating the connection between social and technical resources: for instance, the contact point between a product and a business unit, indicating how dependent that unit is on a specific product or how the product has been modified to fit that specific unit.

During the process of resource combination the interfaces that emerge create interdependencies among companies, both at organizational and technical levels. These resource combinations are moreover characterized by diversity and entail a very large number of possibilities (Dubois and Håkansson, 2000: 6–7): "there are interdependencies between products, facilities, between products and facilities, between business units, between business relationships, between business units and relationships". For instance, Dubois and Araujo (2006) analyze the product development of a new truck by Swedish Scania and the role of one of its suppliers that developed an essential component. These authors analyze technical and organizational interfaces at a network level and find that some key business relationships can be essential for coordinating unexpected interfaces as they emerge in the network.

Why do resource interfaces assume importance when we are investigating a phenomenon such as the implementation, use and effects of a CRM system? Tracing these interfaces enables understanding of the complex mechanisms by which several other resources, both technical/physical and social/organizational, need to be combined with and around the CRM system in order to allow it to produce its effects (cf. Baraldi and Waluszewski, 2005). One can also understand how these resources affect the CRM system and each other in ways that create possibilities or barriers for the adoption of the CRM system, like that of any other innovation.

Box 5.1 summarizes a set of propositions about resources as derived from the works of several IMP scholars. These six propositions are also related to each other.

Box 5.1   Interaction and resources: Key propositions

Håkansson et al. (2009) develop six propositions addressing the process of resource interaction. These propositions are the result of empirical studies carried out by analyzing the resource interaction processes in several areas: product development, innovation, logistics, distribution, supply chain and so on.

1) *The value of a resource is dependent on its connections to other resources*: Moran and Ghoshal (1999) pointed out that the creation of value is a process that involves the use of resources. The value of a specific resource arises from knowledge about what someone can do with it in combination with other resources (Håkansson and Snehota, 1995). As a consequence it is difficult to forecast

how much value might be obtained from resource interaction, since the value will depend also on the type of interfaces emerging between the resources involved. This value in fact changes depending on how the resources are specifically combined. A certain sort of timber can be highly valuable when used in a certain pulping process at a particular factory, but create problems in another one.

2) *A resource changes and develops specific characteristics over time*: the time dimension is an important element when analyzing resource interaction. It is argued that companies can to a certain extent exploit their past achievements, for instance in product development, to influence the way they combine new resources. In fact, the effect of previous interactions influences how each resource can be used. This influence might hinder or make possible new resource combinations.

3) *Every resource is embedded in a multidimensional context*: resources exist in and are related simultaneously to different contexts, where they can be combined in many different ways. Resource combinations accordingly have a different impact in these various contexts. The embedding of resources in multidimensional contexts derives also from the fact that the "resources a company provides or uses are tied directly to those with which the company has direct relationships and also to those that are indirectly connected" (Håkansson and Snehota, 1995: 138).

4) *All changes of a resource create tensions*: the fact that firms depend upon resources owned by others can create not only opportunities for developing products, but it can also lead to contrasts. These contrasts are mostly linked to changes in resource combinations that cause variations in the distribution of economic value among the involved actors.

5) *The intensity of interaction influences the effects of a change in a resource*: changes in resource combinations happen because of interactions between resource providers and users. The intensity of these interactions both makes more changes possible and amplifies their effects. In other words, the higher the intensity of interaction the higher the effects of a specific change in a resource will be.

6) *The broadness of interaction influences the number of resources affected by a change in a resource*: broadness is interpreted here

> as the number of participants (actors) in the interaction process. While involving explicitly the resources of more actors, broader interactions also lead to more consistent effects on resource combinations.

5.4   Resource embeddedness

In order to shed light on such development processes as the introduction of new technologies, especially when they unfold across firms' boundaries, it is particularly important to investigate the context where such processes take place. Moreover, Pettigrew (1992) stresses that an understanding of the context is also necessary when it comes to organizational changes. Expressed in the vocabulary of the resource interaction perspective and the 4Rs model, focusing on the context of a resource or of a resource combination introduces the concept of resource embeddedness (Håkansson and Waluszewski, 2002: 225–226). A specific combination of resources and their use take place or indeed are tied up into a larger structure of resources, which eventually embeds the resources in focus, creating both constraints and possibilities for their combination and use. The concept of embeddedness suggests that each resource is surrounded by others and it is placed in a sort of "interaction space" (Baraldi, 2003: 17–18). For instance, when a new technology is developed it typically results from changing a set of resource combinations, but in order to become eventually a solution being utilized on a regular basis it will need to become embedded within the network, at technical, social and economic level. While embeddedness is a structural concept that can be explicated by looking at the *existing* resource interfaces around a resources, the process of embedding of a new solution into a specific network corresponds to the creation of *new* interfaces between the solution and the surrounding resources (Baraldi, Gregori and Perna, 2011).

Embeddedness depends for instance on the actors participating in a business exchange, the products and technologies exchanged, the problems to be handled and the overall network development (Halinen and Törnroos, 1998). Therefore, in order to favor the embedding process of a new product or of a facility (e.g., of an IT system) many trade-offs as well as balancing acts between conflicting resource combinations will be necessary. At a particular point in time each resource combination will embrace other internal and/or external resources, which can create different or even opposing pressures on it. In terms of the concept of resource interface discussed above, a single resource can be involved in several interfaces at the same time, depending on the resource combinations of which it becomes part.

The notion of embeddedness also enables us to explain the degree of difficulty in combining certain resources: Pardo (2012) analyzes how a resource combines and recombines with other resources, and identifies three different paths of resource combinations. Each path leads to a certain level of capability by a company to identify valuable resource combinations, which in turn also affects the embedding process of the focal resource. In particular, the embedding process of a new product concerns "the creation of interfaces between the four resource types that enable a focal technology (new product) to be developed, produced and used" (Baraldi, Gregori and Perna, 2011: 839). This process stretches from discovery and laboratory development to production, marketing and utilization of a focal technology. Different actors, resources and relationships are involved in different moments of this process, which exposes a new technical solution to different settings.[2] In the next section we will treat CRM explicitly as the focal resource embedded in a specific organizational and inter-organizational context.

5.5 Applying the resource interaction perspective to CRM

Chapter 4 has pointed out that companies implementing CRM need to cope with several potential barriers, but that they can also exploit important opportunities when CRM is adopted. Our literature review about CRM made it clear that companies need to align technology, people and organization in order to make the adoption of CRM possible. Technology allows data and information to be managed more efficiently, eventually including the possibility that IT systems store and spread customer knowledge across the organization. People, as individual users inputting and extracting data from the system, represent the other building blocks of CRM. Therefore, for our research purposes we define CRM systems as devices that interact with people who insert data to receive back processed information which they can use for managing customer relationships (Baraldi, La Rocca and Perna, 2013).

This conceptualization of CRM directly draws upon the resource interaction perspective that we reviewed in the previous sections. In fact, the very processes of implementing and using CRM entail interactions between social and technical resources, namely individual users, their organizations and IT elements. More precisely, the resource interaction perspective allows us to penetrate the interaction between the

CRM system, our "focal" resource and other resources such as other IT systems (defining technical interfaces), and information, individuals, organizational groups and business relationships (defining social interfaces).

Thus, it becomes relevant to understand how the CRM system, which in the terminology of the 4Rs model is a facility that elaborates data to generate digital information (Baraldi, 2003), gets embedded in a network structure that creates both barriers and opportunities for its utilization. Specifically, the embedding of CRM is the creation of social and technical interfaces between the aforementioned resources that enable CRM to be first implemented and then used.

Applying the resource interaction perspective to CRM therefore implies that CRM cannot be considered a context-independent tool or a deterministic platform that automatically gets managerial tasks performed and alone creates its own effects; instead CRM is simply a facility which is greatly dependent on other resources in order to be able to process and spread customer information within and outside the organization. In other words, it is only by interacting with other resources that CRM systems can produce their effects and create value (Baraldi and Waluszewski, 2005). For instance, when actual users interact with CRM certain features of the IT system will become salient or will be affected to the extent that its shortcomings will become evident; or it might be that improving the CRM's performance will be possible only after changing the interface between groups of users (as will be demonstrated by the Loccioni case in chapters 7 and 8). Therefore, whether or not CRM creates effects on the way a company manages its customer relationships does not depend so much on the system itself: it is how CRM specifically interacts with the surrounding resources that determines its use and eventually its effects (cf. Ingemansson, 2010).

5.6   Intra- and inter-organizational effects of CRM embedding

The core research issue for this book concerns the effects of CRM embedding both inside and outside the company that implements such a system. As stated in the previous section, we view CRM as a facility embedded in and interacting with several other resources, which will greatly influence the effects CRM can produce. An important consequence of applying the resource interaction perspective to CRM is that it allows the identifying of many unexpected effects, those deriving from the complex texture of resource interactions, namely not only direct, but also indirect resource interfaces (Baraldi, 2003). And these indirect and unexpected effects clearly impact any assessment of the value and actual contribution of an IT tool such as CRM.

In Chapter 3 we have discussed the effects of IT implementation on for instance employees, organizational culture and ways of working. Our literature review also pointed out that these effects are investigated mostly by taking the perspective of the single firm. Our approach attempts instead to consider how CRM and other resources interact and produce effects both inside and outside the single firm. The effects of an IT system such as CRM can moreover be divided into informative and concrete ones (Baraldi, 2003). Informative effects are the easiest to achieve as they simply derive from providing more qualitative and reliable information that supports decision making. Concrete effects are instead more profound and difficult to both achieve and identify as they imply actual changes in resources, such as faster routines in an organizational unit or improved sales volumes in a business relationship (Ibid: 202–204). The challenge is that the concrete effects of IT are non-linear, typically indirect and even hidden, and require time to emerge as they depend on how resources are utilized in combinations with others.

Generally speaking, the effects of IT are generated when IT systems are regularly utilized and applied in specific managerial tasks (Baraldi, 2003). Therefore, the specific context of utilization greatly matters in shaping the effects of CRM. It is only when users interact with and adopt CRM that its effects can be created. Then, it will typically require some time before the individual use of such systems turns into effects within the whole organization. The intra-organizational embedding and effects of CRM can be identified by analyzing the organizational interfaces that emerge around the focal system.

In this respect, the embedding of a CRM system can affect organizational routines and other internal processes, such as employee evaluation. On the other hand, there are also specific groups of users, such as managers from the marketing and sales divisions, who interact more often than other users with CRM: these advanced users, being more knowledgeable about the system, may in turn affect it, by inducing changes in how the CRM system is constructed, how it actually works or how it is utilized in the organization. Next to the type of users interacting with the IT system, the organizational embedding of CRM also involves the type of information stored and distributed by the system, as well as how this information can be applied for managing the customer relationship, namely the information's value in performing this managerial task.

An important intra-organizational effect emerging from embedding CRM deals with the argument by Homburg, Workman and Jensen (2000) that CRM, like most IT systems, affects employees' ways of working, which may create resistance. For instance, direct users of the system often are required to change their way of storing, processing and obtaining information. Implementing a new centralized CRM system typically breaks the habits of those employees who are accustomed to managing information by means of individualized tools, such as informal notes or local software. Breaking such routines often creates tensions between the involved resources that need to be carefully considered during the implementation of CRM systems.

Another possible effect of CRM at intra-organizational level concerns the interdependences already existent between different groups of users. Typically CRM includes IT tools addressing mostly users within marketing departments (Payne and Frow, 2005), which often results in assigning responsibilities for supervising the system (e.g., overview of information consistency) to marketing employees. Top management also often influences key choices concerning CRM implementation. Consequently, one effect of CRM may well be that users from other departments (e.g., sales or administration) perceive that they are controlled by the CRM system.

As for the inter-organizational effects of CRM, Baglieri, Secchi and Croom (2007) conduct a literature review and find that most contributions investigating how IT impacts supplier–customer relationships take the buyer's perspective and focus on effects at the buyer's organization. Our study takes instead explicitly the *supplier's* perspective, as we focus on whether and how a special type of CRM users, namely Key Account Managers (KAMs), use it for managing customer relationships. However, we bring the inter-organizational context into the picture as well, because we also explicitly focus in our analysis (see chapters 8 and 9) on how certain features of customer relationships (namely their duration and complexity, see Chapter 2) affect how users actually use the CRM system, and thereby which effects the system eventually produces on the relationships being managed by a specific KAM.

The embedding of CRM accordingly has effects also at a broader level: as pointed out by Baraldi (2003), the informative and communicative effects of IT stretch across firms' boundaries and can impact decision making processes at several organizations. But it is even more relevant to capture the concrete economic effects that IT systems, such as CRM systems, have on the other resources (e.g., products, facilities, business units and business relationships) within industrial networks. These concrete economic effects can be more precise product deliveries, more efficient routines of an organizational unit or improved business relationships. However, the emergence of these concrete economic effects greatly depends on how an IT system is embedded within the other resources, both inside the using organization and those widespread in the other units with which this organization interacts.

5.7 Summary

This chapter provided the final conceptual tools necessary for investigating the embedding, use and effects of CRM, both inside and outside the host organization. By applying the "resource interaction" perspective, we provided an alternative view of CRM as a socio-technical resource that interacts with a set of other resources that embed it via specific "resource interfaces" (of both technical and socio-organizational nature). How these other resources (especially organizational units, relationships and other IT tools) embed a focal CRM system will influence the effects it can produce, both the informative and the concrete ones, and both at intra- and at inter-organizational level. At this point the reader is hopefully well equipped to follow both the empirical case (chapters 6–8) and our analysis (Chapter 9), which builds on and applies the concepts presented in this chapter, as well as the previous ones.

6
Introducing CRM in an Industrial Company: The Case of the Loccioni Group

This chapter first introduces the Loccioni Group, its history and current organizational structure (Section 6.1). Then, the production, sales and marketing processes are described (Section 6.2), followed by an overview of Loccioni's customer base (Section 6.3). These three initial sections provide a background for understanding the context in which the CRM system was introduced. The following three sections focus specifically on CRM at Loccioni, from the reasons for introducing it and its origins (Section 6.4), through its development in 2005–2006 (Section 6.5) and finally to its implementation in 2007–2008 (Section 6.6). The concluding section summarizes the key points in this chapter.

6.1 Introduction

6.1.1 Company background

Enrico Loccioni started his career as an electrician in the Italian region of Marche when he was 19 years old. He started his first commercial operations in 1968 when he entered the industrial sector of electrical distribution plants. Since then, Enrico Loccioni has built an international industrial group which is however still run as a family company by the founder, his wife and two sons. Enrico Loccioni's wife is the finance and administrative director, one of his sons leads one of the group's business units, named Human Care, and the other son is in charge of the company's logistic processes.

The first company of the Loccioni Group, General Impianti, was founded in 1974: this company dealt with the production of electrical wirings and all the post-sales and service activities for Loccioni's customers. Six years later AEA (Advanced Electronic Applications), a firm specializing in tests for home appliances and car components, was incorporated. Finally, in 1992 Summa was set up as the holding company of the group. While Loccioni was growing and expanding its business, from 1968 more than 80 employees were helped by the Loccioni Group to start their own spin-off businesses mainly in the areas of information technology (software development for industrial applications) and industrial automation (small test systems for logistics applications).

The Loccioni Group operates today as a systems integrator, mainly of measurement and testing machines for automotive and home appliance components. Each type of solution requires software development and fixtures. According to Enrico Loccioni, the company seeks to develop tailored solutions for industrial customers to help them optimize their industrial processes, save time and money and protect the environment. The Loccioni Group produces only according to customer order and adapts products and solutions to customer needs.

Today, Loccioni operates through several business units relying on core competencies within testing and quality control systems, integrated solutions for industrial automation, and ICT (Information and Communication Technology). Recently, Loccioni also started producing tailor-made solutions to face environmental and eco-sustainability issues, a line of business that was boosted after creating "Leaf House", the very first Italian building with a zero-carbon impact, in 2008 (see Baraldi, Gregori and Perna, 2011). Loccioni's core competencies are applied to solutions for customers in several markets such as automotive and home appliances, ICT, health care and environment. Loccioni's turnover in 2012 was Euro 58 million, 52% of which was achieved abroad; it employed 352 people. R&D investments represent about 5% of its turnover in the last five years. The R&D department is composed of 25 engineers, six of whom hold a PhD.

Loccioni's systems are produced in two manufacturing plants and sold directly to customers without any intermediary involved. Those factories are located in the Ancona province, in an area near the group's headquarters (see Figure 6.1) and close to transport systems. The international operations of Loccioni started already in the beginning of the 1980s and since then the company has installed machines and equipment in more than 40 countries all over the world. Forty percent of the turnover comes from markets such as North America, Germany and China, where in the last four years Loccioni opened three overseas sales offices: the first office was inaugurated in the USA (Washington) in 2009, the second was opened in Germany (Calw) in 2012 and the last one was established at the beginning of 2013 in China (Shanghai).

Figure 6.1   Loccioni's headquarters
Source: Loccioni.

To sum up, Loccioni's activities are primarily based on its distinctive core competencies in mechanical engineering, electronics (mechatronics), controls systems and ICT. These competences are applied to serve diverse markets, to which correspond a number of lines of business and business units: environment/sustainability, energy, home appliances, automotive, industrial operations, community and health (Human Care).

6.1.2   Loccioni's organization: General Impianti, AEA and Summa

In the middle of the 1970s, the first business of General Impianti was focused on developing and producing industrial wirings. By interacting with leading manufacturing companies such as producers of home appliances, General Impianti was able to improve its technological abilities. This company, which today employs around 150 people, develops and delivers solutions that improve the efficiency and effectiveness of customers' operating processes, including solutions for telecommunication, industrial automation and environmental control. Moreover, all Loccioni's post-sales and service activities are grouped and managed by General Impianti. Among its various businesses, in the beginning of the 1990s this company started producing tailor-made solutions for environmental applications: for example, emissions analysis systems for incineration plants, and control and traceability systems for the petro-chemical industry. General Impianti also started to conduct research on the connection between technology, comfort and environmental issues. Since 2007, it has increased its focus on eco-sustainability issues, and in that year it initiated a research project called "Leaf Community". The goal of this project was to create a community in which it would be possible to live in a zero-carbon emission house ("Leaf House"), use electric cars and work in eco-friendly buildings. This new business idea laid the ground to create a dedicated business unit named "Energy" that combined solutions for energy efficiency with renewable energy production.

AEA is a company subject to control and coordination by another Loccioni company, Summa: AEA focuses strictly on manufacturing, while all the functions and activities not directly related to technology and production (i.e., administration, planning of strategic investments and human resources) are managed and provided as a service by Summa. According to Loccioni's managing director, the creation of Summa has provided the whole group with a more flexible and dynamic organizational structure. AEA was founded in 1980 with the aim of innovating the design and development of automatic systems for testing and quality control. AEA was from the start equipped with the capability to define the specifications, to design, to manufacture and to service the special purpose equipment required for automated testing and quality control. AEA now has 172 employees, 20 of whom are involved in the R&D department, ten in the administration office, 47 in the electrical and mechanical technical departments and 20 in the software department. Thirty-one additional project managers work directly for different business units within the Loccioni Group.

AEA describes itself as a "technological tailor workshop", which works in synergy with universities and research centers to develop and set up "all inclusive" high-tech systems for the manufacturing industry, the service industry and public administration. Personnel working at AEA possess skills in measurement and testing for quality control, automation, ICT and service/maintenance. These skills are applied to several fields among which are automotive, household appliances, environment, energy saving and health. The mission of this company is to create innovation by improving product performance through test and quality control. AEA's employees are mostly technicians and engineers focused on finding and develop hi-tech and integrated solutions. The two main markets served are the automotive and household appliance industries. AEA is one of the world leaders in the design and production of quality control systems for home appliances and their components. Among its customers are leading international companies such as Whirlpool and Haier: over 60% of the washing machines produced in Europe are tested with systems by AEA. For the automotive sector, covering more than 50% of AEA's turnover, AEA is a world leader in the design and production of systems for quality control of diesel and fuel injectors. AEA integrates quality control systems with assembling and conveying systems, supervision and control software and the whole industrial automation at the customer's factory, thereby offering a complete automatic manufacturing system (see Figure 6.2).

Figure 6.2   One of Loccioni's "shot to shot" flow meters
Source: Loccioni.

Summa is the third main company in the Loccioni Group: its mission consists of anticipating and supporting the growth of the two operating companies with specific projects and innovative solutions. Summa was in fact founded in 1992 to support AEA and General Impianti, but it later expanded its activities in the territory of Marche by means of the NEXUS network, which connects several local SMEs. Summa can be considered as a "service" company supplying R&D activities and other services (human resources and strategic marketing) mainly to Loccioni's manufacturing companies. For instance, Summa is active in the fields of research, innovative design and development and technology transfer. It also develops continuous training and management education projects. Moreover, Summa takes care of networking activities, both inside and outside the Loccioni Group, in order to connect the companies to universities, schools and centers of research, as well as scientific and technological parks. Summa also engages in joint R&D activities with universities, both in Italy and abroad. In 2006, Summa became the holding company of the group. Today it employs about 30 people, ten of whom are part of the marketing division, which was established in 2005 as a new separate unit. This particular organization of the marketing function was decided by Loccioni's top management, namely the owner, the managing director and the marketing manager. They considered that the key processes of (1) market analysis, (2) development of business plans to enter new markets and (3) customer management needed to be made more visible and centralized for the whole group: therefore a dedicated marketing unit, which also reunited increased competence, was created.

Loccioni's organizational chart for 2012 is presented in Figure 6.3, which indicates also the four business units focusing on the following line of business and customer applications:

Mobility: focuses on assembly, testing and quality control systems for automotive components. This business unit produces measurement instruments and test systems to be installed in customers' production lines.

Home and Industry: this business unit devises and develops testing solutions for electrical and electronic components (motors, pumps, compressors, etc.), home appliances, glass industry, wood manufacturing and food and beverage.

Energy and Environment: develops and integrates environmental and process monitoring systems, combining competences in the areas of measurement, control, automation and data management.

Moreover, this business unit integrates solutions for energy efficiency and energy production from renewable sources. For instance, it develops solutions for waste monitoring as well as for reduction of electricity consumption, and for heating and cooling.

Humancare: provides solutions for the areas of health care and pharmaceuticals, food production and wellness. Its technologies include solutions for production processes, diagnosis, therapy and data management. In 2008 Humancare developed and successfully marketed to several important Italian hospitals an automated system for the mixing of cytostatic drugs.

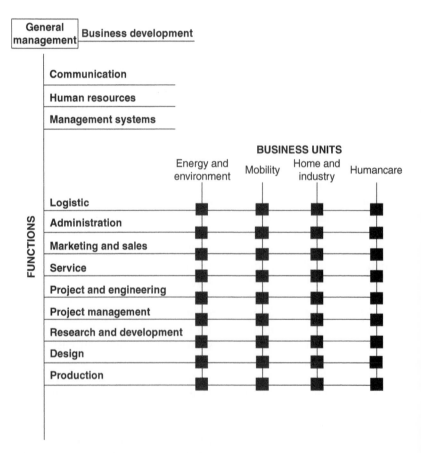

Figure 6.3   Loccioni's organizational chart
Source: Our own elaboration on Loccioni's data.

Table 6.1 Key features of Loccioni's business units, 2012

	Business units			
	Home and industry	Mobility	Energy and environment	Healthcare
Year of birth	1976	1980	1996 (Environment) 2008 (Energy)	2009
Turnover (Millions of Euros)	12	33	7	6
% on total turnover	21	57	12	10
Major customers	BSH, Whirlpool, Haier	Delphi, Continental, Magneti Marelli	Trenitalia, Fileni, Pilkington	Gambro, Glaxo Smith Kline, Cardinal Health

Source: Our own elaboration on Loccioni's data.

Since 2000 Loccioni has adopted this matrix-based organization structure that combines both the functional and business unit-based structures so to facilitate the participation of people from different parts of
the organization in particular projects that need their specialized expertise. Loccioni saw a key advantage of a matrix organization in that it
allows team members to share information more rapidly across unit
and function boundaries, thereby increasing the depth and breadth of
knowledge applicable to specific problems. Table 6.1 below shows the
relevant features of each of the four business units, such as their year of
birth, major customers and total turnover reached in 2012. The selected
customers in Table 6.1 are three major customers for each business unit
in terms of turnover.

6.2 The production, sales and marketing processes

6.2.1 The production process

Loccioni's production activities concern the integration of several components and subsystems into fully customized solutions addressed to its
customers, who operate in various industrial sectors. The group's two
factories today employ about 120 workers. More precisely, Loccioni's
operators design and assemble special machines starting from a

particular requirement or issue of the customer. Moreover, most of the products made by Loccioni include software which Loccioni develops internally. According to the company's president, each product entails a specific project whereby a "tailored solution" is created in order to solve a specific customer problem or issue. In this respect, Loccioni adopts a "job to order" production strategy. A product/solution might require between a few weeks and several months to be delivered to the customer, depending on its level of complexity. Each project is conducted by a specific team of employees who take full responsibility from devising the solution to delivering it to the customer. The team follows a guideline specifying particular tasks to be performed and partial goals to be reached, including several testing sessions, in order to satisfy customer requirements. Some of the workers usually attend training sessions, for instance when software engineers have to develop programs for specific applications, while others have been previously trained on the job.

The organization of the production process follows a set of phases. Each project is assigned to a specific project manager who is responsible for project delivery, coordinating client communication and managing the internal resources assigned to each project. Numerous meetings take place with the client to discuss specific needs, though the most important meeting is the first one, when the two parties discuss the feasibility of the project. A project proposal is drawn up after the first meeting, wherein specific aspects of the project are defined concerning time frames, costs and delivery dates. After having collected all this information the project manager sets up a team composed of workers from several departments such as engineering, production and administration. The project proposal has to be shared among the various parties and assessed before being translated into the technical documentation for the system to be created. This document goes then to the production manager, who is in charge of revising it if necessary and of deciding when the production phase can begin. After the production process is validated, production takes place and then several tests are carried out in order to measure the overall quality of the system. The testing phase can be arranged either at Loccioni's plants or at the customer's premises. Therefore, specialized personnel are very often involved with a product's testing and assembly phases directly at the customer's manufacturing plant, as happened for instance for an injector measuring system called Mexus which Loccioni created for its automotive customer Continental. In terms of services,

Loccioni offers both simple maintenance agreements for individual components and more complex contracts such as long-term service agreements.

Suppliers play an important role in enabling Loccioni to create its integrated solutions, while keeping its production process streamlined and fast. Therefore, Loccioni created strategic partnerships with leading players all over the world, such as National Instruments for automation controllers and Kuka for robots. For example, National Instruments is considered by Loccioni a valuable partner with whom they collaborate for developing new software tools for cutting-edge applications within the automotive industry, such as the already mentioned Mexus system for injector testing (see Perna, Baraldi and Gregori, 2012). Over the years Loccioni moved toward eliminating non-core manufacturing processes, which meant that certain activities have been subcontracted, often to local subcontractors. Some of these suppliers are involved in pre-assembly of components and supply Loccioni's manufacturing plants with modules that are ready to be installed in finished systems. Loccioni adds value by integrating these modules reliably so to deliver exactly the system the customers want.

6.2.2 The sales process

Historically, sales management at the Loccioni Group has been organized with the aim of putting the individual customer in the center, especially the most influential ones. Loccioni never believed in indirect selling strategies, such as distributors or agents, due to the complexity of the technology they develop and offer to customers. On rare occasions some solutions were sold by exclusive agents, but this happened almost solely in cases where the customer was geographically located in particular areas characterized by political instability or somehow difficult to reach (e.g., Israel or some African countries).

During the 1980s there was only one sales manager responsible for a group of six salespeople. These salespeople reported directly to the sales manager who in turn responded to the managing director. At the beginning of the 1990s the sales function was reorganized: The management of relationships with key customers gained such high importance as to induce the introduction of key account managers (KAMs) within Loccioni. This was an important change which also allowed Loccioni to not only improve its offering to selected customers, but also to expand and deepen the relationships with such large customers as Continental, Whirlpool and Ikea so as to include these players also in Loccioni's research and development activities. Thanks to the KAM approach, these major customers became more like partners who play a key role by providing Loccioni with input for the development of future new technologies. Thus, from the beginning of the 1990s Loccioni's sales function was composed of both KAMs and salespeople. Today, 20 years later, the sales organization is shaped in the same way, but the number of employees involved has steadily increased. Now there are about ten KAMs, who coordinate and supervise several salespeople. KAMs are in charge of managing long-lasting business relationships with major customers, especially the most profitable and technology-oriented ones. Those customers may also be important in terms of strategic long-term collaborations. Salespeople, on the other hand, are engaged in developing new relationships with prospects.

Most of Loccioni's sales personnel have technical backgrounds and experience in project management, since they have to sell complex and highly expensive solutions to their customers. There are also many interactions between KAMs, the marketing unit (see below) and the R&D department at Loccioni. Meetings are planned routinely for ordinary sales activities or are set up for discussing specific commercial projects of strategic importance. Loccioni's salespeople need relevant market information and analysis in order to develop their business, including finding new customers: for this type of information they rely on the marketing unit. There are also other important information sources that sales personnel use for expanding sales, such as the personal contacts that KAMs keep in their social networks.

The tasks of KAMs include not only offering a solution for the customer's needs, but also providing an excellent service after the solution is installed at the customer's premises. The cutting-edge technology typically provided by Loccioni's solutions usually lead to improved service levels. However, global clients, such as Continental, Haier and Whirlpool, need a completely different level of service because of their increasingly complex needs. In order to match this complexity, Loccioni has redesigned its sales process, which has been transformed toward a consultative sale, whereby customers can visit Loccioni's plants to discuss openly with Loccioni's managers their needs and challenges. According to Loccioni's managing director, in order to succeed with the consultative selling approach it has been necessary to retrain KAMs: in fact they had to learn that instead of selling solutions, they needed to become better at gathering knowledge about what the customer really needs. Nowadays, it is not only personnel from customer service, technical and field support who are available for supporting and helping the customer with problem solving, but also the KAMs who have explicitly taken on this responsibility.

The selling cycle for Loccioni requires several months, during which Loccioni's salespeople typically maintain telephone contact with customers in addition to paying on-site visits. Following preliminary discussion with a prospect, Loccioni's salesperson arranges for a meeting, usually at Loccioni's premises, in order to let the prospect evaluate the solution. The goal of this meeting is to familiarize the prospect with the product and, as stated by the managing director, "to build trust and credibility".

6.2.3   The marketing process and the evolution of Loccioni's marketing unit

Loccioni's marketing unit was created in 1996, with the primary task of carrying out market research about home appliances. The team at the beginning was very small, composed of just two people, one in charge of external communication activities and the other responsible for business marketing and intelligence, such as market research and customer data analysis. There was no clear strategy and most of the initiatives were developed after suggestions coming directly from the president. But an important marketing tool was the participation in industrial tradeshows and fairs. These were events organized by institutions such as the European Home Appliance Association, where the key home appliances manufacturers and their suppliers participated in order to show cutting-edge technologies. On these occasions, Loccioni would set up their own stand, meet with potential customers, hand out brochures and present their new products.

Over the years, the marketing unit expanded in terms of employees and the activities it undertook aiming to transform Loccioni into a much more customer-focused company. In fact, as the Loccioni Group grew and became more successful, the president recognized the need to increase marketing activities. In 2005, the "Marketing Lab" division was formally created and put under the direction of the manager of business marketing processes. The new division was composed of fresh graduates from universities with business studies backgrounds. This new marketing unit defined the scope of corporate communication activities for the launches of new products and especially it defined the tools for collecting customer information and processing this data. Moreover, one of the key responsibilities of Loccioni's marketing unit became to interact with the sales organization in order to develop lists of potential customers in the so called "scoping phase" of the sales process. In this respect, the marketing team continuously screens the market to identify potential new sales opportunities. In order to manage customer information efficiently and to increase the company's sales and profits, the marketing unit was also a driving actor in the introduction of its own CRM system, which is in focus in this and the next two chapters. Between 2005 and 2008 this CRM system was developed, implemented and launched as "the Loccioni's new marketing tool to improve the management of customer relationships".

Turning to the way of managing potential customers, the marketing unit usually takes responsibility in building the relationship. The potential customer, usually discovered by means of market research, is contacted by the marketing personnel. Alternatively a potential customer could be identified by attending specific trade fairs. In this first approach to the customer, Loccioni tries to assess if the prospect could be strategic or profitable for the company. Then, the potential customer will receive documentation and the contacts of Loccioni's key persons to start to interact with. As the object of the discussion often is a cutting-edge solution, afterward the customer is referred to technical and salespeople. If the interaction begins, Loccioni's sales personnel will prepare a quotation for the potential customer. In the meanwhile, the key technical person with the necessary competences for conducting the potential project may talk to the customer to get information regarding customer needs. Usually there are negotiations up until the signing of the contract. Due to the complexity of the interaction, both in technical and economic terms, the commercial discussion can take months, especially if the customer changes terms and conditions during the process.

It is not easy to identify clearly the boundaries between the marketing and the sales units at Loccioni, due to the fact that marketing people also get involved in sales activities. In fact, the marketing unit is split into two groups: one group of marketers carries out strategic activities in cooperation with Loccioni's top management, while another group operates more on a tactical level. The former activities include monitoring customer needs, both in terms of general trends and within specific customers, as a way to identify information that can help Loccioni develop accurate offers. In these strategic activities, marketing people try to share insights with both top management and the R&D department, supporting them in the development of new products and in improving existing ones. The tactical activities are instead performed to support salespeople in developing and qualifying leads. For instance, as stated before, the marketing unit performs and uses market research and feedback from the sales department to help selling existing solutions to new customers, or they are in charge of developing marketing campaigns and case stories.

6.3 The structure of Loccioni's customer base

"Only by working and collaborating with international big players in the automotive and home appliance business can we grow," Loccioni's president stated at the beginning of the 1980s at a meeting with sales managers of AEA. This focus on having mostly relationships with leading customers, namely large-scale manufacturers, was considered the number one priority of the company and was viewed as one of the most important responsibilities of Loccioni's management. In other words, Loccioni's top management strongly believed, and still does, in building and developing close, long-lasting relationships with large, growing and innovative customers.

According to Loccioni's top managers, information such as customer turnover and installed equipment are also good indicators for the after-sales business, including for instance a continuous stream of sales of spare parts. Moreover, if the customer is growing in an expanding market, this is another positive indicator which identifies a good business opportunity. Third, Loccioni's management views it as necessary to focus on sales potential and cross-selling opportunities to each customer. In this respect, Loccioni prefers customers who have centralized decision-making structures and a business which is stable and viable in the long term.

Loccioni's customer portfolio is composed of 700 customers, among which about 100 are multinational companies for whom Loccioni develops highly specialized solutions. In this respect, fewer than 20% of the customers generate about 70% of revenues. For example, in the automotive market, Loccioni supplies quality testing systems to the automotive divisions of leading companies which are international industrial injector manufacturers, such as Continental Corporation, Delphi, Bosch GmbH and Magneti Marelli. Continental's automotive division in particular has been a Loccioni customer since the 1990s. This strong relationship led to Continental becoming Loccioni's most important automotive customer, accounting for about 25% of Loccioni's automotive turnover. In the home appliances testing market, one of Loccioni's most important customers is Whirlpool. This relationship dates back to 1987, when Loccioni delivered an automatic testing system for washing machines, which it has also subsequently developed continuously. Loccioni also went on delivering several testing systems for other Whirlpool products, such as dishwashers and refrigerators. The automotive and the home appliance businesses are Loccioni's most profitable ones.

The other sectors where the company operates, such as the energy industry, biomedicine and telecommunication, stand for 40% of Loccioni's total income (see Table 6.1). Big customers making up 60% of the sales volume typically stay as good and loyal customers, while the remaining customers usually place more intermittent orders. Looking at the energy industry, the customer base looks quite different from the automotive or the home appliance businesses. Loccioni entered the energy business around 2007, without much experience and with limited competences. Moreover, salespeople had to develop their relationships with customers from scratch. Since this market was and still is populated by leading international competitors, it has been really hard for Loccioni to acquire customers: looking at the composition of the customer base in the energy sector, it appears to be built on small actors with only national reach. The only exception is Italy's largest energy producer Enel, who became a Loccioni customer at the beginning of the 1990s, although not of Loccioni's energy division, but of the "Environment" business unit. Enel was acquired as a customer when they bought solutions for gas analysis emission in their Italian energy production units.

Another important distinction in Loccioni's customer base is between domestic and foreign customers. Italian customers account for 60% and foreign ones for 40% of total incomes. An interesting category of domestic customers in the energy market is local public utilities. Utilities frequently invest in renewable energy resources and may place large orders to purchase Loccioni's solutions not only for energy production, but also for improving their energy utilization efficiency and for monitoring energy consumption. Foreign customers have become more important for Loccioni than Italian ones since the latter have become really demanding in terms of cost cutting. Moreover, since Loccioni's foreign customers continued their international expansion to meet their own growing markets, it turned out to be a good strategy for Loccioni to increase the share of such customers in the customer base as a way to foster the company's growth. Approximately 50% of foreign customers are concentrated in Europe, particularly in Germany, while the other 50% are based in North America (USA) and in Asia (China).

6.4   Introducing the CRM system: The origins

6.4.1   "MDB": The "tricky" marketing database

The origins of the CRM project at Loccioni are linked to the development of the marketing unit and its facilities. In 1996, when the marketing unit was created with the purpose of producing market research, the president of the company, Enrico Loccioni, pushed the marketing manager to create a marketing database (MDB) in order to store customer data. It was an attempt to use information technology as a tool for keeping in an electronic format some key information about customers. Loccioni's desire was to produce a meaningful change toward a more systematic and coordinated way to collect at a single point and to orchestrate the company's overall market insights, which until that point had been widely spread across the entire organization, or indeed in several different sub-units. The majority of customer-related processes were at that time documented, but these documents were dispersed and therefore it was a challenge to get relevant customer information into the hands of the specific employee who needed it from time to time.

Critical customer information was shared within Loccioni through word of mouth, documents, reports, phone calls, e-mails and meetings. As a result, the quality of the information exchanged varied significantly depending on the person who prepared it. Due to the potential problems and inconsistencies that could stem from this situation, the president felt that customer data should be collected and then disseminated through a more reliable and unified technical solution, such as a database system. Afterwards, not only the president but also the CEO of the company and the R&D director recognized that it had become almost impossible, or at least increasingly unreliable, to handle, manage and transfer customer data through the traditional ways. Therefore, Loccioni needed to find other mechanisms for managing customer data and the company's top management found the implementation of a customer database to be the most suitable.

This initiative took time and significant efforts from the marketing manager, who was not sure about how to deal with some of its effects. Several concerns arose, such as the lack of competences in how to adopt information technology to carry out marketing activities and which benefits the company could gain after implementing the marketing database. Heated themes for discussion were the design of the customer database, the parts of the whole organization that would be involved in creating it and the technology evaluation. According to the marketing manager, organizing, codifying and moving data into databases would be a massive job. Moreover, at that time Loccioni was not willing to invest a large amount of money in supporting this initiative due to the fact that the company had a much smaller dimension than today. The result was that the marketing manager had to work together with people from Loccioni's own IT department in order to build and put together a sort of "handmade" database.

The result was not really satisfactory: for instance, purchases made by customers could not be registered automatically in the MDB. In other words the system turned out to be merely an address list. However, this experience led Loccioni to test its IT competences for developing its own software for marketing purposes and to identify a list of shortcomings to avoid in a marketing database. One of the major drawbacks of the MDB consisted in being impossible to access from outside the company's offices for traveling staff members, who therefore could not look up and add information while visiting a customer. Moreover, this database daily shut down when it was accessed by more than four users at once. Despite these problems, MDB was officially launched in 1997 when the IT Loccioni's department and the marketing division opened up the system to the users.

6.4.2   Exploiting the internal IT competences

In 1993, a business unit called TLC (Telecommunications) was created at Loccioni following the initiative of some of its employees who considered creating a new unit as a necessary step in order to enter in a new market, namely solutions for industrial information management. The president, Enrico Loccioni himself, had also fostered for a long time an entry into this market, considering the company's already established competences in integrating software and hardware components for automotive and home appliances applications. The idea was to become able to sell complex, application-specific IT systems to industrial customers: this move would also enable Loccioni to extend its business portfolio in a complex market where the terms "Internet" and "digital" were still quite unknown in the early 1990s.

Over the years the TLC business unit has been growing in both turnover and number of new customers acquired. For instance, in 2005 when Loccioni was approaching the development of its CRM system, this business unit had reached total sales up to 20% of the total company's turnover. The solutions offered by this business unit to the customers have been quite broad, ranging from the creation of telephony and data networks to implementation of various software and

Intranet solutions. More specifically, the TLC business unit was able to provide LANs, wireless data systems, Intranet, Extranet and Internet platforms, video surveillance systems, IP (Internet Protocol) telephony and solutions for building automation. Similarly to the Loccioni Group as a whole, one of the strengths of this business unit consisted in its capacity to integrate different IT solutions and systems supplied by leading multinational companies, such as Cisco Systems, Hewlett Packard and IBM, into the customer's already existing IT infrastructures. In practice, this integration capacity was made possible by particular algorithms which this business unit was able to develop in-house.

At the same time, over the years the TLC unit also increased its technical competences in developing from scratch special software and any type of algorithm for industrial application: for instance for materials handling and automation, or for warehouses and distribution and logistics systems. The employees in this unit emphasized continuous improvements in the software engineering processes and in their project management techniques. In this way, this business unit succeeded in enhancing its processes and methodologies, which made them an appealing partner for collaboration both for other Loccioni units and for external customers. As the business of the unit and the workload was growing, Loccioni's management decided to hire new people. Meanwhile, the unit became certified by national and international expert organizations within the IT sector. At this stage, the team of software engineers designed systems and production processes mostly for clients in the manufacturing and public sectors.

Since 2004, the TLC unit has learnt how to master new technologies applied to business processes such as Data Warehousing and Business Intelligence (B.Int). Learning about these two components, typically combined within Enterprise Resource Planning (ERP) systems, allowed Loccioni to also enhance its capacity for understanding ERP processes as such. In the meantime, in fact, this unit became capable of providing specialized IT consulting services for industrial applications. This type of services gave to Loccioni an opportunity to be even closer to its customers and to eventually create more tailored ICT solutions for them. A staff of technicians was added to the TLC unit with the specific purpose of providing customers with consultancy about how to use their IT systems (such as ERPs) or identify problems and potential for improvements.

As well as generating external revenues, the TLC unit also importantly contributed to increasing efficiency and improving processes within Loccioni. Some projects even combined the two aspects of increased customer value and easier operations for Loccioni's personnel: for instance, in order to provide improved post-sales service, this unit helped Loccioni introduce the "remote assistance" support in 2006. This meant that Loccioni's machines and systems installed at the customer premises can in this way be monitored online from Loccioni's head-quarters, which enables remotely assisting the customer. In this way, Loccioni's technicians can operate without necessarily traveling to the customer's site, while the customer can receive timely support and ser-vice. Since the issue was clearly within the competence area of the TLC unit of Loccioni, it was therefore natural that they became involved first in the aforementioned marketing database project and later on in the CRM project.

6.4.3   Why CRM? Setting the scene

In the spring of 2005 Enrico Loccioni was contemplating the future of his company by considering how to deploy all the extensive mar-ket knowledge which had been gathered over the years by means of the marketing database (MDB) created by the marketing unit. 2005 had moreover been in many respects a breakthrough year for the company's history: this included the creation of the new Marketing Lab division and the reorganization of the sales force by introducing the role of KAMs. Therefore, the strategic plan for the following year, 2006, called for managers to define the business vision of each business unit and to identify how this vision complemented the organizational changes occurring at the level of sales management.

The president felt that customer analytics could become a pillar of Loccioni's marketing strategy, and according to him the company was ready to make a big leap toward the Customer Relationship Manage-ment (CRM) philosophy, that is, the efficient and systematic collection and use of updated information concerning both the past of customer relationships (e.g., contacts, solutions sold, sales turnover, composition of the turnover) and the future opportunities for developing them (e.g., customers' plans to invest in new technologies). The spark which led Enrico Loccioni to believe in the potential of CRM dates back to a meet-ing he attended in 2005 as a member of the board of a local bank. The director of the bank told him that several B2B customers of that bank, mostly small and medium-sized manufacturing firms, had implemented CRM technology in order to improve such processes as product devel-opment, R&D and, of course, their marketing and sales performances. Loccioni was surprised and at the same time became very curious. He did not know much about CRM but he had for many years been involved in creating a similar IT platform for Loccioni, as witnessed by the marketing database launched in the 1990s. A week later the bank organized a meeting on the theme of how to manage business customers fruitfully within "competitive landscapes", and Loccioni took part as a guest. The meeting also included a detailed presentation of a list of CRM's features and functionalities. A demonstration of a CRM software was also given.

It was not difficult for Enrico Loccioni to convince his board of directors of the importance of CRM. Therefore, once Loccioni's board had realized that it was possible to achieve an updated and integrated view of its customer by means of CRM technology, Loccioni's own CRM project was officially launched. In this vein, the company viewed CRM as a strategic possibility, rather than a solution to specific problems: the goal was to offer employees an IT system that would be better than the previous one (the marketing database, MDB) in managing customer information. The potential of CRM technology was also viewed as relevant in terms of cost saving and increased sales efficiency. In fact, Loccioni's president became concerned over the years that salespeople were spending too much time on non-valuable activities, such as the annoying search for customers' profiles, which were distracting them from their main task, that is, selling or at least interacting directly with customers. Basically, a full-blown CRM system promised to make salespeople more efficient. Even if getting there would entail several challenges, customer data could be collected and disseminated through the CRM system instead of using informal mechanisms like "post-its" or "word of mouth".

As stated by Loccioni's Managing Director,

> we need to have a more comprehensive picture of everything related to customers and potential customers. We have to keep track of who we talk to, and how many systems we sell to them. Looking at a unique customer's picture will allow us to be faster than the others in managing customers' issues.

In short, the main reasons for starting a CRM project at Loccioni were the following:

- Despite the existence for several years of a marketing database, this was never really successful as a unifying and central data repository for customer management. Information about customers was instead stored in disparate software applications, such as the company's ERP, the software dedicated to the management of customer complaints and various Microsoft applications (Excel sheets and Access database) which had no digital connections to each other. This customer information from various IT systems needed to be brought together to allow various users, such as marketing and sales team, to rely on a single and "unified" view of the customer.

- By storing in a single well functioning database all relevant customer information, such as locations, cross-selling orientation, volumes of production, purchasing behavior and total investment in production facilities, the sales function could prepare customized offerings in a shorter time. This would lead Loccioni to save money and time, and improve the chance of winning a sale.
- Being a technology-driven company meant that Loccioni should not only sell cutting-edge technologies to its customers, but also adopt and use an intelligent, advanced IT system to manage its customer relationships.
- Finally, learning directly how to perform inside their own organization a complex project for the creation of a complex CRM system would give Loccioni the opportunity of selling this very system as their own product on the market.

At the start of the CRM project in the mid of 2005, there were several important questions to be addressed by Loccioni: "How can we organize our CRM in terms of technology and people to be involved?"; "What could be the potential benefit of a CRM system for the company and for the specific users within the various units?"; "What could be the potential pitfalls of the project and of the IT system?"; "How much would it cost?" Many important choices concerning for instance the system's architecture were also open, while some key decisions were made from the very beginning. For instance, one important standpoint became preventing the CRM system from being able to share valuable information with external companies, such as customers, suppliers or partners: instead it was decided to keep Loccioni's CRM as an internal system. The duration of the project was planned to be two years and a half, including both the development and the implementation of the CRM system. However, due to several unexpected events, the project would eventually take more than three years to complete.

6.5   Developing the CRM system (2005–2006)

The development stage of the CRM project took about one year and a half, from the summer of 2005 to the end of 2006. In order to prepare

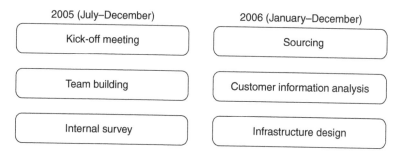

Figure 6.4   Main phases in the CRM development project, 2005–2006

the ground for the development stage of the project several steps had to be defined, as shown in Figure 6.4, in terms of main phases.

The first six months, until the end of 2005, focused on organizing the project team and its initial activities, while throughout 2006 the project team carried out several steps such as the analysis of customer information and the design of the IT infrastructure, which turned out to be important for the beginning of the implementation phase in the year 2007. We will now illustrate separately the two main stages of the development phase. Our review of the first stage emphasizes how an internal survey was made in order to find support for CRM, while in the second stage we will focus on showing the infrastructure design phase.

6.5.1   Preparing for CRM: The internal survey

It is difficult to find an exact date when the CRM project officially started. It was during the summer of 2005 that Loccioni's board involved a team of researchers from the Polytechnic University of Marche, located near Loccioni's headquarters, to complement Loccioni's own competences on organizational and marketing issues. During the first kick-off meeting several discussions took place with representatives from the Faculty of Economics of that university. The Polytechnic University of Marche played a central role in supporting the CRM project, both in the development and in the implementation phase. One of the central issues discussed in the kick-off meeting was the creation of a team of people who should be engaged fully or indeed full-time with the project. A project team was accordingly created and included eight people: two researchers from the university, Loccioni's managing director and five employees representing different functions (marketing, accounting, IT and the TLC business unit). The marketing and communication manager headed the project team. The IT and TLC people would play an important role in transforming abstract CRM models into tools that would work within Loccioni's IT infrastructure. Interestingly, no employee from the sales department, neither a salesperson nor a KAM, was included in the project team. Loccioni's top management did not want to distract them from their selling tasks and considered the implementation of a CRM system mostly as an issue of how to manage and organize marketing information.

This first project step was completed in around two months. During this period, the project team's first activity was to carry out an internal survey among employees, named "CRM's benefits for a customer centric company". This activity turned out to be a critical issue faced by the CRM team, mostly due to the new and unexpected picture of user needs that emerged from the survey.

CRM was not entirely new to most of Loccioni's employees; therefore, rather than evaluating their competence and knowledge of this practice, the project members' survey focused on two key topics: (1) understanding employees' propensity to use IT tools for managing sales and marketing information; and (2) defining employees' needs when adopting IT to manage business relationships. Evaluating their needs was a delicate process, since it related to what information was stored, how it was gathered and how it was translated into inputs inside IT tools. During the survey, people were informed about the significance of CRM and the importance of managing business relationships by using ad hoc software. The data from the employees were collected via a structured questionnaire, which was organized around the following topics:

- Personal knowledge about CRM systems
- Expected role of CRM in employees' daily activities
- Level of utilization of the company's marketing database (MDB), viewed as a sort of precursor of a future CRM system
- Complementary use of other personal IT systems to record sales or marketing data
- Specific needs of valuable information when managing counterparts, such as customers and suppliers. In this respect, some questions were: what decisions do you regularly make for managing the customer? What information do you need to make these decisions? What data do you regularly receive? What information would you like to have available that you are not currently receiving?
- Importance of each specific information need

Out of about 350 employees, the questionnaire was administered to roughly 200 people from different departments, such as marketing, sales, production, administration, R&D and human resources. The decision to involve others in the survey besides personnel from marketing and sales functions was made for two main reasons: to inform as many people as possible about the company's efforts to work on a new IT tool and to gather opinions on the project from people with different backgrounds, including those who do not usually deal directly with customers.

The questionnaire return rate of the questionnaire was quite high, roughly 70%. Among Loccioni's different departments the most responsive was the sales department. Once the data collection was completed, the information was processed in order to be analyzed by the CRM team. One problem in analyzing the survey data was how to deal with the answers received regarding the "specific information needs in managing counterparts", as there was a great variety and complexity of needs expressed by employees. In order to obtain valuable input for continuing the project, these information needs had to be simplified, prioritized and reduced to those considered vital. In narrowing the list of the several needs, the first step was to group those needs that were similar, in order to come up with a summary of the pivotal needs. Then the needs in this list were prioritized depending on the level of importance expressed by the employees and the costs associated with fulfilling through a specific IT solution.

The survey showed a high level of interest by personnel in adopting dedicated CRM software, even though more than 40% were already using their own personal tools to collect and record customer data, such as physical or digital agendas and Excel sheets. By means of the survey another important aspect that arose was the low level of adoption of the marketing database (MDB) that the marketing unit had created a few years before. According to people from the sales department, mostly represented by KAMs, this marketing tool was useless and really complicated, if one even decided to use it at all. Therefore, the potential users of the marketing database were very reluctant to adopt it for their daily routines.

6.5.2 Designing the CRM infrastructure

One important decision that the project team made was how to source the technical solution for the CRM system. The choice was naturally between purchasing an existing system from vendors and developing an in-house system. Several local software producers were invited to present their IT solutions for CRM, but the project team did not find these solutions suitable to the needs of Loccioni. Therefore, the alternative of buying standard software was rejected, but those meetings with CRM systems providers offered Loccioni important knowledge about CRM systems. Instead, it was decided to develop a tailored solution in-house. This task was assigned to Loccioni's IT people, who were assisted by representatives from the TLC business unit, which was specialized in implementing IT business solutions. In fact the company had highly skilled engineers and most of the IT systems they created were using available off-the-shelf IT and software tools.

In the end of January 2006 the project team started to design the infrastructure of the CRM system together with informatics engineers from the TLC business unit, who also shared with the project team a feasibility analysis of the whole project. Before starting the design phase, a few preliminary steps were carried out by the project team:

- A detailed analysis of the customer information needed in order to better manage long-term relationships was conducted.
- All the contact points between Loccioni and its customers were mapped out.
- All the information previously hosted by the marketing database (MDB), which can be viewed as a "legacy system" for the new CRM tool, was revised and updated.

The marketing database was analyzed and a list of customer information considered as crucial was defined. The project team considered as fundamental that this exact list of customer information could be transferred and implemented into the new CRM system. This list included for instance the customer's basic features (addresses, location, etc.), personal contacts, customers' representatives and typologies of products and solutions sold to the customer. Moreover, due to the results of the internal survey carried out in 2005, it was found that users were missing some additional information: (for instance, a customer profile, financial information about customers, about their internal business units and managerial positions) and relevant business relationships in the respective markets, as well as press releases about the specific customer.

The infrastructure design phase lasted around ten months and was a challenging, but critical phase for Loccioni. The design for the overall system infrastructure in fact aimed at integrating the customer information dispersed within the company, by means of a new central database.

This database needed in turn to be connected with all Loccioni's already installed IT tools and systems. The new CRM system was also planned to be easily modifiable so to be able to improve its performance with time, while containing the costs for upgrading and upscaling: the goal of the project team was to develop a new platform that had to be independent from single vendors of software components, flexible to develop further and easy to maintain in the future.

One important decision made by the project team was to develop a CRM system that was Web-based, allowing Loccioni's personnel to access the system from any computer connected to the Internet, not only from the office premises. At the same time, from a technical point of view, the CRM system was designed and set to share the same Web environment as Loccioni's already existing Intranet platform. In other words, Loccioni's IT manager proposed to exploit the Intranet platform in order to access the emerging CRM database.

Therefore, the Intranet system, a key element within Loccioni's IT infrastructure, also played a central role in the CRM project: Loccioni's Intranet would become the Web environment capable of supplying data about customers as well as the system's users, that is, almost all Loccioni's employees (whose basic records such as year of employment, position and role within the company were posted on the Intranet). This Intranet was also connected with the ERP database and with the HDA (Help Desk Assistance) database. Moreover, it was decided later on to connect B.Int software with the Intranet and the ERP, HDA and CRM systems (see Figure 6.5). The B.Int software is a tool that allows operations to be performed on the data stored on all of these systems, such as elaborating customer data so to give the users data representations such as graphics, figures and tables.

Among these IT systems, the B.Int tool was purchased from an external vendor who could make it specifically adapted to interact with a CRM system and database. The ERP and the B.Int systems were physically placed in the TLC business unit, located in Loccioni's headquarters, while the HDA system was placed in the service business unit, located in the General Impianti manufacturing plant. The CRM system, placed in a Web environment rather than within a specific business unit, would receive data from and send updated data to the ERP, HDA and Intranet systems. Figure 6.5 shows how the CRM system was connected with the other IT systems when it was conceived. Information flows from CRM, HDA and Intranet to B.Int are one-sided, as the latter software only queries these databases, without updating them with new information. Instead, the information flows between CRM, HDA and ERP are mutual

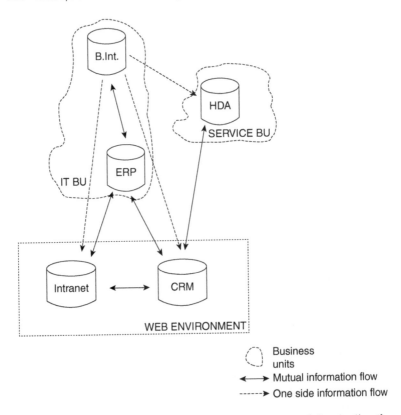

Figure 6.5 The connections between the CRM system and Loccioni's other IT systems

as these systems receive and send back updated data to each other. For instance, both ERP and HDA store data about relevant customer-related tasks: the ERP system keeps financial data about the customers, such as payments made or sales orders, while the HDA system stores after-sales information, such as complaints by a certain customer. All these information pieces residing in other systems were considered to be essential for managing customer relationships and had to be connected with the emerging CRM system.

6.6 Implementing CRM (2007–2008)

Between 2007 and 2008, the CRM system was implemented at the Loccioni Group and was finally officially launched in May 2008. The

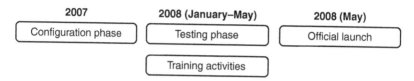

Figure 6.6 Overview of the main stages in Loccioni's CRM project, 2007–2008

main activities carried out in this period are depicted in Figure 6.6. Each of these stages is described below.

6.6.1 Configuring the CRM system

In January 2007 Loccioni's informatics engineers started the configuration phase: this stage of the project addressed the translation of the outcomes of the previous design process into the CRM system. One of the main purposes of the configuration step was to let the CRM infrastructure, designed during 2006, become fully usable. All the existing software containing customer contacts and other relevant information (telephone, mail, e-mail, meetings, etc.) were put together in a single database, so as to avoid duplicating a customer relationship in several data repositories. An important reason for doing this was that having such data recorded in several separate databases would create problems of data inconsistencies if one customer item were changed in one database without anyone remembering to do it in all others. A customer relationship was therefore represented and recorded only in one single central database, the CRM one.

The CRM system was also connected to the existing ERP package, but this was a difficult task and the engineers had to develop special communication and interfacing software. Moreover, the CRM system had to communicate with the company's Intranet and with the company's website as well: in order to achieve this, ad hoc software interfaces were set up. Another technical effort made by the IT engineers was to link the CRM with the B.Int system. It took 12 months to configure the whole architecture. In this period, another project activity was to capture the customer information flow into the CRM database. The very aim of introducing CRM was to be able to process data, by applying the CRM system, so as to deliver information to the users (mainly marketing and salespeople) and, most importantly, to improve their decision-making in relation to customers. Therefore, several user-oriented modules were configured and installed by the project team. Listed below here, these modules are also shown in Figure 6.7, featuring

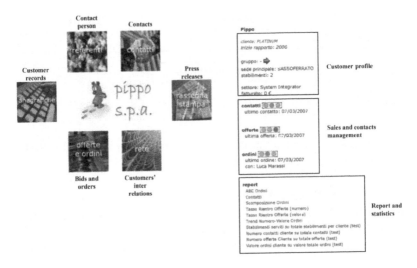

Figure 6.7   CRM's main menu for a demo customer
Source: Our own elaboration on Loccioni's data.

a screenshot of the CRM's entry page to a fictive customer (translated from Italian):

1) "Customer manager": sales processes and the existing marketing database were connected to this module. The project team proposed several sections such as "customer primary data", "contact information" and "account history". In this module, the users would be able to find several pieces of qualitative and quantitative information about Loccioni's customers. For instance, it would be possible for the user to retrieve useful customer information such as investments made by the customer, typology of market served by the customer and customer's market share. Moreover, the specific interactions with each customer were recorded in this module according to a classification into various typologies (meetings, phone calls, e-mails, visits to the customer's premises, etc.). The expected users of the "Customer Manager" module, both in terms of data input and retrieval, were mostly salespeople, KAMs and marketing personnel.

2) "Communication activities": this section of the CRM system was aimed at collecting and storing all Loccioni's data concerning marketing and communication activities for public relations. By means of this module it would be possible to prepare and send out invitations to lists of selected customers, prospects or other contacts for specific events, such as workshop or seminars organized by Loccioni.

The expected users of this module were mostly marketing personnel, and specifically the communication manager, as well as the PR responsible.

3) "Administrative module": this module allowed users, from salespeople to Loccioni's administrative department, to review all the invoices and the payment processes, customer by customer. This module also allowed checking of the financial characteristics and position of an actual or prospective customer.

4) "Production module": in this section of the CRM system, highlighting the importance of an online connection to the ERP system, it would be possible to follow the working progress of each job order of each customer. The users were expected to be mostly KAMs and production personnel. Also people from the "service" unit were interested in using this module, mostly to forecast maintenance activities after the delivery of solutions to the customers.

5) "After-sales and service module": this module allowed users, mostly service people and KAMs, to get customer feedback in a structured way. A systematic use of this module was expected to enable monitoring the reliability of the systems delivered to the various customers. Another interesting feature of this module, expected to be particularly useful to KAMs, concerned new service offerings: KAMs would have important information support to determine how to cross-sell the most profitable mix of product offerings to each customer.

6) "Reports": this module was connected to the smaller software for B. Int that the company purchased in the summer 2006. All the above functionalities and information pieces contained in the previous five modules could be presented in the form of a report created by this last module. For instance, it would be possible to create an "invoice status report", a "costumer's contacts report", a "calendar and tasks report" and so on. Moreover, several different classes of users (KAMs, other salespeople, marketing, R&D, service and administrative personnel or top managers) could produce customized reports by filtering various parameters.

Figure 6.7 shows the home page of Loccioni's CRM, featuring a fictive customer (Pippo S.p.A) and the accesses to the various modules. For instance, the two sections "customer profiles" and "sales and contact management" bring together information described above in the module "Customer Manager" while the module "Communication Activities" is reached by clicking on the sections named "Contacts".

Throughout the configuration phase of CRM, the project team worked hard to design new graphic user interfaces (see Figure 6.7) and to create a new terminology including terms like "contacts," "relationship," "network," "campaign" and "report". Another challenge was the realization of an intelligent and user-friendly search engine. Search functions were broken down into "basic", "simple" and "complex". The "basic" variant would conduct searches based only on company names or last names of individuals at customers, whereas the "simple" variant meant to conduct a search by country or geographical locations. If the user were interested in more complex information or finding particular patterns, it would be possible to rely on the "complex" search engine: this was the case of searches combining multiple choices matched together, such as "location of the customer", "financial profile" and "number of products sold/purchased". Since the CRM system was designed to be accessed from outside Loccioni's offices, the project team also had to create security protocols for all the users. Table 6.2 highlights a list of users divided by functions and business units. Also, within the sales function we have distinguished the KAMs from the salespeople, as well employees working within marketing as opposed to communication. It was decided that all the users had the same level of access, with the exception of the IT engineer who was the developer of CRM, the marketing manager and the manager of the "Connecting" business unit (a new name for the TLC unit applied from the year 2008). These three individuals became the "CRM administrators", and were the only individuals who were allowed to make critical modifications such as canceling ground data or modifying some data entry fields. This decision was made for reasons of security in the CRM software. Basically, it was decided that all the users could input basic data, but only the CRM administrators were allowed to modify the CRM settings, such as adding new functionalities, or to cancel certain information in order to keep the database clean. In this respect, the administrators were enabled to cancel the following:

- Non-active customer profiles
- Duplicated data (contacts and customer profiles)
- Old press releases related to customers

Turning to the information flow from Loccioni's various IT systems to CRM, demographic data about customers come to the CRM system from Loccioni's Intranet, and when a CRM user modifies this data or adds new data, the CRM system sends it back to the Intranet. More specifically, the

Table 6.2 List of CRM users in 2008

Functions	Business units								
	Automotive	Home	Environment	Automating	Connecting	Humancare	Service	Energy	Total
Owners and top management									5
Sales									
KAM	3	2	2	1	1	1	1	1	12
Salesperson	1	3	3	4	4	2	2	3	22
Marketing and communication									
Marketing	1	1	4	0	1	0	1	1	9
Communication									6
Research and development	5	9	6			1		2	23
Human resources									5
Administration									10
Purchasing									7
IT									5
Total									104

Source: Our own elaboration on Loccioni's data.

CRM system receives financial data about the customer from the ERP system and sends this data back to it updated if a KAM or any other user makes a modification to it. The same information flow exists between the HDA system and the CRM system when it comes to after-sales information such as customer complaints. So the resulting CRM system has mutual connections only with Intranet, ERP and HDA (see Figure 6.5). All the IT connections reviewed above were created mostly ad hoc and step by step, as soon as the technical need for each of them was discovered, during the two and a half years of the implementation project. The resulting IT infrastructure around the CRM system comprises many heterogeneous pieces that were combined or even "stitched" together, when Loccioni's IT department designed and introduced several new bridging software items.

6.6.2   The testing phase

The project team organized testing activities to share with personnel's representatives their ideas and to obtain feedback in order to improve the CRM system. "We now have to test if the CRM system is going to work properly," the marketing manager said when the implementation step was accomplished. For a couple of months, from January to March 2008, intensive testing of the system took place under the supervision of the project team. These trials included focus groups with users and face to face meetings with selected individuals. At this stage all the functionalities of CRM were tested several times by personnel from sales (KAMs and salespeople), IT and marketing. IT people were involved mostly in detecting errors: for example they verified the data migration from the previous systems, and the security of the CRM system, reproducing the typical using patterns of most users. People from the Sales and Marketing units were engaged to ensure that system requirements were met: they were invited to test the system by creating demo-customers, about which they could input data and then extract processed information. An initial version of the CRM system had been previously tested by KAMs and salespeople, selected from the three major business units of Loccioni's (Home, Automotive and Environment) in order to be representative of the different types of potential users also in terms of varying technical ability and confidence in using IT systems. All these beta testers from the sales department agreed that the graphic user interface was easy to use, even though it was not really intuitive.

Later on, the testing became focused mostly on the "Customer Manager" module, the one that enabled keeping track of past contacts with the customers and planning future ones. Salespeople and KAMs entered into the CRM system the details about meetings and other contacts they were used to work with: the goal here was to verify if the system worked properly in handling the various types of salespeople–customer interactions. For instance, the details to be included in the contact section of the database included such items as "date" and "time", "subject" of the meeting (for instance, "initial meeting with customer A" or "new system offer to customer A"), "format" of the contact (face to face meeting, phone call, etc.). These testing activities provided significant feedback to the project team in order to solve several technical issues that arose when the system met the users for the first time.

6.6.3 Organizing training activities and the official launch

The project team managed to convince both Loccioni's top managers and the users who got involved in the testing phase of the CRM project that, for the sake of creating a better understanding and widespread use of the system, it would be necessary to organize in-depth training sessions. The project team offered to take care of these courses and the company's management decided to spend time and financial resources on training the staff in how to use the CRM system. Moreover, these extended training sessions would also allow the project team to continue receiving feedback from the users. The training activities were organized by the marketing manager and they involved about 80 employees mostly from the sales, administrative and R&D functions.

Personnel attending the session were divided into ten groups, each one composed of eight people, and each session took about one hour. In total 20 hours of training were conducted, that is, two rounds for each of the ten groups. This training program took place between March and May 2008. The general aim of the training was to spread knowledge concerning the importance of adopting IT systems in managing daily activities. Then, more specifically, the sessions included demo presentations of Loccioni's CRM system and an overview showing how users could interact with the system. In this respect, the sessions covered how a user should feed the system with data: in fact, as data input was a pivotal aspect, this training stressed that data input had to be done in the right way in order for the system to produce the desired data output. Moreover, users were taught how to retrieve customer information and how to make reports. Each session ended with open discussions in order to receive from the audience their first impressions about CRM.

Users had to be assured that it was safe to use the system, in the sense that important items of customer information would not get lost, fall into the wrong hands or be so seriously out of date as to cause erroneous decisions. To counter such risks, the project team suggested that users should use the CRM system not randomly, but systematically, meaning also keeping it updated with regard to the information of which each employee was in charge. An additional important aspect which was stressed during the training sessions concerned the range of advantages that the company and the users could gain from adopting CRM. It was pointed that the company needed (1) a better way to keep track of what the sales and marketing people were doing every day; and (2) a way to avoid losing all the data about specific customers every time one key salesperson left the company, taking with her a lot of tacit information and experience. While these company-wide benefits might not be perceived as so compelling for certain groups of users, and indeed might even be viewed as a sort of imposed control by salespeople, a general benefit was pointed that could accrue to any possible user: using the CRM system systematically (both in inputting and extracting data) would tremendously improve the quality of communication among users, especially from different functions and business units within Loccioni, by making the information exchanged via the system real time and fully updated. The project team underlined several times how important it was for the company that each user put a major effort into approaching the CRM system: the easiest way to approach it for every user was suggested to be viewing it as a useful tool for improving daily activities.

The project team also created a virtual area on Loccioni's Intranet called "CRM and business-to-business marketing management", which included academic literature about the meaning of CRM and how to manage profitable customer relationships, a user's guide to Loccioni's CRM systems and many other resources. The aim was to build up a digital library for improving the CRM culture within the organization.

In May 2008 the project team organized a kick-off meeting at Loccioni's headquarters with the purpose of officially launching the CRM system. People from the various departments involved during the testing and the training phases of the project were invited. Moreover, the company's president, the managing director and representatives from the board of directors also took part in the meeting. The project team developed a detailed presentation for the audience, focusing on the system's long list of features and functionalities. Also, the demo of the system was shown. Concluding the presentation in front of an attentive audience, the project team stated that they would be providing ongoing support after the launch and answering all questions from the users. It now remains to be seen how the CRM system was actually adopted at Loccioni, a topic to which Chapter 7 is dedicated.

6.7 Summary: From complex customer relationships to CRM

The Loccioni Group emerged in the 1990s as a major player in the business of integrating testing and measuring instruments for industrial customers, mainly in the automotive and home appliances markets, but also utilities and the public sector. Loccioni's business model relies on providing customers with fully customized solutions for quality control, industrial automation, energy, environmental tasks and ICT. Most of Loccioni's customers are large multinational companies, with which long-lasting relationships were established in the 1980s or 1990s. These business relationships are extremely important for Loccioni, as customers regularly return to this supplier in order to buy either new tailored solutions or maintenance services for those they already have installed. However, sales processes are lengthy and complex, due to Loccioni's focus on creating unique solutions for each customer. Therefore, Loccioni's customer business relationships turn out to be highly complex, because most customers have multiple sites worldwide, multiple contact points exist between Loccioni and the customer, and the provision of highly customized solutions typically requires Loccioni to initiate complex customer-specific projects.

Since the 1990s Loccioni's customer relationships have become increasingly difficult to manage, overview and trace, due to a huge amount of information and complicated interaction patterns between Loccioni and specific customers: therefore, in 2005 Loccioni's president recognized the need to shift explicitly to a CRM philosophy, that is, an approach to handling sales and customer more explicitly focusing on managing the specific relationship with each single customer. In parallel, the organization of Loccioni as a group of companies had grown increasingly complex since the 1990s, with several business units and functions having contacts with customers, sometimes unaware of each other's interactions with the same customer. The information about single customers was therefore highly widespread across Loccioni's whole organization, which could create inefficiencies and inconsistencies when trying to handle a customer in a consistent way. It was at this point, in 2005, that Loccioni also started looking for IT solutions, that is, the technical tools to support a more explicit and efficient "management" of customer relationships: previously, in the late 1990s, a marketing database (DBM) had been created, but most users and especially KAMs and salespeople were unhappy with it because its information was too little and too rigid. Loccioni decided therefore to "go the whole way" and create a full CRM database and system.

The CRM project included several phases, from an internal survey to infrastructure design and from configuration of modules to testing and user training. The implementation project at Loccioni seems to have followed all the classical phases and principles, such as the building of a project team, in a typical IT system implementation project. Therefore, the CRM project seems to have created the conditions for a successful implementation of the CRM system, with the exception that salespeople/KAMs were not involved in the project team, but only in the internal survey and then in the testing phase. It is therefore time to move to the next chapters and see how the CRM was adopted by its expected users and which effects it created both inside the organization of Loccioni and, outside, on its inter-organizational relationships with customers.

7
Adopting and Using CRM at the Loccioni Group

The purpose of this chapter is to show how the CRM system was utilized by various users in their daily work. In addition to the adoption patterns, the chapter also describes the process whereby this new IT system became embedded in Loccioni's internal organization, that is, which routines and patterns of use emerged around the system, as well as between various groups of users. After a brief introduction (Section 7.1), different paths in using the CRM systems are presented (Section 7.2). Section 7.3 reviews how different groups of users, belonging to different company functions and units, relate to the CRM system, while Section 7.4 presents the barriers and critical factors impacting the use and non-use of the system. The chapter then continues by describing how Loccioni handled several difficulties with the installed CRM system in an attempt to recover it (Section 7.5). Finally, Section 7.6 shows the benefits that eventually started emerging from the system after it became "stabilized" within Loccioni's organization.

7.1 Introduction

Once the CRM system was installed at Loccioni, the users started to approach and use it, but this was not without difficulties and troubles. Just after its launch in 2008 several issues arose concerning the system and the way the users had been using it. The project team was worried that the CRM project might go into the wrong direction and turn out substandard results in the near future. On the other hand, the project team was satisfied that the implementation process had basically followed the initial plan. The biggest challenge was to keep the system reliability high during this early using phase. Similarly to a new technology that appears to be reliable in the laboratory during its development, but might meet resistance and turn into a failure after its market launch, the CRM system at Loccioni was, at the beginning of its adoption journey, indeed in a tricky situation: this system needed to gain user acceptance and widespread use, but some barriers were soon to emerge.

Some months after the launch of the system, the project team carried out another internal survey, after the first one that was conducted in 2005, with the purpose of verifying whether the conditions to continue the project were present. This time the survey was aimed at measuring the effects of the CRM system on its users and also on a sample of relevant customer relationships (presented in detail in Chapter 8). The choice was made to interview directly six of Loccioni's KAMs, as the ambition was to come up with an assessment of CRM in terms of benefits for the users. The survey was based on a questionnaire composed of two sections. The first one included general questions about the origin of the customer relationship and its specific features, such as economic volume of business exchanges, customer's personnel involved in the relationships and contact frequency. The second section of the questionnaire focused on understanding the KAM's interest in and commitment to adopting CRM as a tool to handle the customer relationship. The questions were aimed at discovering the individual KAM's opinions about the usefulness of the system. After collecting the six questionnaires from the KAMs, short individual direct informal interviews were arranged to comment on the results of the survey or, if an answer was not exhaustive, to have it completed.

7.2   Different patterns in using the CRM system

In May 2008, when the CRM system was launched, personnel started to insert data in the system in order to use it to manage customer relationships. Demographic data about customers (location, size etc.) come to CRM from Loccioni's Intranet, while CRM receives financial data about the customer from the ERP. Such data as customer complaints finally come from the after-sales system. CRM sends then these data back to the respective system, when it is updated by its own users. As presented in Chapter 6, the resulting IT infrastructure around Loccioni's CRM system comprises many heterogeneous pieces that were combined or even literally "stitched" together, when Loccioni's IT department designed and introduced several new bridging software items.

Regarding the current use of CRM, individual users can access the system via Loccioni's Intranet. There are at least two different situations

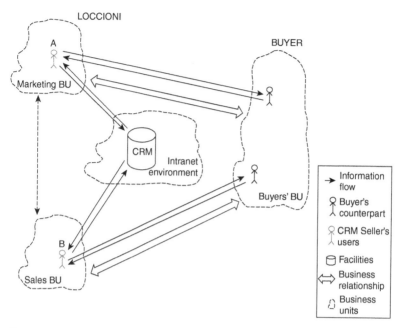

Figure 7.1 Different patterns and information flows in using CRM at Loccioni
Source: Modified from Baraldi, La Rocca and Perna (2013).

describing how CRM is used at Loccioni, depending on which specific users are involved, the patterns of information flows among them
and the purpose of inputting or extracting data from the system (see
Figure 7.1).

Situation 1: User A belonging to the marketing business unit inputs
data into the CRM. This arrangement depends on Loccioni's internal allocation of responsibilities, according to which Loccioni's
marketing unit is in charge of both collecting general market and
customer-specific information, as well as of communicating with
the market via campaigns and other channels. The CRM system
transforms data inputted by this group of users into information
that will be used again by User A, a person belonging to the marketing unit, to handle the relationship. After User A has received new
information from the buyer, she typically puts it into CRM, which
gives her back "processed" information. For instance, the input data
can be all the contacts with a given customer and the activity that
sales people have made with that customer during a certain period

of time. This pattern of use (in terms of both inputting and extracting information) is therefore restricted to the marketing business unit, even if the source of some of the input data can be salespeople (e.g., when it comes to sales activities with a certain customer).

Situation 2: User A belonging to the marketing business unit puts data into the CRM system, but the information produced by the system is used by User B belonging to the sales business unit. This unit includes especially KAMs who are responsible for managing some specific customer relationships and typically have been in charge of doing it for several years. User B will use this information not so much to produce new information or analytics about the customer, as typically User A in the using situation above would do, as to conduct specific and concrete actions to improve the buyer relationship. Only after conducting such an action will the KAM input back in the CRM the information about (1) the action conducted and (2) the reactions received from the buyer. This information might then be used by User B herself, typically a KAM, or by other users, such as User A belonging to the marketing unit. Therefore, this pattern of use crosses the boundaries of Loccioni's internal business units, involving users with different work tasks, expertise and goals when it comes to how the information created by CRM is used.

The information architecture portrayed in Figure 7.1 implies that, when it comes to customer management, the collection, access and retrieval of all customer information is, or should be, centralized around the CRM system. There are also different user profiles inscribed into the system, ranging from Loccioni's top managers to managers from the marketing and the sales units, from KAMs to personnel from the R&D department and the after-sales unit. These different profiles entail different degrees of authorization, with higher level managers and especially executives being granted access to all queries and operations (data input, updates etc.) made within the system by their subordinates, who are formally lower-level users of the system. Therefore, the installation of the CRM system at Loccioni implied not only a centralization of customer information in a single data repository, but also an increased transparency of each user's interactions with the system, mostly in favor of superiors. Moreover, compared to the situation before the advent of the CRM system, when all employees used their own methods to manage customer data (personal notes, commercial software, etc.), now important changes were introduced in the processes of handling customer information, aimed at creating increasingly unified routines.

These changes certainly impacted the 19 KAMs who, between 2005 and 2008, were connected to the system and put in charge of a new task, namely inputting data and using it for conducting sale activities. Each of these KAMs was responsible for managing around ten business relationships with customers, for a total of more than 200 different relationships that were managed according to the KAM approach every year and that from 2008 had to be included in the CRM system. As shown in Figure 7.1, with the new system in place, all customer-related information is expected to be extracted from the CRM system and to be exchanged between personnel involved in customer management primarily via the system, rather than via informal and ad hoc channels. Therefore, CRM assumed a central function in the collection, administration and diffusion of all relevant customer information among all types of users, spread across the various business units of Loccioni's. This centrality of the CRM system greatly increased the visibility and formal requirements of the first activity in this internal process of information exchange, namely data input, which before was an informal and ad hoc activity. In order to guarantee the quality, consistency and timeliness of information, now the input of customer data must be performed according to certain rules and standards, which made some users, especially certain KAMs, reluctant to use the system, at least initially.

7.3 The engagement of CRM users

A few months after the CRM system was launched, the project team identified several different ways of using the system, including basically not using it. It was important for the project team at this stage to verify which interaction existed between the users and the system in terms of which data was retrieved and for which purposes that data was employed in practice. Moreover, it was pivotal to realize which differences existed among various groups of users, depending on their belonging to different business units/functions and hierarchical level. Table 7.1 summarizes these different ways of using (or non-using) Loccioni's CRM system as visible in 2008.

Administration: the interaction between Loccioni's administrative office and the system concerned receiving general information about sales performances and invoices. According to some users from this department, the main value of the CRM system lies in utilizing "financial historical data" to understand the *existing* customers; for instance, the total amount of sales, payments flow

Table 7.1 Connections between CRM's data and different types of use at Loccioni

Business unit, user group	Types of data and information retrieved	Purpose in using the data
Administration	Sales records, terms of payments, actual payments	Understanding existing performances in terms of customer profitability
Top management	Total sales volume for a certain period, total sales volume by product group, sales volume for business area, sales volume by customer, sales budgets	Controlling sales performances and trends. Compare sales outcomes against budget
R&D	Customer geography, customer expenditures in R&D activities, customer propensity in new product development investments, service orders	Getting feedback concerning products issues in order to re-engineer processes
Sales (including KAMs)	Customer profiles, list of customer contacts, orders, deliveries, customer segmentation, financial customer data, press releases	Develop offers and quotations, cross-selling analysis
After-sales	Service contracts and quotations, deliveries and delivery problems	Assigning repair activities, tracking repair activities, spare parts management.
Marketing	Basic customer details, list of customer contacts, volume of orders and quotations, present orders and history of orders, complaints, customer's customers	Building marketing reports, creating new customers profile, build prospect lists
Communication and PR	E-mail addresses, press releases	Building e-mail marketing campaigns, organizing marketing events
ICT	No data retrieved – no use of CRM	None
Production	No data retrieved – no use of CRM	None
Distribution and logistics	No data retrieved – no use of CRM	None

Source: Our own elaboration.

and margins. However, whereas administrative personnel viewed the system as useful in administering existing customers, they considered the system less valuable for attracting *new* customers.

Top management: whereas the top management was highly committed to CRM in the initial steps of the project, they turned out to be interacting much less with the CRM system after it was launched. They were interested mostly in controlling whether the data, particularly sales to individual customers and general sales trends, was inputted into the system. In other words, it was relevant for top managers to know, and to a certain extent to control, how the salespeople's work was proceeding: they paid particular attention to the number of calls and visits made to the customers, and how many orders KAMs and salespeople had obtained from specific customers. This use of CRM by top managers was clearly very oriented toward tracking sales performances, whereas they probably did not believe in, and did not seize the opportunity of gaining, deeper customer knowledge from the system.

R&D: all the new product development activities and investments in research carried out by Loccioni's customers turned out to be interesting information for people from the R&D department. Moreover, they were seeking inside the CRM system data about customer complaints as indications of which aspects of current or new products it might be relevant to re-engineer or develop. Loccioni's R&D group also showed a good level of interaction with the CRM system by uploading on it product development information, which could thereby become available to salespeople, and retrieving reports processed about customer reactions to existing products. The R&D team also retrieved marketing reports about the business relationships between Loccioni, universities and research centers. As described in Chapter 6, over the years Loccioni approached those actors for developing technologies. Therefore, all relationships with key research institutions provided relevant value for people working within R&D. Reports retrieved by R&D contained information concerning research areas, ongoing research projects and key people (professors and inventors) employed at universities and research centers, as well as minutes of meetings arranged with them.

Sales: for the CRM project to be successful, Loccioni's top management had very high expectations that salespeople and KAMs would display the greatest commitment in interacting with the system. Looking at how people from the sales department have been interacting with the system, it is possible to highlight some differences in the use of CRM between salespeople and KAMs: Salespeople used the CRM system to access budgets, recent deliveries and documents regarding history of contacts. The data retrieved was important for salespeople to increase their internal control over quotations. They believed that providing salespeople with models for making quotations could lead them to make more consistent quotations. KAM were interested more in identifying key people in each account (at various organizational levels of the account) and potential opportunities with them. A better overview of a customer's complete range of orders and purchases, in terms of particular products and solutions, would also enable salespeople and KAMs to be better at suggesting new products and solutions, according to the logic of cross-selling.

After-sales: Loccioni's after-sales unit, dealing with providing customers with service on installed products, was interested in obtaining systematic information about deliveries, current orders and delivery problems. This business unit needed to make several analyses regarding accomplished service orders, but also for assigning and planning future service activities. For after-sales it was also necessary to make analysis of how problems were solved. Therefore, they were extracting from the system analytical reports showing such information.

Marketing: people from the marketing unit were among the most active users, when it comes to retrieving detailed data about customers. More specifically, these users viewed it as crucial to have on records the details about the position of the contact person in the customer company: this meant having some personal detail about this person. The marketing unit was also interested in more complex and indirect information: for instance, on what the decision process looks like and the people involved in the customer company; or the identity of a customer's customers, as a way to identify potential prospects for Loccioni.

Communication and PR: the most frequently used function of the CRM system by the communication department was e-mail marketing. The system provides the option of using e-mail addresses to reach customers for any kind of communication, such as new research projects performed by the company. After an e-mail campaign was launched, several kinds of reports with the outcome of the communication activity (e.g., customer feedback) were retrieved and stored by this department.

Production, distribution and logistics and ICT: as shown in Table 7.1, the production, distribution and logistics and ICT unit at Loccioni usually do not access the CRM system for retrieving customer information. These business units do not consider the CRM a useful tool since, according to their representatives, exploiting customer knowledge is not helping them to reach any of their particular goals. As for people from the production area, what they consider pivotal is the information represented by technical knowledge that allows them to be efficient in building a certain solution. The distribution and the logistic function also reckon that information about particular customers, other than orders and addresses, would not support them in reaching their specific job requirements. Also people at Loccioni's ICT, who actually had in-depth knowledge about the CRM system, explicitly stated that CRM was a system developed for purposes that are quite far from their own IT management specific tasks.

In sum, in 2008, the most active users of the CRM system turned out to be people operating close to customers, although there were quite important differences among them. Finding a clear pattern of users might be highly complex: one way has been to look at users' function within the company. For instance, the level of use of CRM by the marketing and communication department was quite high, due to activities carried out by marketers in providing customer insights and discovering potential customers. Also, marketers had to interact with customers for organizing events, meetings and so on. Other users, for instance from the administration, were not so engaged, but still used the system.

It is interesting that the most important users were expected to be salespeople/KAMs, but they showed different ways of interacting with the system depending, for instance, on data availability and reliability. Finally, CRM experienced no use by such departments as production and distribution-logistics. According to people from those divisions, the adoption of CRM does not allow them to achieve any benefits because they are much more focused on using other companies' IT systems that provide them with support in carrying out "technical" activities.

7.4   Critical factors impacting the use of CRM at Loccioni

Informal interviews carried out by the project team member with some representative users identified even more concretely the problems that were afflicting the CRM system at Loccioni a few months after it had been installed. The interviews were carried out with KAMs and sales-people from the Automotive, Home, Environment, Connecting and Automating business areas. Also, some employees from the marketing and communication offices were involved in this round of interviews as well as the responsible manager of the administration office.

In fact, even though CRM was utilized, the picture emerging was not really enthusiastic, mostly due to a diffused organizational iner-tia. In this respect, the deployment of CRM leads the users to interact with a new system and this requires them to move toward new prac-tices. An example of such "inertia" is new data input routines that users were reluctant to follow when they had to learn again how to input data or retrieve it from the system. But quite interestingly, the KAMs, the users interviewed, had very diverging opinions about the CRM system, its usefulness and the very way they were using it. For instance, some employees mentioned that CRM was based on unreli-able and low-quality data and that this was the reason why it was not used. On the other hand, other users stated that they were satisfied with the CRM.

However, the general picture after the implementation of the CRM system was not a completely positive one, as it emerges from the main aspects pointed below here:

1. *Low adoption rate*: the overall use of the system by the various groups of users was less than originally expected. There were no quantitative data available, but the reply to the question "How often do you use the system?" was "little" in most cases. This result led the project team to assume that about 50% of the expected users were de facto not using the system.
2. *Fruitless training activities*: regardless of the extensive efforts in train-ing users at the beginning of 2008, the people interviewed com-plained about the difficulties in using CRM as a tool. A common and general comment was that the CRM system was not really user friendly. Beyond this reason, it was found that only half of the users managed to attend the demo sessions prior to launch.
3. *Data quality and technical issues*: even though during the testing phase (January–May 2008) technical issues did not show up, a few months later several users complained, for instance, about problems in data migration. When data from the old marketing database (MDB) were transferred to the CRM system, it seemed that something went wrong and the users could not find all the customer data they needed. This technical issue was identified by the project team only after

the use and embedding of the CRM system had already begun. One issue was, indeed, the synchronization between the CRM and the old MDB system. The IT manager was quite surprised about this negative result, as the problem was completely unexpected, and it was not possible to find the specific glitch that could have caused this synchronization problem. The worst consequence of these technical problems was that most users now perceived the quality of the data in the CRM system as rather poor. Probably this was the strongest barrier causing the system not to be used. Moreover, there was another problem, this time more human-related, which negatively affected the quality of data: namely the lack of focus and care by the individual user when entering data into the system. Employees made mistakes when inserting data and this inevitably reduced the reliability of this data to other users in general.

4. *Other specific technical problems*: Developing the IT infrastructure internally around the CRM system led to an important problem: the combination of different databases, stitched together with their own software solutions, and the creation of their own algorithm to allow data migration led to a serious instability just after the launch of the system. Another particular technical issue was related to the fact that users were obliged to press the "Save" button on each tab before going to the next window. The probability of forgetting to do this, and therefore missing information, was quite high. This explains why users complained that some information that they were sure they had entered was not captured and registered in the system. Finally, there were several other bugs in the system that contributed to reducing further the users' commitment to using it.

5. *The parallel presence of reporting from the administration*: well after the launch of the CRM system the official sales reporting and forecasting continued to be provided by the Administrative office without using the CRM system for this purpose. More precisely, these reporting documents were sent out by e-mail usually in the form of an Excel sheet produced manually. This issue was a critical one and had not been managed properly during the implementation process, that is, no routine or rule had been specified concerning the dismissal of these weekly reports once the new CRM system would be installed. But another important reason that contributed to this situation was probably the negative attitude of administrative personnel toward the CRM system, which they considered, in spite of some useful items of data they could extract from it, mostly as an "additional useless tool".

6. *The graphic user interface*: a majority of users shared the general impression that the graphic interface displayed a massive amount of information. Although many users who had been involved in the implementation project judged that the graphic interface had been improved a lot compared with previous versions and especially with the original marketing database (MDB), still most users had trouble navigating within it. The suggestion from the users was therefore to remove some information from the screen.

7. *The visibility of user actions and experienced control*: another problem experienced by users, or rather an unpleasant feeling, was related to the fact that the system makes it possible to check exactly which actions every single user performs, or does not perform, on the system and as registered inside the system. This increased visibility concerned for instance who had inputted or omitted to input certain data at a certain moment. Or, concerning actual customer management activities, the system made clearly visible who had made contact with a customer, for what purpose, when and so on. Then, if a superior wanted to inquire about specific actions, the data about each specific user (e.g., a KAM) was easily available, including the possibility of making special queries and even comparing personnel's performance. The visibility of all the actions reported into the system, but also of how each user was using the system (e.g., the quality of data she inputted) was considered a very negative aspect by most users, who felt constantly monitored and controlled by the CRM system.

Among those users who had been expected to receive the greatest advantages from (and thereby to be the most active users of) the system, sales personnel were the most disappointed. As mentioned by one of the KAMs of the company: "the quality and the timeliness of the data are a major issue for being able to process and apply the information from the system. How can I rely on the CRM system if I cannot gain any advantage?" Moreover, it was really the personnel from the sales department, and especially KAMs, who hardly accepted CRM because it made them feel controlled by the system itself or by the management.

Moreover, from several other units and departments of Loccioni a common thought arose that the new system had not streamlined the processes, especially the sales process or the customer management process. Some other users got disappointed when they realized that some of the functionalities that had been promised were not delivered. In fact, functionalities that had been promised were postponed. In this respect, the "smart report" function that would allow users to customize reports on data was not implemented due to some technical issues. Another functionality requested by some users was the integration of Loccioni's VoIP telephone solution with CRM. Unfortunately, after several attempts to add VoIP on CRM, the idea had to be abandoned, once again due to technical issues.

Finally, some users got frustrated since they were not involved in designing or during the implementation process. All in all, there were many reasons for several users to avoid using the newly installed CRM system or use it well below the expected level and extension.

7.5   Recovering the system

Loccioni's president himself was involved by the project team in order to find a solution to the problem of having about only half as many CRM users as expected in mid-2008. It was clearly necessary to enhance the impact of the system on the company and in the late summer of 2008, after a long meeting with the project team, the company's president realized that the CRM project was not really ended and that it now needed to enter a delicate phase, which required bringing substantial improvements to the very system that had just been installed. Both the IT and the marketing managers who were part of the CRM project team reported to him the results of the interviews which had been carried out with the specific purpose of collecting initial feedback from the users (as reported in Section 7.4). This feedback would then be essential to identify the specific areas of improvement to focus on during the further development of the whole project. It became very clear how important it was to put in the hand of the users a fully functioning system. Now, the CRM system that was installed was more than a prototype, but it would have been realistic to think about the possibility of facing unexpected issues. On the other hand, the president was very worried about the initial results of the project, that is, the first users' reactions presented above. Therefore, he suggested that it was necessary to make a considerable effort in order to recover the CRM project, both from a technical and an organizational point of view.

It was decided that one of the first areas to focus upon was to keep the system as simple as possible, with minimal deviation from the prototype created during the design phase. In fact the CRM system became more complex than the prototype in terms of functionalities. A quick solution was to reduce the complexity of the CRM system by making some technical interventions (listed below). The project team clearly decided that they had to focus on the specific suggestions of the users as indicated in the interviews, while the team agreed to keep for a later stage any more encompassing system modification. In this respect the evolution, in terms of refinements, of the CRM system was to be explicitly based on the results of the interviews with users, rather than driven by personal initiatives of project team members.

Several technical interventions were accordingly decided and here follows a list of the most relevant ones: improving data quality, adding alert signals, extending document handling, integration with Microsoft Access, allowing remote access to the system, making available all marketing materials, providing information about prospects and a few other minor changes.

Improving data quality: an address verification system was added to the CRM system to perform data cleansing. This simple tool collected all customers' address details, as recorded in all repositories inside the CRM system, and tested them. In case of inconsistent records an error signal was emitted and a correction was required by the system: if the system assessed that an address might be wrong, it was accompanied by a flag indicating the invalid address. Another small modification made by the IT department allowed the system to eliminate duplications in customer records. This modification was aimed at matching and rechecking the data to keep the CRM system clean.

Alert signals: another improvement concerned adding to the CRM system a function enabling it to trace exactly what is going on with a prospective or a current customer at any time. A set of reminders were added in order to let the user know what to do as a next step in the process of relationship management: for instance, which person at the customer's organization the user could contact or which sales opportunities should be exploited. Following suggestions by the users, another interesting upgrade was implemented that allowed the user to realize that he has not talked to a key customer in the last 15 days.

Document handling: a direct access to some files concerning the final solutions sold to a certain customer was made possible from the customer windows into the CRM system. In this way, when an existing customer was contacted it would be easier for instance for KAMs to get updated on previous selling activities or solutions purchased by that customer. This function was expected to be very useful by the project team and the users themselves.

Integration with Microsoft Outlook: thanks to its easy architecture, Outlook was widely accepted and adopted by salespeople as a tool to organize contacts with customers. Therefore the project team decided to integrate this software directly into the CRM system as a way to enhance contact management by users directly involved in customer relationships. Loccioni's IT manager succeeded in integrating the calendar and e-mail functions, but not other functionalities such as the contacts. The contact functionality of Outlook aims to help users in organizing personal contacts into functional groups, allowing them to send e-mail messages. Since Loccioni's CRM already contained its own list of personal contacts for each user, the integration with Outlook's contacts function clashed.

Remote access: when users worked far away from Loccioni offices, they were facing the problem that it was not possible to connect to the CRM system. Being able to access CRM had actually been a fundamental request by users since the beginning of the project in 2005, but previously it had not been possible to resolve this issue. In 2008, to fix this issue, Loccioni's IT manager decided to apply a set of secure protocols in order to allow users to connect to the company's IT network, and thus to the CRM system, via the Internet. By means of a so-called VPN (Virtual Private Network), users were finally provided with remote access to CRM.

Access to marketing documentation: all Loccioni marketing and communication materials, such as brochures, company presentations and press releases, are placed in an area of the Intranet which was not previously connected to the CRM system. As the importance of having direct access to this material from CRM became clear after the system's launch, a direct connection to the Intranet was made in order to let personnel download this marketing documentation directly from a window of the CRM system.

Information about the potential customer: marketing and sales personnel often organized business trips in order to meet new customers. When visiting these companies, they had to be well updated about the prospect. Therefore, the CRM system was upgraded in order to allow marketing and sales personnel to print out a report with the most important data about each individual prospect. The project team expected that this upgrade would facilitate a direct access to selected and well systematized customer information, to improve the quality of early meetings and communications with a specific prospect.

Other minor changes: in the first few months of using the CRM system the users who were interacting with it also experienced some minor problems. As these were rather simple to solve, the project team decided to address them. For instance, in order to facilitate document search, a free text search function based on keywords was added. Also, the reports about prospective customers were improved in terms of content: the new version included information about the prospect, opportunities to develop projects, opportunities to receive orders and so on.

At the beginning of 2009 an increasing number of users were starting to realize how the CRM system could bring advantages to them. Realizing such benefits was in turn improving their attitude toward CRM. In order to obtain this positive effect on users, the project team had to be efficient in fulfilling the new requirements emerging from users after the implementation of the system. The challenge was to satisfy all the users and their varied needs, which made up a very extensive list of possible improvements to Loccioni's CRM system. Some of the requests were considered so important and were so widespread that the project team had to address them, while others stemmed from personal desires. While excluding this latter type of requests was easy, there were some requests that might be important but not so widespread. As satisfying all requests for changes was not possible, the project team had some difficulties in sorting out the changes to focus upon from the complete list. Moreover, the project personnel had to manage this process with caution, as some users might react negatively and lose motivation in using CRM if their requests were not accepted.

The marketing manager in charge of the CRM project and the IT manager met key users one by one or in small groups in order to discuss openly the issues that appeared when the system was launched. The key users who participated to the meetings were: the KAMs from all the eight business units; all the personnel from the marketing department; some representatives from the administration office; and several R&D managers. A primary goal was to resolve the problems concerning data quality, which represented one of the major problems afflicting the system and had been a hot topic since May 2008. The discussions touched upon several aspects: for instance, how many data sources were to be used or allowed for the various items inside CRM, what level of data quality the system should provide and what data to migrate to CRM from other platforms. As for the level of data quality or data accuracy, it was discussed how to manage the data errors (e.g., wrong records), how to fix incomplete data (e.g., missing records) and how to handle the obsolete information. Another important goal of these meetings between the core project team and key users was to identify and face "hidden" issues, that is, those which were not directly related to flaws inside the newly installed CRM system. One such issue was the skepticism of some users because of their negative experience with the MDB in the past, or other broken down processes (e.g., data input, data recalling and data assessment). A considerable number of these users stated that data entry and feeding the system with customer data was hard work and so time-consuming that they felt that all that work was hardly going to pay off in the end. As a complement to the aforementioned improvements to the CRM system and open discussions on the "hidden" issues, Loccioni's management also decided to invest more in training activities to facilitate the adoption of the system. Eventually skepticism started to decline, while users started to appreciate the benefits derived from the system, especially after the improvements made to the system in 2008–2009.

7.6 Toward stabilized use: Some benefits show up

Since the CRM system gained acceptance, marketing and sales personnel currently use its information outputs typically to obtain a clear customer portrait in order to further develop interactions: information such as financial performance in relation to a customer, sales orders, complaints and contact frequency are the most important data regularly extracted from the CRM system today. Loccioni's CRM can also help managers and KAMs in aggregating and organizing data and information: the system stores customer data and enables users to access sales information at the right time and from any place. For example, KAMs are enabled to input data into the CRM system concerning how sales forecasts have been fulfilled by each customer they will manage within the year. Hence, the CRM can return to the user the outstanding balance of the sales activities planned. Other salespeople can also get information from the beginning of a customer relationship, including either the number of orders placed or the sales opportunities lost.

Other features and outputs of CRM which have gained widespread use consist of customer segmentation regarding sales performances and market shares. Moreover, the communication activities with customers are recorded and added to the customer's contact database in order to be analyzed to plan marketing activities. This means that, after the efforts made in 2008–2009 for recovering the system, the sales business unit and the marketing unit are eventually sharing customer-related information according to the second pattern of using CRM depicted in Figure 7.1.

A highly relevant and appreciated function and information output is the opportunity to track, by means of the CRM system, if a contact person at a customer company is moving to another company. A so-called "Network" folder in the system allows the user to receive information about a contact person's changes of workplace, which is inputted into the system, usually by the marketing office. The "Network" functionality was added to the CRM at the end of 2008 (when several improvements to the system were made: see Section 7.5) upon the initiative of the KAM of Loccioni's Environment business. Looking at how this functionality works, it is necessary that users "link" the contact person to the new company that has employed him/her so that the record will be kept in the system. Afterwards, the system will keep track of this important information by showing the contact both at the "old" company (where the contact is marked with a red line) and at the new one. All the activities done with the contact person (e.g., meetings, projects, quotations) will be automatically stored to avoid losing knowledge. A drawback is that the KAMs or salespeople seldom perform this activity because they consider it valuable but time-consuming, so they empower the marketing office to do it. To sum up, it is of high value to keep in touch with contact persons even though they change company, and the CRM system proves valuable in achieving this goal.

Thanks to these and other benefits that have become increasingly evident, the number of users of Loccioni's CRM system has increased since 2009 to reach about 200 users in 2012. In parallel, a positive view has diffused throughout the company that CRM might be a useful tool to adopt for improving the way in which Loccioni interacts with customers and the way it manages its customer relationships.

7.7   Summary: From skepticism to moderate optimism

Despite extensive preparation work during a two-year project, when Loccioni's CRM system was officially launched in May 2008 it faced several difficulties in gaining acceptance and widespread adoption by users. The goal when implementing the system was that marketing and sales personnel could easily and more reliably start exchanging customer-related information (see Figure 7.1), but poor quality of the data inside the system, time-consuming data input and the feeling of being controlled by the system and superiors made most users dissatisfied with the

CRM system and reluctant to use it. While users from most departments and business units at Loccioni (e.g., marketing, sales, administration, top management, communication and PR) claimed that they could find relevant data and information inside the CRM system, they were not really using it as extensively as the project team expected because they could not yet see direct benefits and advantages from using the system. The reasons for this disappointing level of use, making the benefits hardly visible to users, were a set of challenges and barriers that included the following: inconsistent data found inside the system; tedious procedures for saving data; the parallel presence of other official reporting channels; an overly complicated graphic user interface; and the feeling of being monitored and controlled through the system.

In order to salvage the whole CRM project, Loccioni's management mandated the project team to make the necessary changes to the IT system that could solve at least the technical issues raised by users during a round of in-depth interviews. These technical improvements concerned, for instance, data quality and consistency, alert signals, extended document handling, remote access to the system and access to all marketing materials. However, non-technical issues such as skepticism in using IT tools in general for customer management also had to be addressed. After several months of extensive efforts, including also renewed training sessions, user adoption started to improve as in parallel the first benefits from using the system started showing up.

But even though users are gradually becoming more aware of these benefits, there are still several users who do not recognize them, as the benefits are indeed related to complex factors. As we will point out in the analysis in Chapter 9, the characteristics of a business relationship, the KAMs' attitude toward using CRM and other related dimensions affect both the effects and the very adoption of the CRM system. In order to understand these effects and their complexity, the next chapter will introduce and describe six important customer relationships of Loccioni's.

8
Managing Six Important Customer Relationships: Loccioni's KAMs and CRM

After having presented in the previous chapter how CRM has been adopted and used at Loccioni, we turn now to six important customer relationships of Loccioni's: Magneti Marelli (Section 8.2), Whirlpool (Section 8.3), Trenitalia (Section 8.4), Continental (Section 8.5), Tod's (Section 8.6) and Haier (Section 8.7). These customers vary in terms of industrial sector and solutions they purchased from Loccioni, but are all important customers for Loccioni, even though for different reasons. After an overview of all six customer relationships (Section 8.1), the customer-specific sections first provide background information about each customer and then describe the interaction pattern in the relationship between Loccioni and the specific customer, stressing also the way CRM is utilized in each relationship. This review of each customer relationship and of the role played by Loccioni's KAMs prepares the ground for identifying and analyzing, in Chapter 9, the inter-organizational effects of Loccioni's CRM system, that is, the effects emerging between Loccioni and other organizations such as key customers. By considering first how CRM was embedded inside the host organization (Chapter 7) and then how it influences the interactions between specific key customers and their KAMs, we will then be able to analyze the effects CRM has on customer relationships, considering both their specific characteristics and those of the involved KAM.

8.1 An overview of the six customer relationships

Table 8.1 shows an overview of the six customer relationships, based on two types of features. The first part of the table focuses on basic features, including the following items: the relationship's starting year (corresponding to the date when Loccioni become supplier by selling

Table 8.1 Synopsis of six significant customer relationships of Loccioni's

Relationship start	Magneti Marelli	Whirlpool	Trenitalia	Continental	Tod's	Haier
	1985	1986	1989	1989	1997	2007
Basic features						
Loccioni's business area(s)	Automotive	Home appliance	Environment, Automation	Automotive	Connecting, Automation	Home appliance
KAM's ID (anonymized for confidentiality)	A	B	C	D	E	B
KAM's age	Under 40	Under 40	Over 50	Over 40	Over 40	Under 40
KAM's engagement	Since 2000	Since 1996	Since 1995	Since 1994	Since 1997	Since 2007
System storing customer data	CRM since 2006	CRM since 2006	CRM since 2006	CRM since 2006	CRM since 2006	CRM since 2007
Complex features						
Type of relationship	Continuous	Discontinuous	Discontinuous	Continuous	Discontinuous	Continuous
Top Management involvement	High	High	Medium	High	Low	Low
Sales volume% (share of sales per business area)	8 (2006–2009)	40 (2006–2007)	10 (2006–2009)	55 (2006–2009)	2 (2006–2009)	10 (2007–2009)
Rate of accepted offers%	40 (2006–2009)	60 (2006–2007)	90 (2006–2009)	60 (2006–2009)	60 (2006–2009)	66 (2007–2009)

Source: Our own elaboration on Loccioni's data.

a solution to that customer), the Loccioni business area involved as a provider of solutions to that customer, an identifier of the KAM involved in managing the relationship (including also the age of this person and when the KAM started to manage the relationship) and a final dimension concerning when information about a customer started to be stored in the CRM system. For two relationships, Whirlpool and Haier, the KAM is the same person. The second part of the table, titled "complex features", indicates the following dimensions: continuity/discontinuity over time (in continuous relationships transactions happen regularly, while discontinuous relationships are characterized by intermittent transactions), the level of involvement by Loccioni's top management in developing the relationship (high, medium or low), the customer's importance for Loccioni in terms of sales volumes and finally the customer's reactions to Loccioni's offers.

We have selected these six relationships for a closer analysis because customer data for all of them was expected to be stored on Loccioni's CRM system, as a key tool available to the KAMs and other marketing and sales personnel for managing each of the six relationships. The six relationships are quite different from each other, each one displaying particular characteristics, but all are of strategic importance for Loccioni. Magneti Marelli and Continental are very large players within the automotive industry, while Whirlpool and Haier represent leading producers of home appliances: all four companies are moreover multinational and global in reach. Although Tod's is not an equally large multinational corporation, it is a well-known fashion brand representing "made in Italy" products worldwide. Finally, Trenitalia, the former Italian railway monopoly, may be only a national player, but it is a very large company operating today in several areas of logistics and holding a considerable capacity to invest in cutting-edge technologies.

All of these companies have contributed to Loccioni's development over the years. For instance, a large number of the technologies that Loccioni has introduced in the automotive industry had been developed in cooperation with Magneti Marelli and Continental. By means of the relationships with these two players, Loccioni has also reached a number of car-makers, which are formally customers of these direct customers: in this way, these two customers have opened up new business opportunities for Loccioni with other customers. Whirlpool has been working with Loccioni since the 1980s and has contributed not only to the development of Loccioni's competences in the field of measurement and testing for home appliances, but it also led Loccioni to enter the promising business of eco-sustainability within the frame of the "Leaf

House" project (Baraldi, Gregori and Perna, 2011). Haier, one of the rising Chinese home appliance producers, allowed Loccioni to scale up the cutting-edge Thermovision technology, employed for infrared analysis and testing in refrigerators production lines. The relationship with Trenitalia developed into a more extensive collaboration for product development some years after its beginning in the late 1980s. Partly as an effect of the relationship with Tod's, which can be considered one of the most representative Italian companies in the fashion sector, Loccioni has expanded its business of information technology applications. The origins, the development and the main issues of these six relationships will be presented in the next six sections, after a brief portrayal of the customers. For each relationship we also present a table featuring the interaction patterns between personnel at Loccioni and the customer. In this way we can clearly see who are involved in the interactions and what the interfaces are among them. The description of each relationship also indicates the frequency and intensity of the contacts between Loccioni and these six selected customers, as well as the role of the CRM system in the most recent years. Our review of the six relationships follows their age, starting from the oldest one, between Loccioni and Magneti Marelli (1985), and concluding with the youngest one, between Loccioni and Haier (2007).

8.2 Loccioni and Magneti Marelli

8.2.1 The background of Magneti Marelli

Magneti Marelli is a large Italian company focusing on design, development and production of high-tech systems for the automotive sector. The company is present in 18 countries, with a turnover of €5.9 billion in 2011, about 34,000 employees, 77 production units, 11 R&D centers and 26 application centers. Magneti Marelli is a part of another very large Italian manufacturing giant, Fiat SpA.

In 1919, Fabbrica Italiana Magneti Marelli was established as a joint venture between the two companies Fiat and Ercole Marelli & Co. Magneti Marelli's first business area was the production of full-scale magnetos in 1921. Three years later this company diversified its production into maglights for motorcycles. An important milestone was in 1929 when the company opened a manufacturing facility to produce accumulator batteries for cars. In the same year, the company entered very different business areas, such as the production of televisions and radios, by means of a collaboration with an internationally based company. Between the First and the Second World Wars, Magneti Marelli developed several operations in Europe. For instance, in 1935 it created a joint venture company with the German Bosch to manufacture and market electrical equipment for cars; in 1938 Magneti Marelli gained access, due to another partnership, to light-bulb manufacturing. In 1984 the company moved to Cinisello Balsamo (close to Milan) and two years later, after being restructured, Magneti Marelli became an industrial holding company. Between 1988 and 1994 the Italian company struggled to keep its market position in the following automotive sectors: lighting systems, heating systems and batteries. At the end of the 1980s Magneti Marelli entered two new sectors: the manufacturing of exhaust systems and of oil pumps. This step would mean that Magneti Marelli started to establish its global presence within the Powertrain sector, bringing it closer to an area where Loccioni was operating too.

More specifically, Magneti Marelli entered into the Powertrain sector by purchasing Weber, an established producer of carburetors located in Bologna, Italy. The newly created Magneti Marelli Powertain thus inherited the historical headquarters of Weber in Bologna, dating back to 1923. This division of Magneti Marelli is nowadays an important player worldwide for the development, manufacturing and sale of fuel injection engine control, transmission systems and components. Today the division has three R&D centers, three application centers and 12 plants in seven countries: Brazil, China, Germany, France, Italy, India and the USA. The most important part of the product range is engine control systems for gasoline and diesel engines. Magneti Marelli Powertrain produces hardware components, the electronic control units that steer the engine and their sophisticated software. The customers of Magneti Marelli Powertrain include all the main car manufacturers in Europe and America and the company is moreover the market leader in Brazil.

8.2.2   The business relationship between Loccioni and Magneti Marelli

The relationship was born even before the Powertrain division was created: in 1985 the firm Weber asked Loccioni to supply carburetor test benches for its manufacturing plant located in Bologna. Starting supplies in 1986, in this way Loccioni entered the automotive market for the first time. Then Weber turned into Magneti Marelli at the end of 1989 and the newly started Powertrain division initiated several R&D projects with Loccioni, which entailed close interactions between the two companies. The relationship has been characterized by a high level of commitment and trust, without particular problems. For more than 20 years Magneti Marelli has been among Loccioni's most important customers in terms of profitability and purchase volumes. Moreover, Magneti Marelli also purchased testing systems from Loccioni for automotive components for its manufacturing plants in South America.

A relevant episode which has characterized this relationship was the development of a specific product by Loccioni for Magneti Marelli which had to fulfill the need of one of its most representative customers, Ferrari, the sports car producer. In 1997 Magneti Marelli needed to develop an automatic testing solution for its new inverter that could be mounted inside a new Ferrari model. Magneti Marelli also needed to be able to use the bench to test stand-alone subcomponents of the inverter. In order to shorten the delivery time of this test bench, Loccioni had to start its development before the complete definition of the product and its testing specifications were finished. As a way to accomplish this task, Loccioni decided to start an R&D project in collaboration with Magneti Marelli and the University of Naples "Federico II" to define the test specifications for the new inverter. A joint project team was put together. It consisted of two people from Loccioni's R&D department, one researcher from the university and four people from Magneti Marelli. Both companies wanted to take every opportunity to get to know each other better and enhance the understanding of the technical issues. The biggest task in this phase was to identify a solution for how to manage and test electric components that work with high voltages (600 V) and high current levels (800 A). To accomplish a complete testing of the inverter, Loccioni worked with Magneti Marelli to divide the test into several parts. After several months of development, Loccioni delivered and implemented the bench on the customer's production line. The challenge posed by Magneti Marelli in supplying the new bench for the inverter addressed to Ferrari turned out to be an opportunity for Loccioni to develop a new competence for advanced high-power functional testing of electronics components.

This demanding project, according to Loccioni's KAM "A" in charge of Magneti Marelli, contributed to deepen and enhance the relationship with this customer, which stands for about 8% of Loccioni's turnover within the automotive business. The KAM dedicated to Magneti Marelli is under 40 and has been in charge of this customer since 2000. Next to very intensive interactions during similar joint development projects, the relationship with Magneti Marelli is continuous in terms of supplies and exchanges of information, negotiations and quotations, with about 40% of offers converted into actual contracts. As shown in Table 8.2 this relationship is characterized by highly complex patterns

Table 8.2 Loccioni–Magneti Marelli, pattern of interactions, 2005–2008

		Loccioni					
		Top management	Automotive division		R&D department		Service division	
		President	KAM	Sales assistant	Director	Engineer	Director	Sales person
Magneti Marelli (Powertrain)	Top Management — Managing Director	X	X		X			
	Production — Director		X					
	R&D department — Director		X		X	X		
	Product Development — Director		X			X		
	Engineering — Director		X	X		X	X	
	Purchasing — Director		X				X	X

of interactions between the two companies. In addition to top management involvement from both sides of the relationship, there are many people involved on both sides and there is a lot of information exchange. This interaction pattern reflects the technical complexity and importance of the relationship. More precisely, Loccioni's KAM interacts with all the people involved from Magneti Marelli's side, namely their managing director and their directors of R&D, product development, engineering and purchasing. At Magneti Marelli, a similar role of interacting with most people at the counterpart is played by the purchasing director, who, in addition to Loccioni's KAM, also interacts with its sales assistant, an R&D engineer and people at the Service Division. Finally, a special connection exists between the R&D directors of both companies, as required by the joint development projects conducted between the two companies.

8.2.3   CRM in the business relationship between Loccioni and Magneti Marelli

KAM "A" was quite straightforward in his judgment of the impact of Loccioni's CRM system on the customer relationship with Magneti Marelli:

> CRM has not been useful to handle the relationship itself. It can be viewed just as a database in which financial data about Magneti Marelli are stored and its usefulness consist in being simply a data warehouse. CRM is really a time demanding tool because it requires a lot of time to input data...

"A" was employed by Loccioni in 2000 when he was a young graduate from the university and was therefore accustomed to computer systems, and he was not hostile to the idea of using a CRM system for supporting his tasks in managing customers. However, due to the complex nature of this very old relationship he had no time to input data in the system, which remained accordingly just a repository of static data, mostly taken from the ERP system.

8.3   Loccioni and Whirlpool Europe

8.3.1   The background of Whirlpool Europe

Whirlpool Europe was created in 1985 when Whirlpool Corporation[1] entered the European market. The strategy of Whirlpool to get into the European market was based on the purchase of the appliance division of the Dutch-based company Philips Electronics. As a first step a joint venture company with Philips, Whirlpool International BV (WIBV), was established. WIBV produced home appliances by putting together the Whirlpool brand with Philips. In 1991, due to Whirlpool's goal to be recognized by the market as a European company, Whirlpool became the sole owner of WIBV. Over the years Whirlpool Europe developed three main brands, namely Whirlpool, Bauknecht and Ignis. From a commercial point of view, each of those brands aimed to satisfy different customer segments, defined in terms of price. While Bauknecht served the high-end customer segment, Ignis was oriented to sell low price products, and the Whirlpool brand was positioned somewhere in the middle. As for the organization of Whirlpool Europe, the headquarters were placed in Comerio, located in the north-west of Italy, while the biggest distribution center was set up in central Germany, in Schondorf. In each major European market country sales offices were established: these facilities existed to generate sales and to get in touch with customers. The market for Whirlpool was divided into two main separate markets: consumers, who purchased appliances for their homes, and business customers, mostly building companies, who purchased appliances for new home construction.

Whirlpool Europe's product portfolio ranged from washing machines and dryers to dishwashers, refrigerators and ovens. In order to face the competitors, Whirlpool Europe started big investments in R&D activities. Some examples of product innovations include an increased size of the front-loading opening in washing machines to facilitate loading clothes; moreover, Whirlpool enhanced the life cycle of its products by paying more attention to the quality of critical components. Starting in 1996, this company also expanded its operations in eastern and central Europe, in such countries as Romania and Bulgaria.

8.3.2   The business relationship between Loccioni and Whirlpool Europe

In 1985 Loccioni was looking for customers interested in buying a new testing system for measuring the quality of washing machines. Loccioni took the initiative and got in contact with European home-appliances producers by organizing in its headquarters a marketing and sales event to present innovative testing systems technologies which Loccioni had developed for white-goods producers. Three engineers from Whirlpool attended the event and were positively impressed by Loccioni's technology. Back in Germany, they started to discuss the opportunity to involve that small company, Loccioni, and its technologies in their washing machine business. In 1986 Whirlpool bought from Loccioni an automatic test system for washing machines that was installed their manufacturing plant in Schondorf, Germany. A year later, in 1987, Whirlpool purchased 12 additional test systems from Loccioni. These innovative systems, which Loccioni had developed specifically for Whirlpool, brought Loccioni to the attention of the whole home appliance sector at the international fair "Domotechnica".

In 1989 the relationship between the two companies tightened when Loccioni designed, in collaboration with an Italian research center, six other automatic systems for the testing of washing machines for Whirlpool Europe's manufacturing plant located in Naples, Italy. Following Whirlpool's needs, a set of automatic stations were developed to work simultaneously with two washing machines. The result entailed a considerable reduction of testing time for the customer. During the following years Loccioni carried out a new installation for the Naples plant and refurbished two existing testing lines. In 2004 Loccioni built a data tracking system for the production of washing machines at the Poprad (Slovakia) manufacturing plant of Whirlpool Europe, while in 2006 the Italian company delivered to Whirlpool's German plant in Schondorf a new technology for improving the quality of washing machines. On that occasion Loccioni set up nine testing stations for vibration measurements and two stations for water leakage detection by adopting infrared analysis: this was considered a new cutting edge technology applied for the first time in the area of testing of washing machines. In 2007 Loccioni developed another important technology and then implemented it at Whirlpool: this time the Italian company supplied vision systems to detect, through the use of cameras, the presence or absence of components and their correct assembly. In the same plant in Schondorf a research laboratory was also set up to allow technicians from Loccioni to work together with Whirlpool's engineers for developing hardware for a new line of front loader washing machines.

This review of the history of the relationship between Loccioni and Whirlpool Europe has focused on how Loccioni supported the customer with technologies for their business of washing machines. However, over the years, Loccioni also supplied systems for enhancing the quality of all other product divisions at Whirlpool, namely dryers, dishwashers, refrigerators, freezers and ovens. Here is a brief summary of the major achievements in these product areas:

- *Dryers*: in 2006 Loccioni revamped a laboratory placed in one of Whirlpool's French plants by designing and installing new data acquisition systems.

- *Dishwashers*: Loccioni developed, installed and monitored several testing units for a Polish production facility of Whirlpool Europe. Between 2003 and 2006, about 50 units has been implemented of a system capable of tracking data for controlling dishwashers' doors, for doing audit and for testing of electrical parts.
- *Refrigerators and freezers*: in 2002 Whirlpool Europe involved Loccioni for the first time in testing the quality of its refrigerators and freezers. Loccioni provided several testing units for their biggest manufacturing plant in Europe. The technology adopted for this testing was infrared analysis: by means of this new technology, the testing time was reduced to just a few minutes compared to the two hours of a traditional testing system.
- *Ovens*: in 2004 Loccioni devised and installed a data tracking system for an ovens production line at Whirlpool Europe's plant in Poland.

If we look at how the relationship between Loccioni and Whirlpool Europe developed over the years, it appears to have been intermittent, meaning that the two companies have not been interacting continuously throughout these years. Moreover, it is possible to consider two main periods characterized by closer interactions between Loccioni and Whirlpool: the first one between 1985 and 1989, and the second between 2003 and 2007, when Whirlpool Europe started to buy control systems from Loccioni again. In fact, during the 1990s there was much less interaction between the two parties. After 1992, Loccioni's sales personnel experienced less contact with Whirlpool Europe and perceived that the relationship was less valuable than before. One of the main reasons for the discontinuity of the relationship derives from several substantial changes within the procurement and R&D strategy of Whirlpool Europe which occurred during the 1990s.

The procurement strategy of Whirlpool Europe was characterized before 1992 by decentralization: this meant that all manufacturing plants belonging to Whirlpool Europe and spread across different countries (Germany, UK, etc.) made their purchases even from the very same suppliers without any coordination. Basically, each of Whirlpool Europe's purchasing managers, located in a specific manufacturing plant, was in charge of deciding investments in machinery without coordination with Whirlpool's headquarters in Italy. Loccioni's sales personnel were accustomed with this situation and were used to interacting directly with each of these local purchasing managers. In fact, in order to finalize a sale it was important for Loccioni's salespeople to have good contacts and a common understanding with all the various purchasing managers of each single plant of Whirlpool Europe.

But in the new purchasing organization created after 1992 the responsibility for procurement of important and expensive systems, such as those for testing, was assigned to the purchasing unit in the Italian headquarters. Whirlpool's aim with this reorganization was to create a united front toward all suppliers, as a way to obtain more favorable conditions, and also to increase coordination between various manufacturing plants in search of possibilities of reducing overall procurement costs. This change in Whirlpool's procurement strategy had effects on the business relationship with Loccioni, and did so immediately. All the previous interactions that Loccioni had had with the various local purchasing managers of Whirlpool Europe's had to be cut off, while the new interface for Loccioni in attempting a sale became uniquely the Italian central purchasing unit. This situation made Loccioni lose several contacts that had been established between people who had got to know each other through cooperation over the years. Moreover, before the creation of this new centralized purchasing organization Loccioni had much better access to information on Whirlpool Europe regarding purchasing conditions, orders and production. While the reorganization entailed disadvantages for Loccioni, an unexpected effect of the new purchasing strategy and organization was that many manufacturing plant managers of Whirlpool Europe showed great resistance to accepting the new strategy because each plant had lost autonomy in making key investment decisions.

Another strategic change at Whirlpool that further contributed to the dip in the relationship with Loccioni was the fact that during the 1990s Whirlpool decided to create a new unit in Italy that was in charge of all decisions about R&D projects. Making it even tougher for Loccioni, this unit, considered as the corporate engineering division, produced its own testing systems for quality. Loccioni was rather disappointed with this decision because it implied that Whirlpool Europe would naturally cut off Loccioni as a supplier of quality testing systems. From that moment, every attempt by Loccioni's personnel to contact Whirlpool's plants to propose the joint development of new technologies or systems was ineffective.

However, the situation gradually started to improve for Loccioni from 2003, especially with supplies to Whirlpool's eastern Europe plants. And since 2006 the business relationship between Loccioni and Whirlpool has progressed considerably based on new requirements that Whirlpool put on Loccioni. Interestingly, Whirlpool realized that they lacked internal skills when facing an industrial problem in one of their manufacturing plants located in Schondorf: that was the spark that led to involving Loccioni again in a joint development effort in order to create a new testing system for solving special needs in the customer's production line. An important role in this episode was played by the manager of the German plant, who contacted personnel from Loccioni's R&D department in order to discuss a new complex and high-tech system to detect problems in washing-machine production lines. Of course Loccioni exploited this opportunity to get in contact with Whirlpool again and succeeded in delivering the nine infrared-based testing stations already mentioned.

According to one of Loccioni's salespeople, even during the "dark ages" of this relationship it was important to maintain a direct line of communication with Whirlpool aimed at informing them about Loccioni's progresses in the development and launch of new home appliance testing systems. Another key issue is that this "renewed" relationship entailed a few compromises: Loccioni, in fact, was initially involved in conducting projects regarding just a restricted set of technologies, instead of being involved in all possible testing system solutions. However, the relationship further improved to reach the open collaboration of the 1980s and today, next to routine deliveries of systems, it also includes several important research and manufacturing projects, which were carried out starting from 2010. The most important investments performed by Whirlpool Europe in the last few years were aimed at reducing the defect rates of its washing machines. In this respect, Whirlpool Europe's division in charge of handling the investments for testing activities decided that it was necessary to figure out how far the defect rate would lead to customer losses. Loccioni was also involved in doing the feasibility study taking care of technical activities such as inspections on washing-machine drums and other critical components.

Today there are intense interactions between the two companies: there are daily contacts between the R&D departments and sales/marketing offices of both companies. According to "B", the KAM assigned to Whirlpool Europe, the atmosphere of this relationship can be characterized as good. Despite being under 40, "B has been managing this customer since 1996 and has witnessed the discontinuity in the relationship, which is however still today one of Loccioni's most important: Whirlpool Europe stands in fact for 40% of the turnover within the Home Appliance business area of Loccioni's". Indicating a substantial improvement in the relationship from the dip in the 1990s, today the rate of accepted offers is around 60%.

As shown in Table 8.3, during 2005–2008, the relationship between Loccioni and Whirlpool was characterized by a very complex pattern of interactions. First of all, there is a very large number of people involved from both companies, about ten from Loccioni and at least twice as many from Whirlpool. Moreover, top managers of both Loccioni and Whirlpool intervene in the relationship: Whirlpool Europe's managing director and plant directors are involved in the negotiations every time they are going to invest in new large projects, while Loccioni's President and managing director usually intervene when discussing important and long-term projects or large supplies. Loccioni's KAM "B" is the person having the most contacts with Whirlpool's managers, ranging from their top executives to production directors in single plants, the R&D director, product developers, the quality and testing manager and especially with several directors at the purchasing office. From Whirlpool's side it is purchasing managers who interact with most people at Loccioni: with the KAM "B" and his sales assistant, with the vice director of R&D and with personnel from the Service Division of Loccioni, in charge of delivering maintenance services for the many systems installed at Whirlpool's plants.

8.3.3   CRM in the business relationship between Loccioni and Whirlpool Europe

According to KAM "B" no immediate tangible effects of the CRM system appeared in this relationship. In his words "the CRM system just helps people in organizing data and tracing it". "B" was hired as a sales assistant but he made fast career progress and when he was still very young was assigned the important but challenging task of managing the "giant" account Whirlpool Europe. This is not only an old, but also a very complex business relationship, with a lot of issues to be taken into account for managing and developing it. The limited use of the CRM system by KAM "B" was explained by the fact that he felt that it was really difficult to use the CRM as a way to better approach Whirlpool Europe because no strategic information was held in the system. In this respect, important qualitative customer information, such as the level of satisfaction of individual buyers concerning the solutions Loccioni sold over time, were never made available by the CRM system. And this type of future-oriented information was what "B" would need to improve his way of managing this customer.

Table 8.3 Loccioni–Whirlpool, pattern of interactions, 2005–2008

| | | Loccioni | | | | | | | | |
| | | Top management | | Home appl. division | | Marketing | R&D dept. | | Service division | |
		Presid.	Man.Dir.	KAM	Sales assist.	Mark. manager	Director	Vice director	Director	Sales person
Whirlpool Europe	Top Management									
	Managing director	X	X	X			X			
	Head of Europe's manufact. plants	X	X	X			X			
	Manufact. plant's directors	X	X	X						
	Production Directors			X					X	
	R&D dept. Director			X		X	X	X		
	Product develop. Directors			X				X		
	Quality & testing dept. Manager				X					
	Purchasing Directors			X	X		X	X	X	
	Marketing Office Director					X			X	X

8.4 Loccioni and Trenitalia

8.4.1 The background of Trenitalia

Trenitalia is the leading Italian railway operator, with trains for long and medium distance routes. It is a subsidiary of Ferrovie dello Stato S.p.A, which was established as a public company in 1905. In 2011 the firm employed around 54,000 people with a turnover of about €8 billion. Its long distance passenger division operates about 600 trains per day. In the Italian railway market, the Ferrovie dello Stato Group has a leading position and employs about 90% of the railway workers in Italy. Ferrovie dello Stato was privatized in 1992, although the privatization was only formal, since shares are still owned by the Italian government. In 2000, in compliance with the EU directives on the liberalization of railway transport, an extensive change occurred which led to the establishment of Trenitalia and, the following year, of Ferrovie dello Stato (becoming Ferrovie dello Stato Italiane in May 2011), the parent company, thus completing the reorganization process.

Trenitalia is the main player concerning long distance passenger transport and for its international transport branch it has developed several joint ventures with foreign railway operators. Also, in the segment of freight transport Trenitalia holds more than 90% of the Italian market. Trenitalia's headquarters are placed in Milan and Rome, even though there are 21 regional direction offices.

8.4.2 The business relationship between Loccioni and Trenitalia

The relationship between Loccioni and Ferrovie dello Stato started in 1989 when one of Loccioni's suppliers, Siemens Group, suggested that Trenitalia was looking for suppliers able to rebuild several railway stations. Thus, in establishing this business relationship an important role was played by an engineer from Siemens who concretely connected Loccioni to what would then become Trenitalia. Loccioni was in fact selected as the supplier in charge of devising and delivering an automatic tracking system for an industrial plant. In 1995 Loccioni was again involved directly by Trenitalia in developing tailored solutions for the supervision systems of small plants in their railways stations. Loccioni was able to offer integrated control systems that were the result of several years of studies in the automation sector. The relationship therefore became closer starting from 1995, due to Trenitalia's process of reorganization that led the company to increase its attention to train maintenance. One of the main concerns of Trenitalia was the preservation of the infrastructure of their train systems, including also the cleaning routines of train toilets and the achievement of controlled emissions from these toilets.

Between 1999 and 2003 it was Loccioni's "Automation" division that supplied Trenitalia, but in 2003 it was Loccioni's business division "Environment" that developed automatic systems for toilet sanitation on Trenitalia's trains.[2] More than 15 such plants have been installed on a national scale, according to Trenitalia' needs of sanitizing their different types of trains. Trenitalia was generally satisfied with working with Loccioni, but the relationship over the years has been quite complicated according to "C", Loccioni's KAM belonging to the "Automation" division and in charge of this customer. "C", who is about 50 years old and has been engaged in this relationship since 1995, states that

> To cope with Trenitalia has always been painful, with large investments made by Loccioni in keeping contacts with them. Important characteristics of this business relationship are that it is discontinuous over time and that affairs are intermittent. We really would like to have Trenitalia among Loccioni's most important customers but something should be organized differently.

Consequently, Trenitalia represents only 10% of the revenues of the involved Environment and Automation divisions, even if the greatest majority of Loccioni's offers are usually accepted by this customer (up to 90% in 2006–2009).

Nevertheless, Trenitalia represented and still represents the ideal customer considering its leader position within the Italian railways industry. And most importantly, Trenitalia actually needed continuous maintenance and refurbishing of both trains and railways. In fact, one of the other important problems constantly faced by Trenitalia is associated with safety control of rails, particularly the rail switches that allow a train to be guided from one track to another. The conditions of the rail tracks and their switches represent a critical aspect both for security and punctuality reasons, but such conditions change quickly over the year: in a hot summer, the unconstrained rail lying next to the track is going to expand, while the fixed rail will experience compression. Instead, in extreme cold conditions, the rail will shrink. Therefore, the correct measurement of the exact size of rail switches is pivotal in order to solve this issue.

In 2010, when Loccioni's R&D director and the KAM in charge of Trenitalia convened at one of Trenitalia's premises, the purchase director of Trenitalia explained their need to cope with safety control systems for rail switches. No deal was reached at that meeting, but Loccioni was invited to develop an innovative robot for making diagnosis of tracks and switches' conditions. Mounted on the railway track, the robot was equipped with special tools developed by Loccioni and including a series of vision systems. Specific diagnostic algorithms were also developed in order to process and analyze the acquired data. The main goal of the diagnostic robot was to transmit wirelessly to an operator image and measurement data for further analysis. According to Loccioni's management, who were not however directly involved during the negotiations with Trenitalia, this new technology would turn into a good opportunity to enhance Loccioni's position toward Trenitalia (even if so far the system has been not purchased by Trenitalia). But the management also set an important condition to be met before carrying out the project and all the future investments with this particular customer: before starting large-scale production of those systems, a more comprehensive agreement had to be formalized. Loccioni's management considered this point important in order to avoid misunderstandings that would negatively affect the relationship.

As shown in Table 8.4, which illustrates the pattern of interactions between Loccioni and Trenitalia, this relationship is not as complex as the ones with Magneti Marelli and Whirlpool. First and foremost, this relationship does not involve many functions and individuals from both sides, only about four people from each. Moreover, the top management of Loccioni is only moderately involved in the relationship. In fact, Trenitalia is an important customer at national level, but Loccioni does not have relations with Trenitalia's facilities in Europe. Contacts and

Table 8.4   Loccioni–Trenitalia, pattern of interactions, 2005–2008

			Loccioni			
			Automation division	Environment division	Service division	
			KAM (C)	Sales manager	Director	Sales person
Trenitalia	Top management	Vice-President of R&D operations	X			
	Technical department	Directors	X	X		
		Managers	X	X		
	Purchasing	Directors	X	X	X	X

interactions with all Trenitalia's representatives (top management, technical directors and purchasers) are held mainly by Loccioni's KAM from the "Automotive" division; while from the customer's side it is the purchasing directors who interact with Loccioni's counterparts, including personnel from the "environment" and the "service" divisions. All in all, the complexity of the interactions in this relationship is relatively low.

8.4.3   CRM in the business relationship between Loccioni and Trenitalia

Trenitalia's KAM "C", one of the oldest among Loccioni's KAM, was very skeptical of the effects of CRM and was basically not using it in managing this relationship. He considered that CRM, apart from being an interesting graphic interface, was just another type of IT tool which Loccioni's managers had to use, but that it would not give much value to them. He did not see any positive effects of CRM for relationship management because he generally did not trust IT at all as a tool to manage customer relationships. He was indeed uninterested in adopting any software and IT in general, because he considered only his own skills useful for managing customer relationships. He was hired at the beginning of the 1990s, when IT tools were rather uncommon, and he focused exclusively on Italian customers.

8.5   Loccioni and Continental Automotive Trading (CAT)

8.5.1   The background of CAT

CAT is the Italian subsidiary of the so called "Automotive Group" of the large German conglomerate Continental AG. Continental AG is one of the largest automotive suppliers worldwide with 134,000 employees in 2009 spread across 34 countries. Continental was founded in Hannover, Germany in 1871 as a rubber manufacturer. In fact today Continental is still mostly recognized as a tire producer, and globally it holds the fourth position as manufacturer of tires for the automotive market. However, Continental AG is a diversified conglomerate structured into six different divisions, only two of which deal with tires: "Passenger Car & Light Truck Tires" and "Commercial Vehicle Tires". To these two divisions, one must add Chassis & Safety, Interior, ContiTech and Powertrain. The "Automotive Group" of Continental includes three of the six divisions – Chassis & Safety, Powertrain and Interior – and is one of the leading global automotive suppliers: in 2010, it achieved sales of approximately €16 billion, employing around 87,000 people in more than 170 locations worldwide.

Continental Automotive GmbH manufactures and supplies automotive electronics and mechatronics. It offers replacement parts, diesel repair services and vehicle diagnostics for passenger cars; instrumentation, tachographs, mobile Internet solutions and telematic devices for commercial vehicles. It sells its products through dealers in order to reach final customers, car and truck owners, but also directly to car manufacturers, who include Continental's solutions in their vehicles directly on the assembly line. One of Continental's main areas of expertise, where they are a technological leader, is "fuel consumption reduction", achieved through more efficient fuel injection systems. This business area, which belongs to the Powertrain division, has not been developed from scratch but was developed after Continental took over the automotive division of the German group Siemens, which was named Siemens VDO. The acquisition of Siemens VDO by Continental happened in 2001 for approximately $16 billion. And it is through a previous relationship with Siemens VDO that Loccioni became a supplier to Continental's "Automotive Group".

8.5.2 The business relationship between Loccioni and CAT

In 1989 Loccioni had its first contact with Siemens VDO, which would become fully integrated into Continental in 2008. Loccioni had been one of Siemens VDO's most important suppliers of quality test benches for gasoline engine components since the early 1990s and their business relationship was very close from the beginning. When two former employees of Magneti Marelli, an established customer of Loccioni's (see Section 8.1 for a review of this relationship), received Siemens VDO's support to start their own venture, named Ventek, they also chose Loccioni as a supplier. Ventek was then totally acquired by Siemens VDO and became Siemens VDO Italia. After a long track record of satisfactory joint projects and deliveries, which built a good reputation with Siemens VDO Italia, Loccioni was also able to contact Siemens' headquarters in Germany. Later on, this extended relationship allowed Loccioni to start the supply of testing benches for components also to one of Siemens' most important manufacturing plants in China. A close interaction then started between Loccioni's top management and Siemens' executives responsible for all Powertrain testing systems purchasing: the parties were clearly aiming at finding a deepened and widened way of working together.

This strong relationship led to CAT becoming Loccioni's most important automotive customer, accounting for about 55% of the turnover of Loccioni's "Automotive" division. Continental's manufacturing plants in Regensburg (Germany), Limbach (Germany) and Pisa (Italy) have strong connections to Loccioni: these plants in fact produce gasoline and diesel injectors, for which Loccioni has developed special testing instruments. In particular, Loccioni provides these three plants with quality testing systems. Since Continental's Powertrain division is focused on making fuel systems more eco-friendly, the relationship with Loccioni opened up interesting collaboration opportunities over the years. An important episode that contributed to strengthening the relationship was a research project named "Mexus", which Loccioni performed after the request of its customer Continental (for details, see Perna, Baraldi and Gregori, 2012). In 2005 Continental experienced a serious problem in its injector production line in Limbach, Germany. The technical problem concerned a testing/measuring system that Loccioni had delivered by integrating different solutions. Continental requested that Loccioni not only solve this problem as soon as possible, but also that it find a new technical solution to be used for the long term and which would be a substantial improvement of the previous technology.

This was certainly a challenging request as Loccioni had until then operated mostly as a system integrator of existing components, while Continental's request implied that Loccioni would have to create a new core technology. As Continental was one of Loccioni's major customers, Loccioni agreed to start a specific project with the aim of creating this entirely new solution. Loccioni's team, in collaboration with some external consultants, developed a new algorithm capable of providing a new generation of measurements. When a prototype of Mexus was ready it was time to test it at Loccioni's R&D site. Therefore, for almost six months, between 2006 and 2007, several mechanical and electrical tests were carried out on Mexus. After Loccioni had solved some initial technical problems, Mexus was delivered to Continental's Italian site in Pisa (CAT) to be tested also in their laboratory and production line. This stage of product development unveiled several issues and, in order to recover Mexus, a joint Loccioni–Continental team had to deal with several technical problems, one by one, which led to devising a more complex and sophisticated meter. After the successful completion of the product development project, at the end of 2007 Continental bought several Mexus meters, pointing out Loccioni as one of the most reliable suppliers within their Powertrain division. In fact, about 60% of all offers presented by Loccioni to this customer in the period 2006–2009 turned into a purchase.

In addition to such highly intensive interactions as the Mexus project happening within a restricted period of time, the relationship between

Loccioni and Continental is also characterized by very many continuous interactions: every manufacturing plant of Continental where Loccioni has supplied testing systems is in weekly communication with the sales, technical and service personnel of Loccioni. The resulting pattern of interactions is highly complex in this relationship, as shown by Table 8.5. First of all, there is close involvement from Loccioni's top management, with the president having strong personal relationships with Continental's top management both at local (manufacturing plant) and global level. There are moreover more than ten people involved in the relationship from each side. In particular, Loccioni's KAM, "D", who is in his 40s and has managed this customer since 1994, interacts with all executives, plant managers, the production, the quality, the R&D, the testing and the purchasing directors from Continental. Due to the high research and development intensity in this relationship, the R&D director of Continental is, together with the purchasing director, the person from Continental interacting with most employees at Loccioni.

8.5.3   CRM in the business relationship between Loccioni and CAT

Similarly to Magneti Marelli and Whirlpool, Continental is another important and complex customer of Loccioni's, but CRM is not really applied in managing this relationship. However, Continental's KAM "D" considers CRM potentially useful, but he views only a small part of the available information inside this IT system as really helpful in managing the relationship with Continental. Most of the information inside the system is concerned with the volume of business exchanged with Continental, which allows this KAM to be regularly updated about the transactions done. This type of information creates a good historical overview of the relationship, but it is not so useful for setting up further plans with the customer for future interactions and joint strategic actions. As a consequence KAM "D" regards CRM simply as a data warehouse. In this sense, the CRM system can be useful for retrieving some very detailed information one might not remember exactly, but "D", who has experienced the whole history of this relationship since the early 1990s and is considered to be very competent and precise, would expect some more inspiring information capable of triggering future actions.

8.6   Loccioni and Tod's

8.6.1   The background of Tod's

Tod's SpA is the Italian operating holding of a group which is a leading player in the production and distribution of shoes and luxury leather

Table 8.5 Loccioni–Continental, pattern of interactions, 2005–2008

| | | Loccioni | | | | | | | |
| | | Top managem. | Automotive division | | Marketing | R&D department | | Service division | |
		President	KAM	Sales assis.	Assistant	Director	Engineer	Direct.	Sale sperson
Continental	Top management — Managing director	X	X			X			
	Global purchas. manager	X	X			X			
	Manufact. plants' directors	X	X			X			
Prod.	Director		X						
R&D dept.	Director		X	X	X	X	X		
Testing Division.	Director		X	X	X		X		
Quality dept.	Director		X	X	X				
Purchasing	Director		X	X			X	X	X

goods. In 2010, the group sold for more than €700 million and had 2800 employees. The headquarters is located in the Marche region, in central Italy, not far from Loccioni's headquarters. In the Italian fashion luxury market, featuring a few giants, such as Gucci and Armani, Tod's is considered to be one of the major players.

The company was founded in the early 1900s by Filippo Della Valle, who opened in 1920 a small laboratory where genuine leather shoes were produced. Diego Della Valle, one of Filippo's grandsons, expanded the activity from 1960 in order to turn the small company into an international enterprise. After having realized that the company would be much more profitable by focusing on high fashion products, the company became a leader in special niches. Nowadays, Tod's is the owner of several famous fashion brands: Tod's, Hogan (shoes, hand-crafted shoes, leather goods, accessories and apparel), Fay (casual clothing for men, women and children) and Roger Vivier (shoes, handbags, small leather goods, jewelry and sunglasses). The production is mostly located in the Marche region, while other activities concerning quality control are concentrated in Tuscany. The choice to keep the greatest part of Tod's production in Italy is related to the good availability of sub-suppliers of genuine raw materials. Other critical phases, such as design, are also kept in Italy.

Strategically, Tod's decided not to offshore the production of its branded products and the group has all its manufacturing facilities in Europe, where nine out of ten are located in Italy: at the beginning of 2000 the company's board decided to be listed on the Italian stock exchange. Concerning distribution strategies, Tod's has historically decided to set up its own operating stores in order to get closer to the customer and thereby enhance its brand position. However, worldwide the company's products are distributed through a network, which includes directly owned stores, franchised stores and a selected numbers of independent retailers. Tod's is the owner of more than ten flagship stores in cities like Milan, Paris, Tokyo, New York, London, Düsseldorf and Hong Kong.

8.6.2 The business relationship between Loccioni and Tod's

The business relationship between Loccioni and Tod's was born in 1997. Loccioni was introduced to Tod's thanks to another company, a small consultant firm that had been in contact with Loccioni for several years. This consultant was well aware of Loccioni's capabilities in the area of electrical system design for industry and introduced Loccioni to Tod's in the spring of 1997. At that time, Tod's was building a new manufacturing plant to extend its production capacity and had decided to make large investments in the new plant. Of course, one of the priorities was to set up the electrical and information system infrastructure before starting with the installation of the manufacturing equipment. The consultant firm put the manager of Loccioni's business unit for IT development in contact with one of the responsible persons for Tod's information systems unit. Loccioni viewed the opportunity of entering via Tod's into a new market segment, namely luxury goods producers. Therefore, Loccioni was pleased to start negotiations with Tod's concerning how to develop the project.

After several months of discussions, Loccioni was selected officially by Tod's to supply several electrical systems to be installed in the new facility. As a first step, Loccioni was the supplier responsible for building the whole electrical power supply system. Loccioni appointed as KAM for Tod's the manager of its business unit "Connecting", which started to negotiate with Tod's. The electrical infrastructure turned out to be complex to design and deliver because of the particular layout of the building. Once Loccioni had solved this issue, it received several other assignments from Tod's. Particularly, in the second phase of the project, Loccioni was contracted to integrate solutions for the management of production-related information in the factory: this ranged from the creation of the LANs and WANs to the development of the whole system for wireless data communication. Loccioni also installed the external video surveillance system. More than 8 km of electric cables and 12 km of pipes were installed. This second step was realized within 1998 and was characterized by high interactions between technical people from the two companies.

Three years of the relationship, between 1997 and 2000, were characterized by a high level of collaboration, but in 2001 the relationship became much more complicated. Tod's replaced key people in its IT department and Loccioni had to develop new interactions from scratch. Afterwards, the number of new solutions bought by Tod's dropped and the number of contacts and revenues from this customer stagnated. According to "E", the KAM in charge of the Tod's account since 1997, one of the reasons for this stagnation was the small budget that Tod's invested in IT infrastructure. Moreover, Loccioni did not develop IT systems itself but focused mostly on integrating software and hardware supplied by players such as Cisco Systems, Hewlett Packard and IBM. This way of approaching customers' IT needs implied that Loccioni could not be an innovator but only a system integrator, which reduced Loccioni's capacity to be a technological partner for any customer.

But after several years during which the business relationship with Tod's was dormant, in 2007 it got a new start and considerable development. In those years, Loccioni was experiencing positive technical and sales results in developing and implementing IP (Internet Protocol) telephony systems, in collaboration with Cisco System. In fact, several companies were able to reduce their costs by adopting IP telephony as their platform for telecommunications. Loccioni reckoned that this technology would fit very well in a company such as Tod's, which needs to connect several different facilities – shops, manufacturing plants, distribution centers – by keeping to a minimum the communication costs between them. With a centralized and unified communications system, Tod's would no longer need to purchase and maintain separate voice systems for each of its stores. After discussions between Tod's manager of information and technology infrastructure and Loccioni's IT business unit manager about the feasibility of such a project, Loccioni managed to convince Tod's and was involved in designing and implementing their IP platform. The whole project was delivered after six months and Tod's also signed a three-year service contract with Loccioni for assistance and maintenance activities. Nowadays, Tod's is still a rather small customer for Loccioni, accounting for only 2% of its turnover in the "Automation" and "Connecting" divisions. However, the rate of Loccioni's offers which were turned into orders was as high as 60% in 2006–2009, and contacts are becoming more and more regular between the two companies.

The pattern of interactions with Tod's is much less complex than in the previously reviewed relationships, as they involved only three people from Loccioni and three people from Tod's. Due to the small volumes involved in the relationship, Loccioni's top management is not involved at all in this relationship. There are however two managers of Loccioni who entertain an equal amount of contact with Tod's, namely the official KAM, "E", appointed in 1997 and belonging to the "Connecting" division, and the sales manager from the "Automation" division. From Tod's side, the manager interacting with the largest number of Loccioni employees is the purchasing manager. Still, the relationship includes an important technical dimension which requires involving Tod's IT specialists, though more for short-term issues rather than long-term projects (Table 8.6).

Table 8.6 Loccioni–Tod's, pattern of interactions, 2005–2008

			Loccioni		
			Connecting division	Automation division	Service division
			KAM	Sales manager	Sales manager
Tod's	IT department	Director	X	X	
		Assistants	X	X	
	Purchasing	Manager	X	X	X

8.6.3 CRM in the business relationship between Loccioni and Tod's

According to KAM "E", who is in his 40s, compared to the past and the previous MDB Loccioni now has a useful marketing tool represented by the CRM system. He has used the system for easily processing and sharing information about Tod's with other Loccioni employees. "E" can then use this processed information in order to better prepare, for example, a meeting with the customer. However, according to KAM "E" the system also has two major shortcomings consisting in the lack of reliability of the information contained inside it, as well as in the delays in receiving back information from the system. Therefore, these two aspects turned out to limit the extent to which "E" uses the CRM system for managing the relationship with Tod's. At the same time, there are no direct and clearly identifiable effects coming from the CRM systems on how the Tod's relationship is currently managed. However, KAM "E", who is also a strong expert in IT business applications, underlines the potential of the CRM system as a marketing tool for the future.

8.7 Loccioni and Haier

8.7.1 The background of Haier

Haier, a Chinese household appliance producer, was founded at the beginning of the 1980s and has grown to become a major global player in the production of white goods, in particular refrigerators. Nowadays, Haier sells in more than 160 countries covering North America, Europe, the Middle East, Asia and Africa. In 2011, Haier had global revenues of USD 23 billion and employed more than 70,000 people, including 10,000 employees outside China. The company originated when Mr. Zhang took over a failing refrigerator company in the city of Qingdao: his personal goal was to introduce in China a new generation of high-quality refrigerators very close to the European standards. In order to carry out the project, Zhang realized that it was necessary to set up reliable production lines. Haier imported production lines from Europe, particularly from Denmark and Italy, as well as from Japan. From the beginning, Haier was oriented to commercializing quality and branded products, despite the vast Chinese market's demand for low-cost refrigerators.

In 1986 Haier made a good profit although its refrigerators sold only in three Chinese cities, and in 1988 the company was awarded a prize for the quality level of its products in a national competition. As for the internationalization strategy, by 1990 Haier did not operate in any other market than the Chinese one. Haier was much more interested in keeping its market share in China and the management of the company did not aim to build an international position. In 1991, due to the high demand level for refrigerators in China and the good profit it achieved, Haier became the leading refrigerator producer on the Chinese market. But quite soon Mr. Zhang realized that, in order to preserve the favorable position of the company, it was necessary to adopt a diversification strategy: in fact, almost all of Haier's competitors had developed and commercialized a broader range of home appliances. Therefore, at this point Haier purchased two already existent manufacturing plants committed to the production of freezers and air conditioners: both of those factories were located in Haier's hometown of Qingdao. The manufacturing plants were refurbished by introducing new production lines. Moreover, people with engineering backgrounds and freshly graduated students were hired. Within one year the new division for freezers and air conditioners had become profitable and, in 1992, the Haier Group was founded replacing the former Haier company.

Haier Group grew quickly in terms of profits and number of employees. Moreover, large investments in research and development activities were made and Haier also created a new industrial park in the Qingdao region. Between 1993 and 1997 Haier carried out several important company acquisitions. For instance, in 1995 Haier took over a nearly bankrupt Chinese company involved in the production of washing machines; quite interestingly, within less than two years that company turned out to be among the top-ranked washing-machine producers of China. Another important milestone was reached in 1997 when Haier added televisions and telecommunication equipment to its product range with the acquisition of a company located in the Anhui province. By 1997, Haier had acquired a total of about 17 different companies. In 1998, the Haier Group started a major reorganization into seven different product divisions: refrigerators, air conditioners, washing machines, IT products, kitchen and bath, technology equipment and direct affiliates.

In parallel with the reorganization, Haier also started to look at possibilities to expand overseas. The result is a considerable international presence today: in 2011 Haier had more than 45 manufacturing plants all over the world and from the 1990s it started to build its own factories in South America, Africa, the Middle East and Asia. Haier's global expansion strategy was characterized by different ways of entering the various new markets: for instance, in several countries Haier started as a contract manufacturer for multinational brands and several joint ventures with global leaders were established to explore foreign markets. Haier also made direct investments, such as when in 2001 it purchased a factory in northern Italy. This acquisition turned out to be very important because, when the new company Haier Europe was founded, it was headquartered in Varese, Italy; this company also took responsibility for coordinating sales and marketing of Haier's products in more than ten countries. Haier Europe became responsible for sales and marketing activities in Europe as well as for manufacturing activities of products such as refrigerators by means of its Italian plant.

8.7.2 The business relationship between Loccioni and Haier

Reflecting also the dip in the relationship with Whirlpool Europe (see Section 8.3), at the beginning of the 2000s Loccioni was looking for potential new customers among home appliances producers and started to analyze the Asian market. In that geographical region, the Haier Group was identified as a leading company, along with the South Korean companies LG and Samsung. It took however until 2006 for the marketing office of Loccioni to start collecting more actively information about Haier, LG and Samsung, as a way to evaluate if these could become its customers. This market research showed that all the major Asian producers operated numerous production plants around the world and could be potential customers. As a result of the study it was decided that Loccioni would approach Haier, Samsung and LG to explore business possibilities. The market study identified the refrigeration side of the business of Haier as a potentially interesting and fast-growing business. At an internal meeting between the marketing manager and the sales managers of Loccioni's Home Appliance business unit it was decided to contact the Italian manufacturing plant of Haier and present Loccioni's systems for quality testing of refrigerators.

An e-mail containing a short description of the Loccioni Group, its portfolio of solutions within the home appliance market and some important customer references was sent by the marketing office to the quality manager of Haier's Italian plant located in Padua. Shortly afterwards the plant manager at Haier contacted Loccioni to obtain additional information about the solutions that Loccioni had already offered to other customers. A meeting was scheduled at Haier's plant for January 2007, where the discussion revolved around the investments planned by Haier to enhance the quality of the refrigerators it produced. Haier was particularly interested in the Thermovision technology that Loccioni developed and which they were currently providing to other producers of household appliances. At that time, Haier was aiming at improving its quality as part of its broader company-wide strategic priority and was actively looking for suppliers that could be involved in its efforts to improve the performance and reliability of its products. Loccioni believed that the relationship with Haier would be very important for the future as it could act as a potential gate-opener to other applications in the home appliance industry, in particular in Asia.

It turned out that management at the Haier plant in Italy had had contacts with the production and R&D people of another large producer of white goods located in Northern Italy, and had heard that the management of this producer appreciated and held a high opinion of Loccioni's competence, customer commitment and business approach. Therefore, Haier's managers decided to initiate a project with Loccioni aiming at delivering quality control systems for their plant in Padua, Italy. The implementing phase of the project started in the winter 2007 and in early 2008 the whole system was delivered. Later on, via the relationship with the Padua plant, Loccioni's R&D manager was introduced to Haier's headquarters in China. Since then, Loccioni's business with Haier has been stable and this customer has already reached 10% of the turnover of the Home Appliance division of Loccioni's. From 2007, the relationship appears as rather continuous and the number of interactions has increased; this is especially due to the number of potential opportunities for Loccioni to provide solutions also to Haier's plants in China and the USA. About two thirds (66%) of Loccioni's offers to this customer were turned into deliveries in the period 2007–2009.

Table 8.7 shows the pattern of interactions between Loccioni and Haier. In 2006–2008, only four managers from both sides were involved in the relationship, but this number was gradually increasing. As the customer was not yet a major account, Loccioni's top management was

Table 8.7 Loccioni–Haier Europe, pattern of interactions, 2006–2008

			Loccioni			
			Home appliance division		Marketing department	R&D department
			KAM	Sales assistant	Marketing assistant	Vice director
Haier Europe	Production	Director	X		X	
	R&D department	Director	X			X
	Quality & testing department	Director	X	X	X	
	Purchasing	Director	X	X		X

not directly involved at that point in time. Instead, as the customer was rather new for Loccioni, a marketing assistant from Loccioni's Marketing Department was in charge of several interactions in the first stages of the relationship with Haier Europe. Thereafter, after receiving positive feedback about Loccioni's solution, the interactions with Haier's Italian manufacturing plant became the responsibility of Loccioni's vice director of the R&D Department, and especially of KAM "B", who is also the person in charge of the Whirlpool account. "B" in fact interacts with all relevant managers at Haier involved in this relationship, namely the directors of production, R&D, quality and testing and purchasing.

8.7.3 CRM in the business relationship between Loccioni and Haier

As previously mentioned, the KAM in charge of Haier, "B", is the same person acting as KAM for Whirlpool Europe. But differently from the role of CRM in managing the Whirlpool account, "B" considers CRM a very helpful tool for the relationship with Haier: in particular, in this case "B" claims that the CRM system provides useful data and information to handle the customer Haier. How can this be explained? Isn't the CRM system the very same as the one that "B" considered not useful for managing the relationship with Whirlpool? Does the Haier relationship require more simple information than the one "B" needed for

Whirlpool? Or does CRM include different, indeed more useful information for Haier than for Whirlpool? As it turned out, it is the latter explanation that applies here: for example, under the Haier relationship folder, Loccioni's CRM system includes specific information about Haier's ongoing activities and planned investments, which had been inputted by Loccioni's marketing personnel. Therefore, KAM "B" was able to start interactions with Haier's managers thanks specifically to these pieces of information recorded in the CRM system. All in all, the effects of CRM on the business relationship with Haier were clearly evident, especially during the start up of the relationship and its early development: in fact, at that stage, it was important for the KAM to have real-time and very current customer information in order to facilitate his task of organizing initial meetings with this customer. In other terms, by providing well-structured and future-oriented information about Haier, CRM has contributed to supporting "B" in managing the relationship itself.

8.8   Summary: Looking for CRM's effects on customer relationships

This chapter reviewed six important customer relationships of Loccioni's. They differ greatly in terms of history, continuity and volumes, as well as complexity. The older relationships date back to the 1980s, while the newest was established in 2007, that is, while the CRM system was being implemented. Half of the relationships are continuous, while half are intermittent, in the sense that they were characterized by more or less long periods when the relationship was dormant, with very little interaction between Loccioni and the customer. The importance expressed as percentages of turnover of these relationships varies from just 2% to 55% for the respective business areas. Finally, the complexity expressed as number of people involved varies from about six to 30 people involved in interactions.

When we looked specifically at the use and effects of CRM in these six relationships, the overall picture was disappointing: four relationships (Magneti Marelli, Whirlpool, Trenitalia and Continental) present minimal use by the respective KAMs and little or no effects on both how the customer relationships are managed and their outcomes; while the relationship with Tod's and especially that with Haier showed respectively modest and strong effects from using the CRM system. At a closer look, there appears to be a variegated pattern in how CRM is used and the effects it produces in the six relationships. This pattern may depend on such factors as a relationship's age or stage, or its complexity, as well as the KAM's attitude toward IT tools, which seems to be related to his age, and whether or not he finds inside the CRM system the right type of information he needs to handle the relationship. These dimensions will be analyzed in detail in Chapter 9, which will be specifically looking for the effects of CRM, both inside the host company and on its customer relationships.

9
Case Analysis: The Embedding and Effects of CRM at Loccioni

In this chapter we analyze the embedding of Loccioni's CRM system at both intra- and inter-organizational level. By "embedding" we mean the emergence of connections between the system and the other technical and organizational resources (Baraldi and Waluszewski, 2005). These connections between resources (also known as "interfaces", Håkansson and Waluszewski, 2002; Baraldi, 2003) influence the use of the new IT tool and hence the appearance of its effects both inside and outside Loccioni. Favorable resource connections (or interfaces) positively impact its use and the creation of effects, whereas unfavorable connections hinder its use and effects. To begin with, Section 9.1 focuses on the factors that influenced the installation of CRM at Loccioni, such as top management's visions and the company's attitude toward the use of CRM, aiming to assess how far Loccioni was ready to use such an IT system.

This discussion of the initial context where CRM was installed is followed by an analysis of the effects of Loccioni's CRM after its installation. First, Section 9.2 analyzes the impact of CRM at intra-organizational level, that is, inside the using organization of Loccioni; then Section 9.3 analyzes such an impact at inter-organizational level by considering the effects of Loccioni's CRM on the customer relationships it is expected to influence.

9.1 Factors influencing the installation of CRM at Loccioni

Loccioni's purpose in introducing CRM was to improve the way customer data (e.g., profiles, contacts, financial and marketing data) were stored, shared and utilized among employees. In fact, the Marketing Database (MDB) which for several years had been the only IT tool available had turned out to be often too rigid, imprecise and complex to be used by the employees in charge of managing customer relationships. Loccioni also chose not to purchase off-the-shelf CRM software from specialized vendors but to develop its own CRM system internally. The company's president was clearly a driving force in the decision to develop the system internally. However, the in-house development was characterized by problems and several unexpected barriers emerged.

Due to the decision to develop internally a fully tailor-made CRM solution several interactions had to take place within Loccioni's organization between different organizational entities, such as internal departments (marketing, sales, R&D, IT and the top management), and with one external group (the researchers from the Polytechnic University of Marche). An important internal factor influencing the installation of CRM was then the project created for its implementation and the related project team. This team had in turn to face the rather ambiguous attitude of Loccioni's employees toward CRM.

Most factors or circumstances which led Loccioni to develop and install this system have *internal* origins inside the company, but there are a couple of factors that have *external* origins. We start our discussion with these external factors. A first external factor is the diffusion of CRM, both as a practice and as IT solutions, among Loccioni's competitors. Loccioni's president in fact perceived that other similar companies were introducing CRM and feared that his company could lag behind if it did not do the same. Imitation of competitors' strategies is in fact a rather common factor influencing IT investment decisions (Swan, Newell and Robertson, 2000).

A second important external influence on Loccioni's CRM was the interaction with the team of researchers from the Polytechnic University of Marche. Loccioni already had contacts and had exchanged knowledge with a number of researchers from that university. In order to organize and coordinate the whole flow of activities in the CRM project, Loccioni realized that they needed closer cooperation with these external researchers. In many ways these researchers played a role similar to that of external implementation consultant for off-the-shelf IT solutions. Loccioni also realized that the academicians could help them handle the complex issues in the "intangible" parts of the project, namely those affecting such organizational issues as activity coordination between marketing, sales and IT departments, or the training sessions. The university researchers could also provide Loccioni with knowledge about the complexity of embedding a CRM system, a type of "soft" organizational knowledge that Loccioni hoped to be able to combine with technical capabilities in developing IT systems held by its IT division. Similarly to the traditional steps in purchasing standard systems and their installation consultants (Brandt, Carlsson and Nilson, 1998), Loccioni's choice of the academic team was the result of a selection process where other partners were evaluated according to several explicit criteria. These criteria took into consideration the costs entailed, the potential partner's competence and, most importantly, the partner's willingness to develop a long-term collaboration. In fact, Loccioni wanted to avoid a short-term collaboration, but aimed to build a permanent team of people to involve in future needs related to the CRM system.

The two above factors, competitors' CRM practices and the academic research team, are the only two external factors that clearly influenced Loccioni's CRM project from the start. Other external factors, such as the very customer relationships to be managed via CRM, would also turn out to impact the later stages of the project, and especially the effects of the system. However, these external factors were not visible before starting the project or even before starting to use the system: one of these factors, which will be discussed in Section 9.3, is the age of a business relationship, or rather the start date of the relationship in relation to the installation of the CRM system.

Turning to the internal factors that affected the installation of CRM at Loccioni and the related project development, we can single out at least four main factors: top management support (Chen and Popovich, 2003; Osarenkhoe, 2007); internal IT development skills (Bull, 2003); personnel's attitudes toward CRM (Reinartz, Kraft and Hoyer, 2004); and Loccioni's internal organization (Boulding et al., 2005). A first key internal condition was the fact that the company's president was strongly oriented toward investing in an IT solution to be used as a tool for improving business processes, and especially marketing and sales. In fact, before CRM top managers were dissatisfied with a situation where individuals, for example people from the marketing, R&D and sales divisions interacted with customers but often omitted to report back and share information with other parts of Loccioni's organization. The primary goal of Loccioni's CRM system therefore became to create the conditions for improving the distribution of customer information among people involved in managing customers. Having such information more easily available was expected to support the routine activities of employees: the development of CRM software would make it possible at least to gather data and then to provide to relevant people in the company with some kind of knowledge about the customer. Top managers viewed CRM primarily as an IT system for storing and organizing customer data; they did not explicitly view it as a tool usable for strategic long-term purposes. In fact, from the beginning of the project CRM was conceived as a platform not to be shared with customers for online data exchange.

The second internal factor that influenced, indeed supported, the choice of installing and even developing internally the CRM system deals with Loccioni's previous experience with software development and with customer data management. The MDB system was Loccioni's first attempt at moving toward a customer-centric culture. Moreover, it is important to stress that Loccioni had the skills and internal resources to develop its own CRM application. This situation turned into a further stimulus for the company to pursue its own development of a CRM system. In other words, Loccioni held the capability of developing software by means of its IT business unit. The company's president considered the possibility of internal software development as a way to contain the level of investment, even though a cost evaluation was not explicitly made. Moreover, Loccioni also envisaged a business opportunity for selling CRM systems by designing, implementing and testing the first CRM prototype itself. The goal of becoming a CRM system developer was not officially included in the goals of the CRM project, but the choice of strongly betting on in-house development of the system sent a clear signal that the IT staff would eventually become specialized in building or upgrading such systems.

A third relevant internal factor that influenced the installation of the CRM system, and especially its early adoption, were the individual users' attitudes toward this type of IT tools. Quite importantly, there was a different level of acceptance of such tools among the employees who would become the users of the CRM system. While people from marketing and the younger KAMs were positively oriented toward CRM, senior sales personnel and personnel from the R&D department were skeptical. This latter group did not see how CRM might be useful for their activities. These different attitudes partly depended on prejudices and generalized negative attitudes toward using any kind of IT. But a significant part of Loccioni's staff also perceived that the contribution of this particular technical solution to enhance their working processes was basically absent: in other words, these potential users could not really see the value of this IT system in terms of how they could combine it with other resources in performing their daily activities and various managerial tasks (Baraldi, 2003).

So far, therefore, internal factors include both facilitating and restricting ones: in particular, although Loccioni's president took the initiative of developing the CRM system and was very supportive of it all the time, this corporate decision was going to be met with mixed feelings by the employees. The final internal factor that we identify may in principle be both a facilitating and a restricting one, as we shall soon see.

The fourth and last internal factor that we single out as impacting the installation of the CRM system is Loccioni's particular organizational structure: the Loccioni Group is in fact composed of several separate business units (see Figure 6.3 in Chapter 6), characterized by established information management routines, but also by partly missing communication channels. In particular, the marketing unit and the sales unit were those expected to be affected the most by the CRM system. These two units were those handling the majority of customer-related information, but also those which did not really exchange such information to the extent that Loccioni's management was hoping for. Therefore, the CRM system was viewed by top managers as a way to improve information exchange especially between these two business units, and therefore indirectly also between all Loccioni's other business units possessing or in need of customer information. All in all, installing the CRM system offered an opportunity to re-engineer key business processes (Davenport, 1992; 2000) and to reduce inefficiency in information sharing across different business units: one may therefore expect that the organization as a whole would be positively oriented to a solution helping to improve this type of problem.

However, achieving the potential gains from having a common and reliable data repository would also require some changes in the organizational routines (see Smith et al., 1991). For instance, information flows needed to be remodeled based on how the various parts of the organizations were supposed to exchange information in the future (see Figure 7.1 in Chapter 7) as dictated by the CRM system. A new set of complex computer-mediated organizational interactions (see Suchman, 1987) were expected to emerge after the installation of the CRM system: the various employees and business units would be required to perform new tasks in terms of information management (especially data input) and to do it in a coordinated way. However, the motivation for doing it was not so clear, at least if we compare the cost of changing information management routines and daily working behavior with what people immediately got out of the CRM system. Therefore, the re-engineering of information handling processes could well face a set of barriers in the form of organizational inertia and resistance to changing established routines.

9.2   Intra-organizational effects of Loccioni's CRM

The analysis of intra-organizational embedding implies considering how both technical and organizational resources interact around and get combined with the focal IT system (see Baraldi and Waluszewski, 2005). As for technical resources, our analysis discusses how Loccioni's CRM system is connected to other technical IT resources and which technical interfaces emerged between this type of resources; whereas for organizational resources we discuss the organizational interfaces that emerged between the IT system, the users' routines and the organizational processes. We start by analyzing separately technical and organizational interfaces around Loccioni's CRM, but the identification of the intra-organizational effects of CRM will eventually be based on considering together the technical and organizational interfaces.

9.2.1   Technical resource interfaces surrounding Loccioni's CRM system

Loccioni is a company that can be defined as a system integrator because it has historically good experience in integrating different components to set up technical solutions for its industrial customers. In installing the CRM system, Loccioni's experience in making complex IT systems for its customers was applied to developing the technical side of CRM, even if the whole project originated in the need to handle an internal organizational issue. However, the technical team soon realized they had been too optimistic in terms of how technical issues could be handled. One of the first technical problems was that they did not know in advance what software or IT program would fit with Loccioni's other IT systems already in place.

In combining different technical resources (software, databases and hardware) Loccioni's technical IT personnel tried out several combinations and had to handle adaptations between the single items. They did not have the possibility in advance to anticipate problems and they spent time in finding the right combination to connect, for instance, the CRM with ERP systems (see Figure 6.5 in Chapter 6). The ERP system, the Intranet and the other software already possessed its own configurations and interfaces, which could create problems if a new element such as CRM was to be connected with the others. The search for a good combination between all these technical resources was thus an important activity for Loccioni during a long period. A lot of attempts were made but these did not lead to the kind of configuration that would produce the effects necessary for a successful architecture. Through trial and error between 2006 and 2007, Loccioni was able to come out with a prototype only after several months. And starting to embed the system, that is, approach actual use of the final version of CRM, took several more months, going into 2008. However, the final version of the system that was presented to the users was afflicted by some technical problems that required the IT team to solve these unexpected issues quickly. As often happens with any innovation, including IT systems, meeting the users in actual using situations entailed further adaptations of Loccioni's CRM to the using context (Akrich, Callon and Latour, 2002; Van de Ven et al., 1999): hence, the process of assembling different resources for developing the new IT system and embedding it at technical level was costly, time-consuming and non-linear (Ciabuschi, Perna and Snehota, 2012).

In building a bridge between technical resources (software and hardware) and organizational ones, such as information, users and customers themselves, the technical team had to handle the key issue of which kind of data would be inserted in the CRM system and in which format. This issue dealt with how to create a model (Nilsson, 1999) which would represent the customer and the customer relationship by means of digital data in a database (cf., Baraldi, 2003). While defining the characteristics and the various entry points in the database comes close to combining *technical* resources, when the project team moved to defining which kind of customer information to collect, which user and when had to input the related data into the system, they started combining more and more *organizational* resources. In particular, when the team started discussing what a typical CRM user should do with the information extracted from the system, in terms of the decisions they could make, then the team was fully embracing organizational resources: for example, how should users utilize that information to manage a customer? Should they look for meeting alerts to plan new customer meetings? Structuring and partly re-engineering these information management processes was demanding and time-consuming, but it also created the premises for the organizational embedding to follow, including barriers and possibilities for it.

9.2.2 Organizational resource interfaces surrounding Loccioni's CRM

The organizational interfaces around CRM indicate how the CRM system, especially when it enters into use, relates to the users' routines and to broader organizational processes. As typically happens with key administrative and information management systems spread across the whole organization (see Smith et al., 1991), most users at Loccioni changed their work routines and processes in some way when the CRM system was implemented. Chapter 7 of our empirical case indicates that CRM is utilized by almost all Loccioni's organizational units except the production and the distribution and logistics units. Employees of the sales unit (especially KAMs) and of the marketing unit were highly involved and indeed direct users, both in terms of data input and extraction. The changes in routines that had to accompany the embedding of CRM in the organization can be considered substantial. Especially, the direct users of the system had to change their way of handling customer data: from a very heterogeneous set of individual approaches, with informal notes and ad hoc software solutions, to a common set of templates and steering procedures, which gave the system itself a lot of power and control over the workflow (cf. Zuboff, 1988).

It is not strange then that some among Loccioni's personnel reacted negatively to CRM, especially the KAMs, who felt supervised and controlled by the system and their superiors, in a sort of panoptical mechanism (Ibid: 320–360). KAMs also felt that due to the CRM system they were giving up their flexibility in handling customers. As the CRM system became embedded within Loccioni's organization some activities, such as data input, required standardization and control so to avoid duplication and mistakes that would make the information provided by the system less valuable. But at the same time, these forms of control made these activities more scrutinized and evident to everybody than in the past.

While these organizational interfaces concern the single user (and her routines) and the system, there are also more complex organizational interfaces involving several organizational resources at once: for instance, many KAMs felt they were losing their independence if they shared customer information with other people in the organization. In a similar vein, another complex organizational interface surrounding the CRM system appeared as KAMs became all of a sudden dependent on somebody else for key informational input in their work: marketing personnel was in charge of inputting into CRM customer data that would then be processed and transformed by the system into information that was supposed to be used by KAMs. Marketing personnel may even occasionally change key customer-related information about a KAM's "own" customers without informing the KAM in charge: this made KAMs wary and suspicious about what information was to be found inside the CRM system, a system where the same "customer meeting" may have been entered twice. Basically, KAMs did not trust the system as much as their own personal way of keeping track of customer information. Therefore some KAMs were reluctant, at least in the first period, to use CRM.

All in all, the CRM system made two previously relatively separate business units, sales and marketing, become more dependent on each other, creating or making more salient an organizational interface between them and the system itself, an interface which it now became necessary to handle. In fact, the marketing unit, on behalf of Loccioni's president, had to engage in convincing KAMs that the advantages of an increased level of information management efficiency due to CRM outweighed the loss of control deriving from sharing information with the other users.

9.2.3 Identifying the intra-organizational effects of CRM at Loccioni

Both technical and organizational resources were involved in the development, implementation and use, framing the embedding of Loccioni's CRM system. The intra-organizational effects of CRM derive from how CRM is embedded into the host using organization by means of the technical and organizational interfaces shown in Figure 9.1. The embedding of CRM happened as a complex, non-linear process which allowed several technical and organizational interfaces to emerge and which showed its effects over time (cf. Baraldi, Gregori and Perna, 2011). While we have so far kept separate in our discussion the technical and the organizational interfaces, we can now analyze them together in order to grasp the effects of the CRM system on the using organization. In fact, the organizational and technical interfaces around CRM also influenced each other during the embedding process.

Loccioni's CRM emerged as a functioning IT system from the combination and interfacing of such resources as technical facilities (hardware, software and databases), competences and skills in the area of IT and system integration, organizational teams and the engagement of specific business units (see Figure 9.1). All these resources were internal to Loccioni, except for a group of university researchers who contributed competence in the area of marketing and organization/management. These various resources were combined as shown in Figure 9.1 by means of the interfaces represented by double headed arrows. The challenge for Loccioni's CRM project team was that, when the various resources were combined and connected to each other, the exact shape of these interfaces could not be anticipated: the consequence was that the effects of CRM were highly unpredictable.

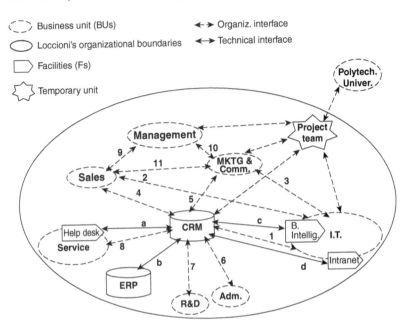

Figure 9.1   Resource combination and interfaces involved in embedding CRM at Loccioni

The interaction between Loccioni's top management and the other business units, such as sales, and marketing and communication (MKTG in Figure 9.1) was pivotal for deciding on the development of the CRM approach and system (see interfaces 9 and 10 in Figure 9.1). Also the interface with the Polytechnic University of Marche played an important role in influencing the functions that the CRM system should later perform. This external organizational unit was also involved in coordinating numerous project activities, especially in training users. At the very start of the CRM project, Loccioni's management set up the CRM team, a group of eight people (Loccioni's managing director, five functional managers and two university researchers). This team also included the necessary IT development competences to create an in-house CRM solution. The CRM team itself can be viewed as a specific organizational resource, indeed an organizational unit by itself: however, the major difference from the CRM project team and the other business units was that the former was a temporary organization, created in order to reach a specific purpose within a specific timeframe (Packendorff, 1995; Turner and Müller, 2003; Söderlund, 2004). It is important to stress that most members of the project team were fully dedicated to the specific task at hand. Even though the project team did not use this terminology, they were highly engaged in identifying and forging the technical and organizational resource interfaces necessary for embedding the CRM system. However, in order to achieve this result the project team had itself to build its own interfaces with several organizational resources, namely the competences of Loccioni's IT developers and various groups of internal users, who represented the users' needs of more accurate and on-time customer information (see the interfaces surrounding the star symbol in Figure 9.1).

The various organizational interfaces mentioned so far influenced how the CRM system was developed from a technical point of view: in particular, the organizational interfaces (such as the combination between IT and marketing competences within the CRM team, and existing/expected communication flows between Loccioni's business units) had an effect on how CRM was combined and connected with Loccioni's other IT systems (see the technical interfaces a, b, c and d in Figure 9.1). For instance, interface "d" between CRM and Intranet was created in order to make CRM accessible to all users belonging to Loccioni's various business units that relied on the project team's specific competence about these systems and on an analysis of the needs of these various users. Creating this specific interface (CRM-Intranet) also reflected the expected organizational interfaces according to which all business units should exchange customer data in a more efficient way.

In turn, how CRM was designed, developed and connected to the other facilities would clearly also affect the users. During the project phases of "infrastructure design" and "system configuration" (see Sections 6.5 and 6.6 in Chapter 6), the CRM project team addressed the key issue of how to properly translate information and business processes into the CRM system. In other words, CRM would represent, model and orient such key organizational interfaces as the processes through which Loccioni's users communicate and interact every day with each other and with the customers. It was therefore a challenging task to select what kinds of data, information and routines had to be turned into digital data and automatic processes (Nilsson, 1999; Baraldi, 2003). The project team addressed this issue by closely interacting with the users in order to receive feedback, via surveys and in-depth interviews, about which kind of information would be relevant to have digitalized inside the CRM system.

After the launch, when the users from the various business units started interacting regularly with the CRM system (see organizational interfaces 1, 4, 5, 6, 7, 8 in Figure 9.1), the system also started producing concrete effects as it was applied to handle certain tasks such as customer data entry, and a number of internal routines in customer information management were changed due to the system. However, users' knowledge of and commitment to CRM, both at individual and business unit level, were generally low, which also translated into a rather limited use of the CRM system. It was at this stage, a few months after the system's official launch, that users could in turn considerably influence the further development of CRM, in terms of a set of improvements that made the system more attuned to their actual needs and thus more valuable and eventually adopted. In particular, KAMs from the sales unit and personnel from the marketing unit interfaced with the IT unit (see interfaces 2 and 3 in Figure 9.1) and provided concrete specifications for new and improved features which the IT engineers added to the earlier version of CRM (see interface 1 in Figure 9.1).

Therefore, not only did the CRM system require Loccioni's organizational routines to be changed to be adapted to the system, but the organizational context also required the IT system to be changed to eventually better fit the needs of important groups of users. The adaptations between the CRM system and the using organization by means of the resource interfaces we have reviewed so far were therefore mutual (Akrich, Callon and Latour, 2002; Van de Ven et al., 1999). Moreover, inscribing the new routines into CRM and transforming the already existent routines turned out to be a continuous and time-consuming process. As it is becoming increasingly used, the CRM system is also producing, in the long term, an effect on the organizational interface between the Sales and the Marketing units (see interface 11 in Figure 9.1); after all, it was exactly the communication patterns between the two units more directly concerned with customer relationships that CRM was expected to improve. There are indeed two ways of analyzing this interface: either as an *indirect* interface, mediated by the CRM system (i.e., as the result of interfaces 4 and 5 in Figure 9.1) without the need of closer or personal interactions between the two units, or as a *direct* interface between personnel from Sales and Marketing, who need to coordinate their processes more closely, including meeting and interacting with each other also outside the IT system. In either case, the increased visibility or improvement of this interface is an important intra-organizational effect of CRM.

All in all, the key intra-organizational effects deriving from the embedding of CRM at Loccioni include the following:

- *Digitalized routines*: the CRM system has had an impact on the specific activities, processes and routines to which it is applied. These activities and routines became by and large more automatic and digitalized, as they were performed within the IT system. After the installation of the system, certain activities, such as organizing a marketing campaign, can be performed only by means of CRM. This role of the system can in turn lead to both positive and negative effects. Positive effects could be gained either by reducing the difficulty or increasing the speed and precision in doing a certain activity whenever CRM is utilized daily as a valuable information source. For instance, CRM has made it easier to find information about customers' organization charts and it has improved the spreading of sales reports among individual users. On the other hand, users have to rely and become more dependent on the system and, in case the data it contains is incorrect or delayed, the processes it is utilized for can be jeopardized. However, for these effects to be produced, the level of adoption of the CRM system needs to reach a certain threshold, which has proved to be problematic in the case of Loccioni, where the commitment of several users to the system has been shifting or at worst weak.

- *New interaction patterns*: another effect arising from the embedding of the CRM system is the development of new interaction patterns, including informal ones, within Loccioni's organization. Especially personnel from the IT, the marketing and the sales business units were all involved in joint discussions concerning the introduction of CRM, both as a managerial practice and as an IT solution. Ideas, proposals and suggestions for improving the system turned out to be possible by means of this intra-organizational effect. Moreover, the CRM system, once installed, also created the effect of making various business units, such as the sales and the marketing units, more aware of the importance of coordinating their activities and of the quality of their information exchange.

- *Impact on parallel processes*: The exchange of information among users that was driven by the CRM system also enhanced parallel processes and activities to which the CRM system is not directly applied. For instance, the administrative unit gained in terms of flexibility from the new logic behind order management (see Section 7.3 in Chapter 7): for example, they could retrieve in real time information concerning customers' profitability. It is important to stress that the interfaces between technical and organizational resources played a pivotal role in producing these first three types of effects.

- *Trade-offs and compromises*: installing and embedding the CRM system made several trade-offs emerge inside Loccioni's organization; these required a set of compromises and in turn also influenced the embedding process. For instance, in order to gain users' acceptance and stimulate their willingness to adopt CRM, several training sessions were held. However, training sessions were arranged during working hours, which diverted people from their normal duties. A compromise was reached by holding a limited number of training sessions, which were probably not enough to gain rapidly the widespread acceptance that was necessary. Another trade-off emerged in the composition of the project team: the ambition of being representative of key users and also including the necessary IT and organization/marketing competences led to a rather large group of eight members, but KAMs, who are probably the most important user group, were not involved in the project team because this would distract them too much from their daily selling activities. A compromise was reached here by involving KAMs as key respondents to provide feedback and suggestions for improvements, but such involvement came only after the CRM system had already been installed and was meeting serious problems blocking its adoption. Finally, because of users' diverging needs and suggestions for improvements, a set of technical and functional trade-offs were faced in the choice of which specific features, functions and data the CRM should include. Here, IT developers and the project team had to negotiate with users in order to find compromises as to which functions to include and which routines to digitalize. All in all, the CRM system installed and currently in use at Loccioni is the result of several compromises caused by the diverging pressures posed by the heterogeneous technical and organizational resources which affected its development and which are involved in its daily utilization.

9.3 Inter-organizational effects of CRM

In this section we first discuss the difficulty of tracing inter-organizational effects of a CRM system and then we analyze the specific ways in which the KAMs in charge of the selected customer relationships use the CRM system (Ehret, 2004). These first two parts prepare a more detailed discussion of possible explanations behind the different effects of CRM on how customer relationships are handled at Loccioni.

9.3.1 Overview: The indirect nature of the inter-organizational effects of CRM

Investigating the effects of CRM on Loccioni's customer relationships is challenging because, even though the six customer relationships presented in Chapter 8 have been affected in some way, it is very arduous to trace specifically these effects. At a general level, the CRM system processes data that can be then utilized by Loccioni's personnel as a better support in managing the relationships than the previously scattered, ad hoc and sometimes inconsistent information. However, the case study reveals that there are no direct effects and interfaces from the CRM system to each single customer relationship. Next to a limited use by KAMs, this lack of direct effects also depends on the choice made by Loccioni to exclude customers from having a direct, online IT connection to the CRM system.

The effects produced on Loccioni's customer relationships are instead mediated by the effects of CRM at intra-organizational (Steel, Dubelaar and Ewing, 2013) level that we discussed in the previous section, such as on Loccioni's internal routines, communication flows, personnel's interest and attitude toward the technology. As it appeared a couple of years after its installation, the CRM had not contributed to improving Loccioni's customer relationships in any evident and substantial manner. However, this lack of strong effects does not mean that the contribution of this technology is negative or the same for all business relationships. It is in fact quite difficult, as we will see in Section 9.3.3, to generalize about the effects of CRM on customer relationships, because the six relationships that we considered present slightly different effects. Moreover, each relationship has a history of its own and a different level of complexity than the others, and is managed by a KAM who might be more or less favorable to using CRM. It is therefore useful to start by summarizing the standpoints of the five KAMs about the impact of CRM on how they handle the six customer relationships. We will then turn in the following section to an analysis of which factors are behind the effects of CRM at inter-organizational level.

9.3.2 The KAMs' use of CRM and its effects on customer relationships

An important condition for CRM to produce any effects on customer relationships is that KAMs consider it a useful tool and regularly utilize it in handling them. The review of the six customer relationships (Magneti Marelli, Whirlpool, Trenitalia, Continental, Tod's and Haier) in Chapter 8 provides mixed if not disappointing evidence of the extent to which KAMs utilize the CRM system as a tool for managing relationships.

KAM "A", a relatively young manager in charge of Magneti Marelli, did not make much use of the CRM system in actively and strategically handling this relationship because he viewed CRM as a simple repository of mostly financial data. KAM "B", another relatively young manager, provided instead a more complex view of the effects of CRM on customer relationships: he was in charge of two accounts, Whirlpool and Haier, for which CRM played clearly different roles and produced different effects. While for Whirlpool, a very large, complex and established relationship, KAM "B" could not see any immediate tangible effects, for Haier, a smaller, less complex and very new relationship, CRM was a very useful tool in handling the relationship. For the complex and old relationship with Whirlpool, the CRM system was not so useful because it did not include the strategic and future-oriented information that KAM "B" needed for approaching this customer in new or better ways; while for the simpler and newer relationship with Haier, CRM did include current and future plans related information (inputted by the marketing unit's personnel), which the KAM could use for starting the very first interactions and meeting with the customer during the relationship's development stage (Ford, 1980; Ford et al., 2011).

The relationship with Trenitalia is probably the one where CRM is utilized the least, mostly because of the negative attitude of KAM "C", one of Loccioni's oldest KAMs, toward any type of IT tools for managing customer relationships. On the other hand, KAM "D", another middle-aged manager, is a bit more positive on the role of CRM in handling his account, Continental, one of Loccioni's largest and most complex and established relationships. However, KAM "D" considered the CRM system limited because just a small part of the information it included, namely volumes exchanged, was helpful in managing the relationship with Continental, and mostly as a tool for tracing past transactions. Therefore, similarly to KAM "A" in charge of Magneti Marelli, KAM "D" viewed CRM mostly as a historical data warehouse, not so useful for setting up further plans and interactions with the customer.

Finally, KAM "E", another middle-aged manager but with an extensive IT competence, considered the CRM system rather useful for managing the Tod's relationship, of which he is in charge. This KAM could identify positive effects in terms of more easily arranged meetings with the customer thanks to customer information made more easily available via CRM. However, "E" complained that accessing required customer information via the system was still time-consuming and that clearer effects on the customer relationship may only become visible in the future.

A common theme emerging from the opinions of the KAMs is that they do not find useful a CRM system which is a simple data repository, storing historical financial data, or which is a tool for simply "organizing better" the existing data: the Magneti Marelli and the Whirlpool KAMs, two young users, wish that the CRM enabled them to do something more than tracing historical performances. They would appreciate it if CRM allowed them to do something ideally future-oriented, but the lack of strategic information about these two relationships and customers makes the CRM system less than useful. And also the older KAM in charge of Continental complains that, while it can be partly useful to have historical information, Loccioni's CRM was just a data repository, lacking the type of information to support future plans and interactions in the relationship with Continental. An "extreme" situation is represented by Trenitalia's KAM, the oldest in terms of age, who is skeptical of any IT tool for managing customer relationships and considers himself the only reliable source of knowledge for doing it: this implies that for this user CRM is not even good as an historical data repository that may facilitate remembering key past aspects of a business relationship. Delayed or overly time-demanding information response from the system are other problems indicated by Tod's KAM, which made the CRM system only partly useful and produced only partial effects in the relationship with Tod's.

All in all, it seems like the use and effects of CRM at interorganizational level are related both to features of the customer relationship, such as its history (Reinartz, Kraft & Hoyer, 2004) and complexity (Steel, Dubelaar and Ewing, 2013), and features of the KAM in charge of it, such as his age and the information needed to handle a relationship. In particular, as we shall discuss at the end of the next section, the type of information needed (historical vs future-oriented), its quality (reliable or not) and its easiness of acquisition (in terms of, e.g., time response from the system) are key aspects which, when matched with the specific tasks in managing a certain customer relationship, strongly impact the extent of use and the effects of CRM at inter-organizational level.

9.3.3 Framing the inter-organizational effects of CRM

Why do certain customer relationships of Loccioni's present strong use and effects of CRM, while others just minor or no use and effect at all? Which dimensions of the resources involved in the embedding of CRM at Loccioni and of the relationships that this system is expected to influence can account for this variation of effects? Based both on the concepts presented in our theoretical chapters and on the evidence from the case study, we propose three dimensions that can help frame whether or not and how CRM affects Loccioni's customer relationships: two of these dimensions are basic characteristics of the customer relationship itself, namely its history/start date and its level of complexity, while the third dimension is a characteristic of CRM users, namely the age of the KAM, which indicates the users' willingness and attitude toward using IT tools in performing their managerial tasks.

History and start date of customer relationships: If we look across the six customer relationships it appears clear that the history, and even more precisely the start date, of a relationship, is a key dimension when it comes to the actual use and effects of CRM on the relationship. In particular, the CRM system has definitely been a source of useful information for managers who approach a new customer, such as Haier. More precisely, the start date of the relationship in relation to the date of installation of the CRM system seems to be pivotal here: a customer relationship that starts after the introduction of a CRM system does not meet the same barriers to the use of CRM as relationships that preceded its installation. The latter, older relationships face in fact the problem of legacy information (Baraldi, La Rocca and Perna, 2013) and of digitalizing and representing the whole history of a relationship for the first time in a computer system (cf. Baraldi and Nadin, 2006). In fact, the relationship with Haier was born in 2007, when Loccioni's CRM system was basically ready to install: therefore, almost all the information about this customer was collected for the first time in a structured way in order to be digitalized inside CRM, instead of being scattered in many places across Loccioni's organization. Such key information about Haier as turnover, number of employees, manufacturing plants' locations, investment plans and number of contacts (meetings, e-mail exchanges, phone calls) could be collected within the CRM system. Making this information available was an important precondition for CRM to become truly useful to keep track of interactions with Haier and to produce benefits for users, including supporting the KAM in interacting more efficiently with this counterpart and in developing the customer relationship. In particular, the KAM in charge of Haier received from CRM information about Haier's current and future needs, which was inputted in the system by Loccioni's marketing unit, and could really use this high-quality information to make strategic decisions concerning the relationship.

The CRM system has made a much less positive contribution in supporting Loccioni's customer relationships that predated the installation of CRM, and especially the most long-lasting ones. The KAM in charge of Haier is also handling Whirlpool, a relationship dating back to 1986: as demonstrated by his use of CRM in the interactions with Haier, he is willing to use CRM, but its lack of strategic information about Whirlpool convinced him not to use the system in managing the Whirlpool relationship. In fact, in 2006 not all historical information about this customer was inputted inside the CRM system, which moreover did not include information about Whirlpool's R&D plans and product development projects. As the particular rationale of the Whirlpool relationship is conducting joint R&D projects, the lack of that type of information limits the opportunity for the KAM to handle and develop the relationship by means of CRM. As for Magneti Marelli, another very long-lasting customer, the KAM only rarely inputted customer data in the CRM system: instead he often distributed information via memo or protocol, which tends to disappear before they are "digitalized" inside CRM. This is not an unusual situation when it comes to registering information on complex processes into IT systems, as shown by Baraldi and Waluszewski (2005) for IKEA's product managers.

Complexity of business relationships: The complexity of buyer–seller relationships can be assessed by means of several elements (see Håkansson and Snehota, 1995), but in our case we focus on the following ones: number of persons involved and contacts (i.e., interactions from both sides of the relationship), sales volume and top management involvement. Each of these three complexity-related facets of a business relationship impact the amount and type of information created within the relationship: for instance, numerous people and interactions make communication and information grow exponentially, and large sales volumes are typically associated with many transactions, each one carrying several pieces of information. Top management involvement also makes the relationship more informal, as opposed to the daily routine work conducted by lower-level managers; and with greater informality in the relationship comes information which is less structured and systematic, and thereby more difficult to digitalize inside a CRM system. All in all, the more complex a business relationship is the more information it entails, especially unstructured and informal information, which is likely to make it more difficult to digitalize very complex relationships (cf. Baraldi and Nadin, 2006). But how does this connection appear in the six relationships we examined? In other words, how are the effects of CRM on business relationships related to their level of complexity?

The relationships with Magneti Marelli, Whirlpool and Continental are Loccioni's most complex ones, characterized by a vast network of interlocking contacts between people from different departments and different hierarchical levels. Top management is also highly involved in these three relationships. Even though, due to their age, these three relationships include several routines resulting from institutionalization processes (Ford, 1980), the three relationships also experienced several changes due to the customers' recurrent organizational changes, and remain relatively informal. At the opposite end of the continuity spectrum are the business relationship with Trenitalia and Tod's, which present a low level of complexity, with much fewer interconnections, minimal involvement of Loccioni's top management and modest sales volumes. The complexity of the relationship with Haier is, finally, somewhere in between the two previous groups: a rather large number of interactions and involved people during the first negotiations, as well as a growing exchange volume characterized this relationship, even though Loccioni's top management has not yet been directly involved in it.

Looking across the six relationships it is not really possible to find a clear pattern between the use and effects of CRM on the one hand, and the complexity of each relationship on the other. While for three out of four complex customer relationships (Magneti Marelli, Whirlpool and Continental) there are no evident effects of CRM, the relationship with medium level of complexity (Haier) presents strong effects of CRM. In fact, while for Haier the KAM could use the data inside CRM to organize the first visit to Haier's facility for introducing Loccioni and its solutions, for the other three complex relationships most of the really valuable customer data remains stored in the KAMs' personal documents or is somehow spread around Loccioni's organization. Relationship complexity seems to be unable to explain the use and effects of CRM also for the low-complexity relationships (Trenitalia and Tod's): in fact, one simple relationship (Tod's) does present some modest effect of the CRM system, thanks to the KAM's propensity for using some of its information for preparing meetings, while the other simple relationship (Trenitalia) is the one where CRM is used the least, because of the KAM's total distrust of the system.

Summing up, relationship complexity does not seem to be a factor explaining the use of CRM, and consequently its effects on customer relationships. A possible explanation is that a relationship's complexity entails two opposing forces on the use and effects on CRM. A force that stimulates the use and effects of CRM on complex relationships is the fact that relationship complexity means increased amounts of information and therefore IT tools can theoretically provide important efficiency gains in handling automatically these larger amounts of information. There is however also a contrary force associated with complex relationships, which obstructs the use and effects of CRM: complex relationships, especially old ones, include a lot of widespread, unstructured and informal information. This "legacy" and diffused information is highly costly first to find (as it is spread across the many people involved in a complex relationship) and then to digitalize at once. Long-lasting and complex customer relationships are often managed without CRM. We also found less utilization of CRM because the digitalization of informal information is very complex. Further, complex relationships involving several managers in many interaction episodes require that all these people make explicit and input their information into the system, which is very difficult to achieve: if someone involved in the relationship omits to input data in the system (or making her knowledge explicit to those who are in charge of data input), this is enough to make the customer-specific information stored in the CRM system become less than useful as it is not updated or comprehensive. This obstructing force in complex relationships derives from the *intra*-organizational embedding of CRM, namely from the interfaces between various users inside the host organization, and shows how the *inter*-organizational effects of CRM are closely related to the intra-organizational ones. This obstructing force reduces the value of information about complex relationships and thus also the usefulness of the CRM system for all potential users: basically, the potential of the IT system to improve efficiency in handling large amounts of information is undermined by the fact that much of such information never reaches the system.

The age of the KAM: So far, only one of the two relationship-specific dimensions we selected, namely its start date, was found capable of explaining the use and inter-organizational effects of CRM, whereas relationship complexity could not explain them. What about our third dimension? How are the effects of CRM on business relationships related to the age of their KAMs?

Looking across the six relationships, we find that this dimension also is only partially capable of explaining the use and effects of CRM on customer relationships. In fact, two of the three older KAMs perceive the control deriving from using CRM more strongly than younger KAMs, which reduces their willingness to use the system. In particular, the oldest of all the KAMs, the one in charge of Trenitalia, completely avoided the CRM system, based on his belief that his own knowledge of the customer relationship could not be matched or supported by the IT tool. However, there is also one older KAM, the one in charge of Tod's, who embraced the use of CRM, which produced some effects in this customer relationship.

Coming to the younger KAMs (Magneti Marelli, Whirlpool and Haier), their attitude toward CRM may be potentially more positive than that of older KAMs; but when it comes to their actual utilization of the system, and its inter-organizational effects, a great variation appears: one of them (Magneti Marelli) does not really use CRM, while the other uses it in one relationship (Haier) but not in the other (Whirlpool). All in all, the age of the KAM seems to be unable to fully explain the effects produced by CRM on a specific customer relationship.

We can now bring together the three dimensions (relationship history/start date, complexity and KAM's age), which we have so far discussed separately into a comprehensive frame to try and explain the use and effects of CRM on customer relationship. Table 9.1 reviews our findings relationship by relationship and in connection to the three dimensions.

The only dimension which has a consistent impact on the use and effects of CRM on customer relationships is their history, and especially their start date in relation to the installation of the IT system. By contrast, complexity and KAM's age indicate mixed results when it comes to the use and effects of CRM in each single relationship.

Business relationships 1 and 2 have not been affected by CRM, despite the young age of their KAMs, which suggested openness to using CRM: probably the influence of the other two dimensions (established and complex relationships with a lot of hard to codify and digitalized legacy information) is stronger than that of the KAM's age. The lack of use and effects of CRM in the Trenitalia relationship can be explained by the fact that although it is not highly complex, it has a long history predating the CRM system and a KAM with a strongly negative attitude toward CRM: here the two latter dimensions offset the first and inhibit the CRM system's effects. All three dimensions seem instead to move in the same direction and block completely the use and effects of CRM

Table 9.1 Three dimensions of customer relationships and the effects of CRM

Business relationship	History/Start date	Complexity	KAM's age	Effects of CRM	Information needs
1) Magneti Marelli	Established (1980s)	High	Young	No	Not matched
2) Whirlpool Europe	Established (1980s)	High	Young	No	Not matched
3) Trenitalia	Established (late 1980s)	Low	Middle aged	No	Not matched
4) Continental	Established (late 1980s)	High	Middle aged	No	Not matched
5) Tod's	Relatively new (1997)	Low	Middle aged	Modest	Partly matched
6) Haier	Newest (post CRM)	Medium	Young	Yes	Matched

in the relationship with Continental: this relationship is an old one, characterized by high complexity, and is managed by a middle-aged KAM. As for business relationship 5, the effects, although modest, of CRM seems to derive from the low complexity of the relationship and its short history, while the older age of the KAM does not affect negatively the use and effects of CRM as the person in charge is highly IT skilled. Finally, the young age of the KAM and its very recent start date (post-CRM) support the extensive use of CRM and its clear effects on the relationship with Haier, thereby offsetting the potentially negative impact of the complexity in this relationship.

There are however a few questions concerning the use and effects of CRM that remain unanswered by applying only the three dimensions of history/start date and complexity of relationships, and KAM's age. For instance: why is the effect of CRM in the relationship with Tod's only "modest" and not full? And why are the effects in the relationship with Haier so strong despite its being a complex relationship? Is there some other relevant dimension which can explain this variation and also the overall pattern? As mentioned at the end of Section 9.3.2, the type and quality of information provided by the CRM system, its easiness of acquisition and how it matches the information needs of IT users does influence the use and effects of CRM on customer relationships, to the point that we can single out a fourth dimension called "matching of informational needs" (see the last column in Table 9.1). The logic behind this dimension is straightforward: if the user (e.g., a KAM) easily obtains from CRM the type of information that satisfies her need in handling a customer relationship, she will use the system which in turn can produce its effects (Shum, Bove and Auh, 2008), whereas she will avoid it in the opposite case, that is, if the available information does not match her informational needs in terms of content, quality and accessibility. Content, quality and accessibility are in fact some of the key features of information that we presented in Chapter 3, Section 3.2.2 (cf. Baraldi, 2003; Ramström, 1973; Anthony, 1965).

The relevant types of information that appeared in our case were *historical* information, which covers past events in a relationship or past behaviors and features of the customer, as opposed to *future-oriented* information, which covers future interactions and plans of the customer (Anthony, 1965). Depending on the specific tasks and goals pursued by a KAM in a business relationship, both the historical and the future-oriented type of information contents can be valuable. However, the information type in focus in a customer relationship becomes valuable only if it is reliable (Reid and Catterall, 2005 and easy to acquire, for instance in terms of response time from the system. "Matching of informational needs" thus includes three elements: information content, quality and accessibility. This fourth dimension refers to the extent to which the CRM-borne information (1) corresponds to the type of information (historical vs future-oriented) needed to handle a relationship, (2) is reliable and (3) is easy to acquire. Let us see how the "matching of information needs" dimension applies in order to explain the pattern of CRM's use and effects in the various customer relationships.

Starting from relationship 6, with Haier, the one where CRM is used the most and produces the strongest effects, it appears clear that the degree of matching of informational needs by the CRM system plays a pivotal role for this outcome: CRM in fact included the future-oriented information about the customer (production and new plants plan), which is so important for, and badly needed by, the KAM to plan future interactions with this customer. The degree of matching of informational needs also plays a key role in explaining the non-use of CRM by the very same KAM, but in another relationship, the one with Whirlpool; whereas the future-oriented information he needed for handling Haier was reliably inputted and available inside CRM, for Whirlpool CRM included only historical information, which does not provide much value to the KAM's task and goal of planning future activities and joint R&D projects with this customer. Therefore, since the needed future-oriented information is easily available inside CRM for Haier, KAM "B" uses CRM for Haier, whereas he does not use it for Whirlpool because that type of information is not available in the system for Whirlpool.

What about the role of "matching of informational needs" in the other four relationships? Our fourth dimension is certainly low in three of them, even though for different reasons, and therefore explains well the missing use and effects of CRM: in the Magneti Marelli and Continental relationships, it is the lack of future-oriented information inside CRM that blocks its use and effects; while in the Trenitalia relationship the KAM's negative attitude toward any IT-borne information, including the historical type, makes it hard for even high-quality and easily accessible information to match his informational needs. Finally, the matching of informational needs increases from relationships 1 to 4 and is at least partial in the relationship with Tod's, but here the low reliability and the time-consuming means of accessing information reduce the use of CRM and makes its effects only modest.

Summing up, as shown also by the last two columns of Table 9.1, the dimension "matching of informational needs" seems to correlate strongly with the use and effects of CRM on customer relationships (Kaila and Goldman, 2006). This fourth dimension also provides a better explanation of these inter-organizational effects compared to the other three dimensions of relationship history/start date and complexity, and KAM's age. This dimension did not appear immediately from the empirical case and its analysis because it is a rather complex one, compared for instance to the relationship's start date or the KAM's age. In fact, the matching of informational needs in relation to the specific tasks in managing a customer relationship is the result of a highly complex resource interface between as many as four resources (see Figure 9.2): (1) Loccioni's organization (and namely the communication routines between the marketing and the sales units behind the type and quality of information made available); (2) the CRM system itself (as the vehicle providing or not providing information of a specific content, quality and accessibility); (3) the individual KAM (who has particular informational needs depending on her goals and tasks in relation to a specific customer); and (4) the very business relationship (whose past, present and future interactions influence the KAM's goals and tasks).

The salience for the inter-organizational effects of a complex dimension such as "matching of informational needs" by the CRM system further indicates that the *inter*-organizational effects of CRM are tightly connected with its *intra*-organizational effects and embedding. This fact switches the attention from the characteristics of the customer relationship to be affected by CRM, or those of the KAM who is expected to directly use it, to another part of Loccioni's organization, namely the

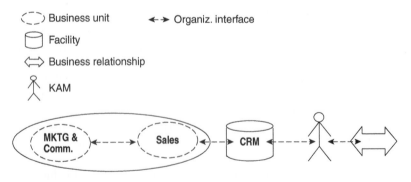

Figure 9.2   A complex resource interface impacts the effects of CRM on customer relationships

marketing unit. It is in fact this very organizational unit which one can thank for having inputted inside CRM the future-oriented information about Haier, which turned out to be so valuable for the KAM. This recognition also raises the question: why doesn't Loccioni do the same for every customer? Would the currently limited use of CRM increase in other relationships as well if CRM included more future-oriented information for each of them? The marketing unit is a clear candidate for screening even more closely the informational needs of each KAM in relation to each customer relationship they handle, and then intervening to collect and input inside the CRM system information that matches such needs. There is however a slight risk here that, even when the "right" type of information is included and easily available inside CRM, other barriers might appear, such as the reluctance of some KAMs to use CRM because of a negative prejudicial attitude or fear of being controlled by the system.

9.4 Summary

This chapter has analyzed and discussed the embedding of Loccioni's CRM system and its intra- and inter-organizational effects. Four main intra-organizational effects of CRM we identified at Loccioni are: digitalized routines; new interaction patterns among different organizational units; an impact on parallel processes separate from customer management via CRM; and a number of trade-offs that required compromises during and after the installation of the system. The inter-organizational effects, namely those on how Loccioni's customer relationships are managed, appear instead to be rather limited: only two out of six examined relationships were affected by CRM, while in the other four relationships CRM is not really utilized by the involved KAM. This pattern of use and effects of CRM in the six relationships can be explained by the extent to which the CRM system is capable of matching the specific information needs expressed by the KAM within each single customer relationship. A shorter history and recent start date of a relationship also favors the use and effects of CRM in that relationship. The complexity of a relationship and the age of the KAM in charge of it do not instead explain univocally the use and effects of CRM.

Finally, it is important to stress that intra- and inter-organizational effects are intertwined. In particular, the creation of inter-organizational effects on customer relationships by CRM depends on the previous emergence of intra-organizational effects and resource interfaces that embed the CRM system. These connections between various types of resources (e.g., organizational units in charge of data collection/input, individual users, the IT tool and customer relationships) become pivotal in enabling the CRM system to match the informational needs of KAMs/users whenever they appear in relation to specific customers.

10
Conclusions: Results, Managerial Implications and a Research Agenda

In this chapter we first summarize and discuss the results of our research (Section 10.1) and its contribution (Section 10.2). We then derive from our results a set of managerial implications for firms who aim to implement and use CRM (Section 10.3). The chapter concludes with the formulation of a further research agenda about CRM (Section 10.4).

10.1 The findings of this study

By applying the "resource interaction" perspective (Håkansson and Waluszewski, 2002; Baraldi, Gressetvold and Harrison, 2012) to the Loccioni case, this research shows the complex interplay among resources involved in the implementation and use of CRM systems. Overall, the most evident effects are at *intra*-organizational level, whereas at *inter*-organizational level CRM has had a modest impact. Let us now review the effects at both levels.

10.1.1 The effects of CRM at intra-organizational level

The Loccioni case highlights that even if a company holds in-house technical competence on IT systems, the implementation of CRM can become problematic because it entails not only technical interfaces, but also social and organizational ones. Project management tools, such as the creation of dedicated project teams with ample mandate and representativeness, may help address some of the social interactions that influence CRM implementation, but certainly not all of them. A main reason is that the social interactions that embed the CRM system are highly complex, as they involve the single user, groups of users and the connections between different groups of users, usually belonging to different hierarchical levels inside the host organization.

Starting from the single users, their perception of CRM and its impact on their working routines frames the way in which they will interact with the system, thereby influencing its adoption and the intra-organizational effects if can produce. As for groups of users, the case highlights that every organizational unit of Loccioni's has different goals when interacting with the CRM system, which creates different and sometimes conflicting pressures on CRM that cause delays and subop-timal solutions to information management issues. Interestingly, our analysis shows that it is not only the routines of single users or of a group of users that are influenced by the implementation of CRM, but also the degree of coordination and interdependences among different groups of users: for example, CRM made Loccioni's KAMs become more depen-dent on the marketing business unit. An important finding in this regard is that CRM can make some social interactions become so strong and evident that tensions and barriers arise during the embedding process: for instance, Loccioni's KAMs felt controlled by their superiors and other functions since the CRM system was also open to other users. Thus, the emerging inter-organizational effect was somehow the opposite of the expected centralization and coordination of customer knowledge which was at the origin of the entire CRM project: indeed, right after the system's launch, KAMs became more reluctant to share customer information with people from different divisions.

Since the overall purpose of Loccioni's CRM system was providing users with well organized information for managing customer relation-ships, it became crucial to increase the coordination between different groups of users, each one performing different tasks in terms of informa-tion collection, input and use. Then, when the CRM system is installed and fully embedded, it has the power to frame how users systemati-cally interact with each other by using it. Even if it is clearly advisable that all actors involved in CRM implementation (users, IT developers, consultants and top management) are aware of the social interaction patterns which the CRM system will consolidate inside the organiza-tion, planning entirely the intra-organizational effects of CRM is not possible because the embedding of CRM is a non-linear and unpre-dictable process, often accompanied by unexpected effects. For example, organizational resistance can suddenly appear for unforeseen reasons and from users who had been proactively involved in the imple-mentation project, such as Loccioni's KAM. In this sense, our study confirms previous research on IT and organization: embedding CRM takes time for both individuals and organizations, because learning and profound organizational adaptations are required (Leonard-Barton, 1988; Orlikowski et al., 1995).

10.1.2 The effects of CRM at inter-organizational level

Our case shows that even if the technical embedding of CRM proceeds smoothly, the effects on customer relationships can be weaker than expected. A main reason can be the limited adoption of CRM by some categories of key users in the host company, such as KAMs, who are expected to apply CRM in their daily interactions with customers. This result indicates a more general issue, namely the fact that the *inter*-organizational effects of CRM are closely related to, and to some extent rely on, its *intra*-organizational effects. First of all, a lack of user adoption reduces the use of the system to below a threshold, enabling even external effects only to appear sporadically. Moreover, the creation of inter-organizational effects by CRM relies on a broader organizational context inside the host organization; more precisely, such external effects on business relationships depend on well functioning intra-organizational interactions inside Loccioni, where different users (namely KAMs and marketing personnel) trust each other's inputs into the CRM system. If this intra-organizational embedding does not happen, it is even more difficult for CRM to create *positive* external effects. But producing no effects at all – basically lack of use by KAMs – is probably a better option than having that CRM produce *negative* effects on the customer relationship. It is probably this fear of negative effects on their customer relationships that restrains some KAMs from using CRM (cf. Baraldi, La Rocca and Perna, 2013; Baraldi, Gregori and Perna, 2011).

In general, we can state that the effects of CRM on customer relationships are mediated by the intra-organizational embedding of the system. However, as our case demonstrates, some characteristics of customer relationships themselves also affect the creation of inter-organizational effects. Our major findings are that CRM can affect customer relationships depending on four specific dimensions (see Table 10.1): two dimensions are related to customer relationships, namely their history/start date (established vs newest) and their level of complexity (low vs high). While our results show clearly that newest customer relationships are associated with more intense use and effects of CRM, the complexity dimension does not provide clear results. This is a puzzling finding to which we will return later on.

The other two dimensions are connected to features of the individual KAM and of other resources involved. The first dimension is the

Table 10.1   Inter-organizational effects of CRM

Resource	Dimensions	Instances and results/effects of CRM
Customer relationship	History/start date	*Newest*: strong tendency to use CRM in the relationship *Established*: minimal use or avoidance of CRM
	Level of complexity	*Low to medium*: some use of CRM in the relationship *High*: no use of CRM in the relationship
KAM	Age	*Young*: positive attitude toward using CRM *Senior*: negative attitude toward CRM
	Matching of informational needs	*Yes*: willingness to apply CRM in the relationship *No*: avoidance of CRM in managing the relationship

age/experience of the KAM (young vs senior) and indicates a positive or negative attitude toward IT, with younger users being more positive than older ones (even though older age can be compensated by strong interest and experience in IT tools). The second KAM-centered dimension is the matching of informational needs of the KAM: this is a more complex dimension focusing on how well the information provided by the CRM system, thanks to the input by other organizational users, satisfies the specific information needs of a KAM for performing a particular task in managing a customer relationship: different tasks and relationships entail different needs in terms of quality, reliability, accessibility and timeliness of information, but typically the higher these features of the information provided by CRM about a relationships the more willing a KAM is to use CRM in managing that relationship.

Combining the four aforementioned dimensions, the case of Loccioni clearly shows the presence of two different patterns behind the appearance of the effects of CRM at inter-organizational (see Figure 10.1).

Pattern 1: *CRM produces (positive) effects in newest and low/medium-complexity customer relationships, which are managed by younger technology-oriented KAMs, whose information needs are matched by the CRM system.* A new customer relationship (especially if initiated after the installation of CRM) managed by a young, technically confident KAM provides the ideal situation for CRM to be applied and yield positive effects, especially if the relationship is not very complex and the CRM-based information matches the informational needs of the KAM in charge.

Pattern 2: *CRM produces no effects in established and high-complexity customer relationships, which are managed by senior and non-technology oriented KAMs, whose informational needs are not matched by the CRM system.* The long-term and historical nature of these relationships apparently creates barriers to adopting CRM. There are several reasons for this situation. Usually senior KAMs are in charge of older relationships, which tend to be more institutionalized than new ones. In turn, senior KAMs, who are typically more technology averse also perceive as risky using CRM to handle these relationships. In fact, these senior KAMs often prefer to use and exchange informal information and tacit knowledge that tend to be difficult to be digitalized into an IT system (Baraldi and Nadin, 2006). These KAMs also have problems finding inside CRM the type of information that can match their informational needs.

Patterns 1 and 2 indicate the already mentioned puzzling result that CRM is not applied in highly complex relationships, characterized by broader patterns of information exchange between the counterparts. There appears to be a paradox here: in fact, one can expect that CRM would offer the greatest gains in efficiently handling and automating the large amount of information that characterizes long-lasting and complex customer relationships. However, our case shows that, on the contrary, CRM is primarily adopted and produces effects in new and relatively simple relationships, with much less information involved. This apparent paradox depends on the fact that old and

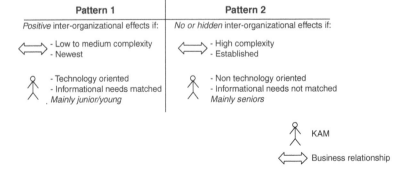

Figure 10.1 The effects of CRM on customer relationships, two patterns

complex relationships also involve a large amount of "legacy" information which is difficult to digitalize: this information is often informal and related to tacit knowledge, which makes it very costly and time-consuming to find and convert it into digitalized information inside the CRM system. It is instead easier to start digitalizing a new customer relationship from the very beginning, when there is not much widespread, hidden and tacit information to be chased across the organization. There is, finally, another possible explanation for this puzzling result, which relates to the specific content of some of Loccioni's relationships and the related informational needs: CRM systems may be better as tools to handle short-term, sales-related interactions rather than such long-term and complex cooperation as R&D projects, which character-ize Loccioni's most established relationships (see Magneti-Marelli and Continental).

Our findings concerning the four dimensions affecting the use and effects of CRM on customer relationships can also be viewed as barriers to CRM, which we can now also "rank" in terms of importance and seriousness of impact on the use of CRM:

1) The age or, better, the IT attitude of the KAM is the most important dimension and barrier, because a KAM refusing in principle to use the CRM system makes it virtually impossible to initiate the adoption process which is a precondition for producing effects on customer relationships later on;

2) The matching of informational needs is the second most important dimension: in fact, even if a KAM is willing to use CRM in prin-ciple, she would eventually start avoiding it if it does not provide information which is specifically useful for her managerial tasks;

3) Relationship age correlates strongly with the lack of use and effects of CRM (see Table 9.1 in Chapter 9), with the older and more estab-lished relationships representing a barrier to using CRM. But the fact that a relationship predating the installation of CRM was affected (Tod's) indicates that established relationships too can be influenced by CRM provided that barriers 1 and 2 above are overcome, that is, the KAM is positively oriented toward IT tools and her informational needs are matched by the CRM system;

4) Relationship complexity appears to be the least strong of all the four barriers to using CRM, because complexity does not have a clear-cut role in systematically blocking the use of CRM, nor does the sim-plest relationships seem to favor the use of CRM (see Table 9.1 in Chapter 9).

Finally, one should not forget that these inter-organizational effects of CRM are dependent on CRM becoming first of all embedded at intra-organizational level, which is facilitated if CRM does not break the daily routines of users. If CRM requires changes in such routines and additional efforts in the form for instance of tedious data input, then it becomes even more pivotal that CRM does provide information that perfectly matches the informational needs of users, as a way to counterbalance the sacrifices users have to make when they start using CRM.

10.2 Key contributions

This book provides a set of contributions visible at different levels. Firstly, from an empirical point of view, this volume investigates CRM in a B2B context. There is a dearth of studies that investigate CRM in this type of context, and even fewer that explicitly reveal the conditions that can facilitate the implementation and effects of CRM at both intra- and inter-organizational level. Moreover, another main empirical contribution of ours is that we highlight the technical and social complexities involved in the embedding of CRM.

Secondly, from a theoretical point of view, by applying the "resource interaction" perspective (Baraldi, La Rocca and Perna, 2013; Håkansson and Waluszewski, 2002), this study provides a new understanding of the critical interactions around the implementation and use of CRM. This new understanding relies on conceiving CRM as a focal resource that has to interact with others in order first to be adopted and then to improve customer relationships. Therefore, our theoretical and analytical stance is that CRM cannot be considered a context-independent tool or a deterministic platform that automatically gets managerial tasks performed and creates its own effects alone: instead, CRM is simply a facility which is greatly dependent on other resources in order to be able to process and spread customer information within and outside the organization. This study also demonstrates how the effects of CRM can be traced by investigating the resource interactions involving the CRM system: in fact, it is only by interacting with other resources that CRM systems can produce their effects and create value (cf. Baraldi and Waluszewski, 2005). As for these effects, our research stresses their non-linear and unpredictable nature, due to the specific combinations of the resources surrounding a particular CRM system. Therefore, the effects of CRM on customer relationships do not derive from a sequence of planned activities: they emerge instead from coping with barriers and triggers which stem from the patterns of interactions between IT tools, individual users and other social and organizational resources.

Finally, this study is also unique from a methodological point of view, as we observed the phenomenon of implementation and use of CRM through a real-time longitudinal case study (Yin, 1994), conducted also as action research (Coughlan and Coghlan, 2002) for a period of three years. This methodological approach, including the possibility of observing a complex phenomenon from "behind the curtain", was pivotal for gaining the deep insights into the complex interactions mechanisms that are the basis of our contribution.

10.3   Managerial implications

Our study suggests a set of managerial implications for companies that aim to implement CRM. This section distinguishes between (1) implications for companies when coping with the embedding of CRM at intra-organizational level and (2) implications when dealing with CRM at inter-organizational level, namely in managing customer relationships.

10.3.1   How to cope with CRM at intra-organizational level?

At a general level, companies implementing CRM have to cope with organizational barriers such as employees' resistance in adopting CRM for managing customer information. Therefore, managers in charge of a CRM project should motivate and support sales and marketing personnel to use CRM first and foremost by communicating to them its benefits and advantages. Negative organizational reactions by users can be reduced by directly involving in the project team the users who are more directly affected by CRM. A key principle is that a widespread adoption of CRM systems can be achieved only if that CRM provides value to the users. A first way to provide such value relates to the technical side of CRM: companies should devise CRM in such a way that it can be technically modified or adapted following the emergent user needs. However, this technical flexibility and adaptability may risk pulling the CRM system into inconsistent directions if user needs greatly diverge. Therefore, it is important to appoint a CRM leader who has a good overview of the overall, company-wide information flows and needs and who can accordingly act as a mediator between the pressures coming from different user categories. Moreover, this leader should be in charge of constantly evaluating the level of users' trust in the CRM system, which is a necessary condition for easing the adoption of CRM by individual users.

We reckon that convincing *all* users of the advantage and value of CRM can be challenging: in fact, centralizing information and enabling comparison, reporting and measurement of relationships over time might provide great value to top management, but it might not create enough value for single users (e.g., KAMs) in their daily duties, or it might even entail threats to their autonomy and creativity. While the feeling of being controlled by the CRM system can hardly be totally eliminated, it can be alleviated (1) by empowering users to influence the features of the CRM system via their direct involvement in the CRM project, and (2) by shifting attention to how individual sacrifices can contribute to overall organizational advantages. In fact, at the intra-organizational level, social interfaces between users from different areas play a critical role: for example, more timely and updated customer information inputted in the system by marketing personnel can enable KAMs to be more responsive and improve coordination in the relationships they handle.

Moreover, training sessions embracing simultaneously all relevant categories of users should be organized. However, such sessions need to take into account the new routines and inter-organizational connections that the CRM system will create: in practice, the users who will become dependent on each other after the implementation of CRM have to be trained together in order to become more aware of such dependence, and their specific role in overall information management, in addition to becoming more confident with the data entry procedures which will influence the quality of the information made available to the rest of the organization. Even though these sessions are time- and resource-consuming, the pay-off is anticipating the sudden emergence of intra-organizational inconsistencies in the actual use of the CRM system.

10.3.2 How to cope with CRM at inter-organizational level?

The effects of CRM on customer relationships are greatly unexpected due to opportunities and obstacles created by the surrounding resources in which the CRM system is embedded (Baraldi, 2003; Baraldi and Waluszewski, 2005). Therefore, our suggestions for managers in this regard are not intended to provide concrete solutions, but to indicate areas of concern that will most likely need to be addressed. As a matter of fact we prefer to formulate our inter-organizational implications as a set of key questions that emerge from our case study.

A first key question is: which events, stages or periods of a customer relationship should be digitalized inside a CRM system? A risky assumption in this regard is thinking that today's IT systems are so sophisticated and capacious to be able to contain all the customer information that a company can possibly possess, both formal and informal. However, pursuing such a goal would make CRM too cumbersome in terms of data input and, after all, some pieces of information will remain extremely difficult and costly firstly to find and secondly to codify. Instead, companies need to be selective with the customer information they choose to digitalize inside CRM.

But how can a company select the most relevant information to be included inside CRM? A starting point is asking users exactly which goals and functions (e.g., type of interaction) they expect to achieve and conduct via the CRM system. In case users were not aware of all the potentials of CRM technology, they would need close guidance from technology experts. But the key point is that users from sales and marketing should orient the implementation process by helping IT developers define a model for representing customer relationships that extracts the right amount of information and no more. Companies should accordingly analyze which elements belong to the "strategic information" that several users conceive to be relevant for managing customer relationships. Our case shows clearly that important features of such information are not only reliability, accessibility and timeliness, but also that it is future-oriented.

There is no doubt that in B2B settings information such as a customer's planned plant openings or future product launches is strategic for a supplier. But then the thorny issues arise of how to find this information, how often to input it inside CRM and how to validate it, especially as this future-oriented information is to some extent also speculative. All in all, another key question for managers is: how to make the management of all this future-oriented information automatic, efficient and reliable inside the CRM system? Such information is often informal, taking the form of rumors, or tacit or even confidential information. Therefore, there is a challenge in turning it into a formalized record inside an IT system. The chain "from rumors to forecasts to facts" is a difficult process to handle in a CRM system, but this type of information seems to be the most valuable according to the KAMs involved in our study, much more so than static historical records. Finding methods and routines to accomplish this conversion process is therefore pivotal in enabling first intra-organizational CRM use, and then inter-organizational effects on specific customer relationships.

Our final issue concerns to what extent companies should digitalize their customer relationships, especially depending on their age and level of complexity. When relationships are old and established it is almost impossible to collect digitally their entire "memory". In fact, our results suggest that CRM is more easily applicable to and works better for new customer relationships. But there are situations in which the CRM system is required to play an important role also for established customer relationships: for instance, CRM can facilitate the complex task of a new KAM taking over an established relationship from a previous KAM. What is then the ideal type of information which the new KAM would need in order to start managing the relationship? Answering this question could act as important guidance for defining standards and procedures about what minimal information should be used to model and represent all customer relationships of a company.

10.4   Suggestions for further research

This book opens up intriguing issues to be further researched, some of which are related to the limitations of this research. One avenue for further research concerns the difference between CRM in a B2C and in a B2B context: within consumer markets, individual customers are managed based on patterns extrapolated at segment level from the whole populations, which is clearly different from managing specific business relationships based on their own constituent features. The findings of this volume indicate that for B2B relationships the most valuable information for account managers is not so much about past behavior or episodes in the relationship, but is future-oriented in nature. It would be interesting to identify which is the corresponding type of most valuable information in CRM as applied to consumers.

We also suggest further research about the concrete effects of CRM on customer relationships, which were not covered by this study. Or more precisely, we could not trace these concrete effects in our case because the CRM system was new and not so widely used. However, after years of regular use a CRM tool is also likely to produce concrete inter-organizational effects. Therefore, it is advisable to focus research explicitly on investigating the impact of CRM on volumes of transactions, profitability, relationship quality, investments and level of collaboration. Ideally, this research on the concrete effects of CRM should also switch the focus from the supplier to the customer: a central aspect that deserves attention is whether or not customers notice at all that they are being "managed" with a CRM system. Do they perceive any improvement or other effects in the relationship as viewed from their perspective? A fully comprehensive study would accordingly need to take into account both the buyer's and the supplier's perspective when investigating the effects of a certain CRM tool.

Our research also points out that the embedding of CRM entails a non-linear process with unexpected effects. However, comparing, by means of several case studies, the processes and experiences of several firms, with similar or dissimilar characteristics, might help in finding common patterns and salient differences. Finally, as this research was limited to the Italian context, cross-country investigations on CRM might make it possible to identify the impact of the cultural dimension on the embedding and use of CRM.

Notes

2 Customer Relationships in Industrial Networks

1. This book does not cover consumer markets, where buyers are individuals, but only industrial or "business to business markets", where buyers are companies or other types of organizations.
2. A relevant aspect concerning the origin of customer relationships is the reasons that lead a supplier to assess a potential relationship with a new customer. In other words: what are the antecedents of customer relationships? Answering this question is challenging because behind the birth of a relationship there are typically both individual reasons and reciprocal motivations, most of which become visible only when the parties start interacting. Both the customer and the supplier have to gain something from the interaction with each other. The IMP "interaction model" (Håkansson, 1982) shows that the interaction process is important for the dynamics of the relationship and for how the parties to a relationship develop. This model describes the business relationship between organizations in terms of mutual (interactive) exchange episodes. These exchange episodes, when repeated, constitute an exchange process, which can have different objects: products and/or services, information and financial resources. A fourth type of exchange process is represented by the personal relationship that is created between the people taking part in the economic exchange: this last type of exchange is explicitly of social character.
3. It is beyond the scope of this book to compare the IMP approach to relationship management with the "Relationship Marketing" school (Gummesson, 1997; Brodie et al., 1997). However, it is important to stress that, despite some partial overlap, the two perspectives are quite distinct in terms of origins, key assumptions, philosophy and contributions in the study of relationships in industrial markets. A comparison between the two approaches is presented in Ford et al. (2006:132–133).

5 Conceptualizing CRM as an Interacting Resource

1. There are many IMP-inspired contributions which focus on resources and their relevance for businesses. The "resource interaction" perspective in particular has been the object of a special issue of *Journal of Business Research*, dedicated to the theme of resource interaction in inter-organizational networks (Baraldi, Gressetvold and Harrison, 2012). Focusing on resources and their role in business networks corresponds to penetrating one of the three layers of the ARA model (see Chapter 2 in this book), the other two being actors and activities (Håkansson and Snehota, 1995). The resource dimension can therefore be seen simply as one of the dimensions of interactions in

business relationships and networks. The IMP studies focusing on resources show that resource interactions affect technological development (Håkansson and Waluszewski, 2007; Baraldi, Gregori and Perna, 2011) and the firm's economic efficiency and strategic development (Baraldi, 2003; Ford and Håkansson, 2006), as well as new business formation (Ciabuschi, Perna and Snehota, 2012).

2. Several studies (e.g., Håkansson and Waluszewski, 2007; Ingemansson and Waluszewski, 2009; Ingemansson, 2010; Baraldi, Gregori and Perna, 2011) have focused on the conditions, mechanism and resource patterns emerging when new technologies are embedded. New solutions have to be embedded in networks to be accepted by the market. The embedding process needs to occur across three different contexts or settings, namely the "developing", the "producing" and the "using" settings. The developing setting refers to actors such as universities who develop something new by combining resources in new ways (Håkansson and Waluszewski, 2007); the producing setting refers to actors such as manufacturers or logistics firms, who transform an innovation into a product that can be produced and sold on a large scale; lastly, the using setting refers to direct and indirect users of a technology, spanning from companies to consumers.

8   Managing Six Important Customer Relationships: Loccioni's KAMs and CRM

1. Whirlpool Corporation is one of the world's leading manufacturers and marketers of home appliances. In 2011 this company reached a turnover of more than $19 billion, and it employed 68,000 people in 66 manufacturing plants and technology research centers. Whirlpool markets several brands such as Whirlpool, Maytag, KitchenAid, Jenn-Air, Brastemp and Bauknecht.

2. All the main activities concerning the treatment cycle were managed by the central logic unit which is placed in the control room; the latter is expected to perform treatment functions according to the time and modes set beforehand or later on. The plant starts and ends the sanitization cycle automatically. The emptying out and sanitization plant allows the treatment on more railway tracks to take place, thanks to a series of on-site stations, spaced out so as to ensure the emptying out and the sanitization of all kinds of trains.

References

Aarikka-Stenroos, L. 2008. *What Really Happens in Initiation? Investigating the Subprocesses and Features of Emerging Buyer-Supplier Relationships*. In Proceedings of the 24th IMP Conference, Uppsala, Sweden.

Ackoff, R. L. 1996. On learning and the systems that facilitate it. *Center for Quality of Management Journal*, 5(2), 27–35.

Ahearne, M., Rapp, A., Mariadoss, B. J. and Ganesan, S. 2012. Challenges of CRM implementation in business-to-business markets: A contingency perspective. *Journal of Personal Selling & Sales Management*, 17(1), 117–129.

Akrich, M., Callon, M. and Latour, B. 2002. The key to success of innovation: The art of interessement (Part1)/The art of choosing a good spoken person (Part 2). *International Journal of Information Management*, 6(2), 187–225.

Alshawi, S., Missi, F. and Irani, Z. 2011. Organisational, technical and data quality factors in CRM adoption – SMEs perspective. *Industrial Marketing Management*, 40, 376–383.

Ang, L. and Buttle, F. 2006. CRM software applications and business performance. *Journal of Database Marketing*, 14, 4–16.

Anthony, R. N. 1965. *Planning and Control Systems: A Framework for Analysis*. Harvard University Press: Boston.

Araujo, L., Dubois, A. and Gadde, L.-E. 1999. Managing interfaces with suppliers. *Industrial Marketing Management*, 28(5), 497–506.

Ata, Z. and Toker, A. 2012. The effect of customer relationship management adoption in business-to-business markets. *Journal of Business & Industrial Marketing*, 27(6), 497–507.

Avgerou, C. 2000. IT and organizational change: An institutionalist perspective. *Information Technology & People*, 13(4).

Avlonitis, G. J. and Panagopoulos, N. G. 2005. Antecedents and consequences of CRM technology acceptance in the sales force. *Industrial Marketing Management*, 34(4), 355–368.

Baglieri, E., Secchi, R. and Croom, S. 2007. Exploring the impact of a supplier portal on the buyer–supplier relationship: The case of Ferrari Auto. *Industrial Marketing Management*, 36, 1010–1017.

Baraldi, E. 2003. *When Information Technologies Faces Resource Interaction*. Doctoral Thesis, Uppsala University: Uppsala.

Baraldi, E. and Bocconcelli, R. 2001. The quantitative journey in a qualitative landscape: Developing a data collection model and a quantitative methodology in business network studies. *Management Decision*, 39, 564–577.

Baraldi, E., Gregori, G. L. and Perna, A. 2011. Network evolution and the embedding of complex technical solutions: The case of the leaf house network. *Industrial Marketing Management*, 40(6), 838–852.

Baraldi, E., Gressetvold, E. and Harrison, D. 2012. Resource interaction in inter-organizational networks: Foundations, comparison, and a research agenda. *Journal of Business Research*, 65, 266–276.

Baraldi, E., La Rocca, A. and Perna, A. 2013. Intra- and inter-organizational effects of a CRM system implementation. *Mercati e Competitivita'*, 1, 13–34.

Baraldi, E. and Nadin, G. 2006. The challenges in digitalising business relationships: The construction of an IT infrastructure for a textile-related business network. *Technovation*, 26, 1111–1126.

Baraldi, E. and Strömsten, T. 2006. Embedding, producing and using low weight: Value creation and the role of the configuration of resource interfaces in the networks around Holmen's newsprint and IKEA's Lack table. *The IMP Journal*, 1(1), 52–97.

Baraldi, E. and Waluszewski, A. 2005. Information technology at IKEA: An "open sesame" solution or just another type of facility? *Journal of Business Research*, 58, 1251–1260.

Barney, J. B. 1986. Strategic factor markets: Expectations, luck and business strategy. *Management Science*, 32, 1231–1241.

Barney, J. B. 1991. Firm resources and sustained competitive advantage. *Journal of Management*, 17, 99–120.

Barrett, J. 1986. Why major account selling works. *Industrial Marketing Management*, 15, 63–73.

Batonda, G. and Parry, C. 2003. Approaches to relationship development processes in inter-firm networks. *European Journal of Marketing*, 37(10), 1457–1484.

Beged-Dov, A. G., Ehrenfeld, S. and Summer C. E. 1967. An overview of management science and information systems. *Management Science*, 13(12), 817–837.

Benjamin, R. I. and Levinson, E. 1993. A Framework for managing IT-enabled change. *Sloan Management Review*, Summer, 23–33.

Berkley B. J. and Gupta, A. 1994. Improving service quality with information technology. *International Journal of Information Management*, 14, 109–121.

Berry, L. L. 1983. Relationship marketing. In Berry, L. L., Shostack, G. L., Upah, G. D. (eds), *Emerging Perspectives of Service Marketing*. American Marketing Association: Chicago.

Bhattacherjee, A. and Premkumar, G. 2004. Understanding changes in belief and attitude toward information technology usage: A theoretical model and longitudinal test. *MIS Quarterly*, 28(2), 351–370.

Blattberg, Robert C. and Deighton, J. 1991. Interactive marketing: Exploiting the age of addressibility. *Sloan Management Review*, 33, 5–14.

Boddy, D., Boonstra, A. J. and Kennedy, G. 2002. *Managing Information Systems: An Organisational Perspective*. Prentice Hall: New York.

Bose, R. 2002. Customer relationship management: Key components for IT success. *Industrial Management and Data Systems*, 102(2), 89–97.

Boulding, W., Staelin, R., Ehret, M. and Johnston, W. J. 2005. A CRM roadmap: What we know, potential pitfalls, and where to go. *Journal of Marketing*, 69(4), 155–166.

Brady, M., Saren, M. and Tzokas, N. 2002. Integrating information technology into marketing practice: The IT reality of contemporary marketing practice. *Journal of Marketing Management*, 18, 555–577.

Brandt, P., Carlsson, R. and Nilsson, A. G. 1998. *Välja och förvalta standardsystem*. Student-litteratur, Lund.

Brodie, R., Coviello, N., Brookes, W. and Little, V. 1997. Towards a paradigm shift in marketing? An examination of current marketing practices. *Journal of Marketing Management*, 13, 383–406.

Brynjolfsson, E., and Hitt, L. M. 2000. Beyond computation: information technology, organizational transformation and business performance. *Journal of Economic Perspectives*, 14(4), 23–48.

Bull, C. 2003. Strategic issues in customer relationship management (CRM) implementation. *Business Process Management Journal*, 9, 592–602.

Buttle, F. 2004. *Customer Relationship Management: Concepts and Tools*. Oxford: Elsevier Butterworth Heinemann.

Campbell, A. J. 2003. Creating customer knowledge competence: Managing customer relationship management programs strategically. *Industrial Marketing Management*, 32, 375–383.

Campbell, N. G. C. and Cunningham, M. T. 1983. Customer analysis for strategy development in industrial markets. *Strategic Management Journal*, 4, 6–18.

Chang, W., Park, J. E. and Chaiy, S. 2010. How does CRM technology transform into organizational performance? A mediating role of marketing capability. *Journal of Business Research*, 63, 849–855.

Chen, J. I. and Popovich, K. 2003. Understanding customer relationship management (CRM): People, process, and technology. *Business Process Management Journal*, 9(5), 672–688.

Ciabuschi, F., Perna, A. and Snehota, I. 2012. Assembling resources in the formation of a new business. *Journal of Business Research*, 65(2), 220–229.

Clegg, C., Carey, N., Dean, G., Hornby, P. and Bolden, R. (1997). Users' reactions to information technology: Some multivariate models and their implications. *Journal of Information Technology*, 12, 15–32.

Corey, R. E. 1976. *Industrial Marketing*. Prentice-Hall: Englewood Cliffs, NJ.

Coughlan, P. and Coghlan, D. 2002. Action research for operations management. *International Journal of Operations and Production Management*, 22 (2), 220–240.

Coughlan, P., Coghlan, D. and Lombard, F. 2003. Managing collaborative relationships in a period of discontinuity. *International Journal of Operations & Production Management*, 23, 1246–1259.

Cova, B. and Ghauri, P. 1996. *Project Marketing: Between Mass Marketing and Networks*. The European Seminar on Project Marketing and System Selling (Working Paper).

Cova, B., Mazet, F. and Salle, R. 1996. Milieu as a pertinent unit of analysis in project marketing. *International Business Review*, 5, 647–664.

Coviello, N. E., Brodie, R. J. and Munro, H. J. 1997. Understanding contemporary marketing: Development of a classification scheme. *Journal of Marketing Management*, 13(6), 501–522.

Cunningham, M. T. 1982. An interaction approach to purchasing strategy. In Håkansson, H. (eds.), *International Marketing and Purchasing of Industrial Goods: An Interaction Approach*. Wiley: London. 345–358.

Cunningham, M. T. and Turnbull, P. W. 1982. Inter-organizational personal contact patterns. In Håkansson, H. (ed.), *International Marketing and Purchasing of Industrial Goods: An Interaction Approach*. John Wiley and Sons: Chichester, New York, Brisbane, Toronto, Singapore, pp. 304–316.

Darrell, R., Reicheld, F. F., Schefter, P. 2002. Avoid the four perils of CRM. *Harvard Business Review*, February 2002, 101–109.

Davenport, T. H. 1992. *Process Innovation. Re-engineering Work through Information Technology*. Harvard Business School Press: Boston, MA.

Davenport, T. H., 2000. *Mission Critical: Realising the Promise of Enterprise Systems*. Harvard Business School Press: Boston, MA.

Davenport, T. H. and Prusak, L. 1998. *Working Knowledge: How Organizations Manage What They Know*. Harvard Business School Press: Cambridge, MA.

Davenport, T. H., De Long, D. W. and Beers, M. C. 1998. Successful knowledge management projects. *Sloan Management Review*, 39(2), 43–57.

Davis, F. D. 1989. Perceived usefulness, perceived ease of use, and user acceptance of information technology. *MIS Quarterly*, 13(3), 319–340.

De Burca, S., Fynes, B. and Marshall, D. 2005. Strategic technology adoption: Extending ERP across the supply chain. *Journal of Enterprise Information Management*, 18(4), 427–440.

Delone, W. H. and Mclean, E. R. 1992. Information systems success: The quest for the dependent variable. *Information Systems Research*, 3(1), 60–95.

Dewett, T. and Jones, G. R. 2001. The role of information technology in the organization: A review, model and assessment. *Journal of Management*, 27(3), 313–346.

Diebold, J. 1953. Automation – The new technology. *Harvard Business Review*, November–December 1953, 63–71.

Diller, H. 1992. Euro-key-account-management. *Marketing ZFP*, 14, 239–245.

Dube', L. and Pare', G. 2003. Rigor in information systems positivist case research: Current practices, trends, and recommendations. *MIS Quarterly*, 27, 597–635.

Dubois, A. 1994. *Organising Industrial Activities. An Analytical Framework*. Doctoral Thesis, Chalmers University of Technology: Gothenburg.

Dubois, A. and Araujo, L. 2006. The relationship between technical and organisational interfaces in product development. *The IMP Journal*, 1(1), 28–51.

Dubois, A. and Gadde, L.-E. 2002. Systematic combining: An abductive approach to case research. *Journal of Business Research*, 55, 553–560.

Dubois, A. and Håkansson, H. 2000. *Technical Development in Networks: The Importance of Third Parties*. Paper presented at 4th International Conference on Chain Management in Agribusiness and the Food Industry, Wageningen, The Netherlands.

Dwyer, F. R., Schurr, P. H. and Oh, S. 1987. Developing buyer–seller relationships. *Journal of Marketing*, 51, 11–27.

Easton, G. 2010. Critical realism in case study research. *Industrial Marketing Management*, 39, 118–128.

Easton, G. and Araujo, L. 1994. *Discontinuity in Networks: Initiators, Issues and Initiative*. In: Proceedings of the 10th Annual IMP Conference, Groningen.

Edvardsson, B., Holmlund, M. and Strandvik, T. 2008. Initiation of business relationships in service-dominant settings. *Industrial Marketing Management*, 37(3), 339–350.

Ehret, M. 2004. Managing the trade-off between relationships and value networks: Towards a value-based approach of customer relationship management in business-to-business markets. *Industrial Marketing Management*, 33, 465–473.

Eisenhardt, K. M. 1989. Building theories from case study research: Academy of management. *The Academy of Management Review*, 14, 532–550.

Emery, J. C. 1964. *The Impact of Information Technology on Organization*. In: Proceedings of the 24th Annual Meeting, Academy of Management, Chicago.

Evans, P. and Wurster, T. S. 2000. *Blown to Bits*. Harvard Business School Press: Boston, MA.

Finnegan, D. J. and Currie, W. L. 2010. A multi-layered approach to CRM implementation: An integration perspective. *European Management Journal*, 28, 153–167.

Finnegan, D. J. and Willcocks, L. P. 2007. *Implementing CRM: From Technology to Knowledge*. John Wiley & Sons: Chichester.

Fiocca, R. 1982. Account portfolio analysis for strategy development. *Industrial Marketing Management*, 11, 53–62.

Ford, D. 1980. The development of buyer–seller relationships in industrial markets. *European Journal of Marketing*, 14, 339–353.

Ford, D. 1990. *Understanding Business Markets: Interaction, Relationships and Networks*. Academic Press: San Diego.

Ford, D., Gadde, L-E, Håkansson, H., Lundgren, A. Snehota, I, Turnbull, P. and Wilson, D. 1998. *Managing Business Relationships*. John Wiley & Sons Ltd: Chichester.

Ford, D., Gadde L.-E., Håkansson H. and Snehota, I. 2003. *Managing Business Relationships*. 1st Edition, Wiley: Chichester.

Ford, D., Gadde L.-E., Håkansson, H. and Snehota, I. 2006. *The Business Marketing Course. Managing in Complex Networks*. 2nd Edition, Wiley: Chichester.

Ford, D., Gadde, L.-E., Håkansson, H. and Snehota, I. 2011. *Managing Business Relationships*. John Wiley & Sons: Chichester.

Ford, D. and Håkansson, H. 2006. IMP: Some things achieved, much more to do. *European Journal of Marketing*, 40, 248–258.

Ford, D. and Rosson, P. J. 1982. The relationships between export manufacturers and their overseas distributors. In Czinkota, M. R. and Tesar, G. (eds.), *Export Management: An International Context*. Praeger Publishers: New York, pp. 257–275.

Foster, L. W. Flynn, D. M. 1984. Management information technology: Its effects on organizational form and function. *MIS Quarterly*, December 1984, 229–235.

Fournier, S. and Avery, J. 2011. The uninvited brand. *Business Horizons*, 54(3), 193–207.

Gadde, L.-E. and Håkansson, H. 2001. *Supply Network Strategies*. John Wiley: Chichester.

Gadde, L-E. and Håkansson, H. 2008. Business relations and resource combining. *The IMP Journal*, 2(1), 31–45.

Galbraith, J. R. 1980. *Strategy Implementation: The Role of Structure and Process*. West Publishing Co.: St. Paul, MN.

Gersick, C. 1991. Revolutionary change theories: Multilevel exploration of the punctuated equilibrium paradigm. *Academy of Management Review*, 16(1), 10–36.

Glazer, R. 1997. Strategy and structure in information-intensive markets: The relationship between marketing and IT. *Journal of Market Focused Management*, 2(1), 65–81.

Goodhue, D. L. 1995. Understanding user evaluations of information systems. *Management Science*, 41(12), 1827–1844.

Gorry, G. A. and Scott Morton, M. S. 1971. A framework for management information systems. *Sloan Management Review*, Fall 1971, 55–70.

Grandon, E. E. and Pearson, J. M. 2004. Electronic commerce adoption: An empirical study of small and medium US businesses. *Information & Management*, 42, 197–216.

Grant, R. M. 1991. The resource-based theory of competitive advantage: Implications for strategy formulation. *California Management Review*, 33 (Spring), 114–135.

Greenberg, P. 2010. The impact of CRM 2.0 on customer insight. *Journal of Business & Industrial Marketing*, 25, 410–419.

Gressetvold, E. 2001. *Technical Development within the Industrial Network Approach as Interaction between Four Resource Entities*. In: Proceedings of the 17th Annual IMP Conference, Oslo.

Grönroos, C. 1990. *Service Management and Marketing. Managing the Moments of Truth in Service Competition*. Free Press/Lexington Books: Lexington, MA.

Grönroos, C. 1994. From marketing mix to relationship marketing: Towards a paradigm shift in marketing. *Management Decision*, 32(2), 4–20.

Grönroos, C. 1996. Relationship marketing: Strategic and tactical implications. *Management Decision*, 34(3), 5–14.

Gummesson, E. 1997. Relationship marketing as a paradigm shift: Some conclusions from the 30R approach. *Management Decisions* 35(4), 267–272.

Gummesson, E. 2004. *Many-to-Many Marketing*. Liber: Malmö, Sweden.

Gummesson, E., Lehtinen, U. and Grönros, C. 1997. Comment on Nordic perspectives on business marketing. *European Journal of Marketing*, 31, 10–16.

Hadjikhani, H. 1996. Project marketing and the management of discontinuity. *International Business Review*, 5(3), 319–336.

Hadjikhani, H., Lindh, C. and Thilenius, P. 2012. The impact of discontinuity on firms' business relationship behavior. *European Business Review*, 24, 134–150.

Haigh, T. 2011. The history of information technology. *Annual Review of Information Science and Technology*, 45(1), 431–487.

Håkansson, H. 1982. *International Marketing and Purchasing of Industrial Goods*. John Wiley & Sons, Chichester.

Håkansson, H. (ed.). 1987. *Industrial Technological Development: A Network Approach*. CroomHelm: London, Sidney, Dover, New Hampshire.

Håkansson, H. and Johanson, J. 1988. Formal and informal cooperation strategies in international industrial networks. In Contractor, F. J. and Lorange, P. (eds.), *Cooperative Strategies in International Business*. Lexington (MA): Lexington, pp. 369–379.

Håkansson, H. and Johanson, J. 1992. A model of industrial networks. In Axelsson, B. and Easton, G. (eds.), *Industrial Networks: A New View of Reality*. Routledge: London. 28–34.

Håkansson, H. and Snehota, I. 1992. *Developing Business Relationships in Industrial Networks*. Thompson Learning: London.

Håkansson, H. and Snehota, I. 1993. *The Content and Function of Business Relationships*. In: Proceedings of the 9th Annual IMP conference, Bath, UK.

Håkansson, H. and Snehota, I. 1995. *Developing Relationships in Business Markets*. Routledge: London.

Håkansson, H. and Snehota, I. 2000. An IMP perspective. In Jagdish, N. S. and Parvatijar, A. (eds.), *Handbook of Relationship Marketing*. Sage: Thousand Oaks, pp. 69–93.

Håkansson, H. and Waluszewski, A. 2002. *Managing Technological Development: IKEA, the Environment and Technology*. Routledge: London.

Håkansson, H. and Waluszewski, A. 2007. *Knowledge and Innovation in Business and Industry: The Importance of Using Others*. Routledge: London.

Håkansson, H., Ford, D., Gadde, L-E, Snehota, I. and Waluszewski, A. 2009. *Business in Networks*. John Wiley & Sons: Chichester.

Halinen, A. and Törnroos, J-Å. 1998. The role of embeddedness in the evolution of business networks. *Scandinavian Journal of Management*, 14(3), 187–205.

Halinen, A. and Törnroos, J-Å. 2005. Using case methods in the study of contemporary business networks. *Journal of Business Research*, 58, 1285–1297.

Hart, L., Emery, P., Colomb, R., Raymond, K., Chang, D., Ye, Y., Kendall, E. and Dutra, M. 2004. *Usage Scenarios and Goals for Ontology Definition Metamodel*. Lecture Notes in Computer Science.

Hartley, R. 1976. Use of customer analysis for better market penetration. *Industrial Marketing Management*, 5(1), 57–62.

Hedberg, B. and Jönsson, S. 1978. Designing semi-confusing information systems for organizations in changing environment. *Accounting, Organizations and Society*, 3(1), 47–64.

Hedman, J. and Kalling, T. 2002. *IT and Business Models: Concepts and Theories*. Copenhagen Business School Press, Copenhagen.

Henderson, J. and Venkatraman, N. 1993. Strategic alignment: Leveraging information technology for transforming organizations. *IBM Systems Journal*, 32(1), 4–16.

Hevner, A., March, S., Park, J. and Ram, S. 2004. Design science in information systems research. *MIS Quarterly*, 28(1), 75–105.

Hill, J. and Scott, T. 2004. A consideration of the roles of business intelligence and e-business management in management and marketing decision making in knowledge-based and high-tech start-ups. *Qualitative Market Research*, 7(1), 48–57.

Hitt, L. and Brynjolfsson, E. 1996. *Productivity without Profit? Three Measures of Information Technology's Value*. Working Paper Series 190, MIT Center for Coordination Science.

Holmen, E. and Pedersen, A-C. 2001. *Knowledge and Ignorance of Connections between Relationships*. In: Proceedings of the 17th Annual IMP Conference, Oslo.

Holmen, E., Roos, C., Kallevåg, M., Von Raesfeld, A., De Boer, L. and Pedersen, A.-C. 2005. *How Do Relationships Begin?* In: Proceedings of the 21th Annual IMP Conference, Rotterdam.

Holmlund, M. 2004. Analyzing business relationships and distinguishing different interaction levels. *Industrial Marketing Management*, 33, 279–287.

Holmlund, M. and Törnroos, J. Å. 1997. What are relationships in business networks? *Management Decision*, 35, 304–309.

Homburg, C. Workman, Jr. J. P. and Jensen, O. 2000. Fundamental changes in marketing organization: The movement toward a customer-focused organizational structure. *Journal of the Academy of Marketing Science*, 28(4), 459–478.

Hoos, I. R. 1960. When the computer takes over the office. *Harvard Business Review*, 38(4), 102–112.

Huber, G. P. 1990. A theory of the effects of advanced information technologies on organizational design, intelligence, and decision making. *The Academy of Management Review*, 15(1), 47–71.

Ingemansson, M. 2010. *Success as Science but Burden for Business? On the Difficult Relationship between Scientific Advancement and Innovation*. Doctoral Thesis, Uppsala University: Uppsala.

Ingemansson, M. and Waluszewski, A. 2009. Success in science and burden in business: On the difficult relationship between science as a developing setting and business as a producer-user setting. *The IMP Journal*, 3(2), 20–56.

Ingram, T. N., Laforge, R. W. and Leigh, T. W. 2002. Selling in the new millennium: A joint agenda. *Industrial Marketing Management*, 31(7), 1–9.

Johnston, R. and Vitale, M. 1988. Creating competitive advantage with inter-organizational information systems. *MIS Quarterly*, June 1988, 153–165.

Kaila, I. and Goldman, M. 2006. *Eight Steps to Implementing a Successful CRM Project*. Gartner Group report series, Gartner, London.

Kallinikos, J. 2001. *The Age of Flexibility – Managing Organizations and Technology*. Academia Acta: Lund.

Keen, Peter G. W. 1991. *Shaping the Future: Business Design through Information Technology*. 1st edition. Harvard Business School Press: Harvard.

Keramati, A., Mehrabi, H. and Mojir, N. 2010. A process-oriented perspective on customer relationship management and organizational performance: An empirical investigation. *Industrial Marketing Management*, 39, 1170–1185.

Kettinger, W., Grover, V., Guha, S. and Segars, A. H. 1994. Strategic information systems revisited: A study in sustainability and performance. *MIS Quarterly*, 18(1), 31–58.

Kevork, E. K. and Vrechopoulos, A. P. 2009. CRM literature: Conceptual and functional insights by keyword analysis. *Marketing Intelligence and Planning*, 27(1), 48–85.

Kumar, V. and Reinartz, W. 2012. *Customer Relationship Management: Concept, Strategy and Tools*. Springer: Verlag-Berlin.

Lado, A. A. and Zhang, M. J. 1998. Expert systems, knowledge development and utilization, and sustained competitive advantage: A resource-based model. *Journal of Management*, 24, 489–509.

Lambert, D. M. 2010. Customer relationship management as a business process. *Journal of Business & Industrial Marketing*, 25, 4–17.

Landry, T. D., Todd, J. A. and Arndt, A. 2005. A compendium of sales-related literature in customer relationship management: Processes and technologies with managerial implications. *Journal of Personal Selling & Sales Management*, 25, 231–251.

Langefors, B. 1995. *Essays on Infology: Summing up and Planning for the Future*. Studentlitteratur: Lund.

Langerak, F. and Verhoef, P. C. 2003. Strategically embedding CRM. *Business Strategy Review*, 14(4), 73–80.

Laplaca, P. J. and Katrichis, J. M. 2009. Relative presence of business-to-business research in the marketing literature. *Journal of Business-to-Business Marketing*, 16, 1–22.

La Rocca, A. 2011. *Interaction and Actors' Identities in Business Relationships*. Doctoral Thesis, Usi: Lugano.

Lawler, E. E., Mohrmann, S. A. and Ledford, G. E. 1998. *Strategies for High Performance Organizations: The CEO Report*. Jossey-Bass: San Francisco.

Leek, S., Turnbull, P. W. and Naude, P. 2003. How is information technology affecting business relationships? Results from a UK survey. *Industrial Marketing Management*, 32, 119–126.

Leidner, D. E. and Elam, J. J. 1993. *Executive Information Systems: Their Impact on Executive Decision Making*. In: Proceedings of the 26th Annual Hawaii International Conference on System Sciences.

Leonard-Barton, D. 1988. Implementation as mutual adaptation of technology and organization. *Research Policy*, 17(5), 251–267.

Levin M. and Greenwood, D. 2001. Pragmatic action research and the struggle to transform universities into learning communities. In Reason, P. and Bradbury, H. (eds.), *Handbook of Action Research: Participative Inquiry and Practice*. London: Sage, pp. 103–113.

Lindgreen, A., Palmer, R., Vanhamme, J. and Wouters, J. 2006. A relationship-management assessment tool: Questioning, identifying, and prioritizing critical aspects of customer relationships. *Industrial Marketing Management*, 35, 57–71.

Lucas, H. C. and Olson, M. 1994. The impact of information technology on organizational flexibility. *Journal of Organizational Computing*, 4(2), 155–176.

Markus, L. M. and Robey, D. 1988. Information technology and organizational change: Causal structure in theory and research. *Management Science*, 34(5), 583–598.

Mclean, E. R. 1979. End users as application developers. *MIS Quarterly*, 3(4), 37–46.

Meadows, M. and Dibb, S. 2012. Progress in customer relationship management adoption: A cross-sector study. *Journal of Strategic Marketing*, 20, 323–344.

Melville, N., Kraemer, K. and Gurbaxani, V. 2004. Review: Information technology and organizational performance: An integrative model of IT business value. *MIS Quarterly*, 28(2), 283–322.

Mendoza, L. E., Marius, A., Pérez, M. and Grimán, A. C. 2007. Critical success factors for a customer relationship management strategy. *Information and Software Technology*, 49, 913–945.

META Group. 2001. *Integration: Critical Issues for Implementing of CRM Solutions*. META Group.

Millman, T. and Wilson, K. J. 1996. Developing key account management competences. *Journal of Marketing Practice*, 2, 7–22.

Mintzberg, H. 1972. The myths of MIS. *California Management Review*, XV(1), 92–97.

Mithas, S. Krishan, M. S. and Fornell, C. 2005. Why do customer relationship management applications affect customer satisfaction? *Journal of Marketing*, 69, 201–209.

Moran, P. and Ghoshal, S. 1999. Markets, firms and the process of economic development. *Academy of Management Review*, 24(3), 390–412.

Morgan, R. and Hunt, S. 1994. The commitment-trust theory of relationship marketing. *Journal of Marketing*, 58, 20–38.

Mulligan, P. and Gordon, S. 2002. The impact of information technology on customer and supplier relationships in the financial services. *International Journal of Service Industry Management*, 13(1), 29–46.

Ngai, E. W. T. 2005. Customer relationship management research (1992–2002): An academic literature review and classification. *Marketing Intelligence & Planning*, 23, 582–605.

Nilsson, B. E. 1999. On why to model what and why: Concepts and architecture for change. In Nilsson, A. G. et al. (eds.), *Perspectives on Business Modelling: Understanding and Changing Organisations*. Springer: Berlin, pp. 269–303.

Nonaka, I. 1991. The knowledge-creating company. *Harvard Business Review*, 69, 96–104.

Nonaka, I. and Takeuchi, H. 1995. *The Knowledge-Creating Company*. Oxford University Press: New York, Oxford.

Nord, J. H. and Nord, G. D. 1995. MIS research: Journal status assessment and analysis. *Information & Management*, (29), 29–42.

Ojasalo, J. 2001. Key account management at company and individual levels in business-to-business relationships. *Journal of Business & Industrial Marketing*, 16, 199–218.

Orlikowski, W. J. 1993. CASE tools as organizational change: Investigating incremental and radical changes in systems development. *MIS Quarterly*, 17(3).

Orlikowski, W. J. and Barley, S. 2001. Technology and institutions: What can research on information technology and research on organizations learn from each other? *MIS Quarterly*, 25, 145–165.

Orlikowski, W. J. and Gash, D. C. 1992. *Changing Frames: Understanding Technological Change in Organizations*. CISR WP, No. 236: MIT.

Orlikowski, W. J. and Iacono, C. 2001. Research commentary: Desperately seeking the "IT" in IT research – A call to theorizing the IT artifact. *Information Systems Research*, 12, 121–134.

Orlikowski, W. J. and Robey, D. 1991. Information technology and the structuring of organizations. *Information Systems Research*, 2(2), 398–427.

Orlikowski, W. J., Walsham, G., Jones, M. R. and Degross, J. I. (eds.). 1995. *Information Technology and Changes in Organizational Work*. Proceedings of the IFIP WG8.2 working conference on information technology and changes in organizational work.

Osarenkhoe, A. 2007. *What Characterises the Culture of a Relationship-Oriented Organisation Applying a Customer Intimacy Strategy?* In: Proceedings of Networking and Electronic Commerce Research Conference, Lake Garda, Italy.

Osterman, P. 1991. The impact of information technology upon employment. In Scott Morton, M. S. (ed.), *The Corporation of the 1990s: Information Technology and Organizational Transformation*. New York: Oxford University Press.

Packendorff, J. 1995. Inquiring into the temporary organization: New directions for project management research. *Scandinavian Journal of Management*, 11(4), 319–333.

Pardo, C. 2012. *From Internal Knowledge to Customer Offering: The Combination Trip of a Resource*. In: Proceedings of the 28th Annual IMP conference, Rome.

Pardo, C., Salle, R. and Spencer, R. 1995. The key accountization of the firm. A case study. *Industrial Marketing Management*, 22, 123–134.

Parvatiyar, A. and Sheth, J. N. 2001. Customer relationship management: Emerging practice, process, and discipline. *Journal of Economic and Social Research*, 3(2), 1–34.

Paulissen, K., Milis, K., Brengman, M., Fjermestad, J. and Romano, N. 2007. *Voids in the Current CRM Literature: Academic Literature Review and Classification (2000–2005)*. In: Proceedings of the 40th Annual Hawaii International Conference on System Sciences.

Payne A. and Frow, P. 2005. A strategic framework for customer relationship management. *Journal of Marketing*, 69, 167–176.

Penrose, E. 1959. *The Theory of the Growth of the Firm*. Reprint 1995, Oxford University Press: New York.

Peppers, D. and Rogers, M. 1993. *The One to One Future*. Currency Doubleday: New York.

Peppers, D. and Rogers, M. 2004. *Managing Customer Relationships: A Strategic Framework*. John Wiley & Sons: New Jersey.

Perna, A., Baraldi, E. and Gregori, G. L. 2012. Exploring the conditions for marketing an innovative and unique customized solution: Mexus case study. *The IMP Journal*, 6(1), 1–16.

Perna, A., Runfola, A., Guercini, S. and Gregori, G. L. 2012. *A Resource Network View of Relationship Beginning: A Case Analysis in the Mechanical Industry*. In: Proceedings of the 28th Annual IMP conference, Rome.

Perna, A., Cardinali, S. and Gregori, G. L. 2013. Coping with alternatives in sales organisations: Experiences from an Italian company. *Journal of Business Market Management*, 3, 107–122.

Pettigrew, A. M. 1992. The character and significance of strategy process research. *Strategic Management Journal*, 13 (winter special issue), 5–16.

Piccoli, G. and Ives, B. 2005. IT-Dependent strategic initiatives and sustained competitive advantage: A review and synthesis of the literature. *MIS Quarterly*, 29(4), 747–776.

Porter, M. E. 1980. *Competitive Strategy*. New York: Free Press.

Ramström, D. 1973. *The Efficiency of Control Strategies Revisited*. University of Umeå Department of Business Administration.

Rapp, W. V. 2002. *Information Technology Strategies: How Leading Firms Use IT to Gain an Advantage*. Oxford University Press: New York.

Reid, A. and Catterall, M. 2005. Invisible data quality issues in a CRM implementation. *Journal of Database Marketing & Customer Strategy Management*, 12(4), 305–314.

Reinartz, W., Krafft, M. and Hoyer, W. D. 2004. The customer relationship management process: Its measurement and impact on performance. *Journal of Marketing Research*, 41(3), 293–313.

Richard, J. E., Thirkell, P. C. and Huff, S. L. 2007. An examination of Customer Relationship Management (CRM) technology adoption and its impact on business-to-business customer relationships. *Total Quality Management & Business Excellence*, 18, 927–945.

Rigby, D. K., Reichfeld, F. F. and Scheffer, P. 2002. Avoid the four perils of CRM. *Harvard Business Review*, 80, 101–109.

Robey, D. 1977. Computers and management structure: Some empirical findings re-examined. *Human Relations*, 30, 963–976.

Rodriguez, M. and Honeycutt, E. D. 2011. Customer Relationship Management (CRM)'s impact on B to B sales professionals' collaboration and sales performance. *Journal of Business-to-Business Marketing*, 18, 335–356.

Runfola, A., Guercini, S., Gregori, G. L. and Perna, A. 2013. Discontinuity in interaction. Findings from two cases in the Italian context. *Mercati e Competitivita'*, 1, 53–72.

Ryals, L. 2005. Making customer relationship management work: The measurement and profitable management of customer relationship. *Journal of Marketing*, 69, 252–261.

Ryssel, R., Ritter, T. and Gemunde, H. G. 2004. The impact of information technology deployment on trust, commitment and value creation in business relationships. *Journal of Business & Industrial Marketing*, 19(3), 197–207.

Rytkönen, M. H. and Strandvik, T. 2005. Stress in business relationships. *Journal of Business & Industrial Marketing*, 20(1), 12–22.

Salle, R., Cova, B. and Pardo, C. 2000. Portfolio of supplier–customer relationships. In Woodside, A. J. (eds.), *Getting Better at Sensemaking (Advances in Business Marketing and Purchasing*, Volume 9, pp. 419–442). Emerald Group Publishing Limited, London.

Salojärvi, H., Sainio, L.-M. and Tarkiainen, A. 2010. Organizational factors enhancing customer knowledge utilization in the management of key account relationships. *Industrial Marketing Management*, 39, 1395–1402.

Sambamurthy, V., Bharadwaj, A. and Grover, V. 2003. Shaping agility through digital options: Reconceptualizing the role of information technology in contemporary firms. *Information Systems Quarterly*, 27(2), 237–263.

Schwartz, M., Schliebs, O. and Wyssusek, B. 2002. *Focusing the Customer: A Critical Approach towards Design and Use of Data Warehousing in Corporate CRM*. DMDW Workshop at Caise, Toronto.

Selnes, F. and Johnson, M. D. 2004. A dynamic customer portfolio management perspective on marketing strategy. In Håkansson, H., Harrison, D. and Waluszewski, A. (eds.), *Rethinking Marketing: Developing a New Understanding of Markets*. West Sussex, UK: John Wiley & Sons, pp. 117–135.

Shannon, C. E. and Weaver, W. 1949. *The Mathematical Theory of Communication*. University of Illinois Press: Urbana.

Shapiro, B. P. and Moriarty, R. T. 1984. *Organizing the National Account Force*. Report, 84–101. Cambridge: Marketing Science Institute.

Shapiro, B. P. and Posner, R. S. 1976. Making the major sale. *Harvard Business Review*, 54 (March-April), 68–78.

Shum, P., Bove, L. and Auh, S. 2008. Employees' affective commitment to change: The key to successful CRM implementation. *European Journal of Marketing*, 42, 1346–1371.

Simon, H. 1977. *The New Science of Management Decision*. Prentice Hall: Englewood Cliffs, N.J.

Skaates, M. A. 2000. *Actor Bonds in Situation of Discontinuous Business Activities*. In: Proceedings of the 16th Annual IMP Conference, Bath, UK.

Smith, K. G., Grimm, C. M., Gannon, M. J. and Chen, M.-J. 1991. Organizational information processing, competitive responses, and performance in the U.S. domestic airline industry. *The Academy of Management Journal*, 34(1), 60–85.

Snehota, I. 1990. *Notes on a Theory of the Business Enterprise*. Doctoral Thesis, Uppsala University: Uppsala.

Snehota, I. 2004. Perspectives and theories of market. In Håkansson, H., Harrison, D. Waluszewski, A. (eds.), *Rethinking Marketing: Developing a New Understanding of Markets*. Wiley: Chichester, pp. 15–32.

Söderlund, J. 2004. Building theories of project management: Past research, questions for the future. *International Journal of Project Management*, 22, 183–191.

Spencer, R. 1999. Key accounts: Effectively managing strategic complexity. *Journal of Business & Industrial Marketing*, 4, 291–309.

Srivastava, R., Shervani, T. A., Fahey, L. 1999. Marketing, business processes and shareholder value: An organizationally embedded view of marketing activities and the discipline of marketing. *Journal of Marketing*, 63 (Special issue), 168–179.

Stein, A. and Smith, M. 2009. CRM systems and organizational learning: An exploration of the relationship between CRM effectiveness and the customer information orientation of the firm in industrial markets. *Industrial Marketing Management*, 38, 198–206.

Stein, A., Smith, M. and Lancioni, R. 2013. The development and diffusion of CRM knowledge. To appear in *Industrial Marketing Management*, http://www.journals.elsevier.com/industrial-marketing-management/

Steel, M., Dubelaar, C. and Ewing, M. T. 2013. Developing customised CRM projects: The role of industry norms, organisational context and customer expectations on CRM implementation. To appear in *Industrial Marketing Management*, http://dx.doi.org/10.1016/j.indmarman.2012.08.009.

Stone, M., Woodcock, N. and Wilson, M. 1996. Managing the change from marketing planning to customer relationship management. *Long Range Planning*, 29(5), 675–83.

Straub, D., Limayem, M. and Krahanna-Evaristo, E. 1995. Measuring system usage: Implications for IS theory testing. *Management Science*, 41(8), 1328–1342.

Suchman, L. 1987. *Plans and Situated Action*. University Press: New York, Cambridge.

Swan, J., Newell, S. and Robertson, M. 2000. The diffusion, design and social shaping of production management information systems in Europe. *Information Technology & People*, 13(1), 27–45.

Swift, R. S. 2001. *Accelerating Customer Relationships Using CRM and Relationship Technologies*. London: Prentice Hall.

Tanner, Jr. J., Ahearne, M., Leigh, T., Mason, C. and Moncrief, W. 2005. CRM Sales intensive organizations: A review and future directions. *Journal of Personal Selling & Sales Management*, 25(2), 169–180.

Tikkanen, H. 1998. Research on international project marketing. A review and implications. In Tikkanen, H. (ed.), *Marketing and International Business, Essays in Honour of Professor Karin Holstius on her 65th Birthday*. Turku School of Economics and Business Administration: Turku, Finland, pp. 261–285.

Turnbull, P., Ford, D. and Cunningham, M. 1996. Interaction, relationships, and networks in business markets: an evolving perspective. *Journal of Business & Industrial Marketing*, 11, 44–62

Turnbull, P. and Zolkiewski, J. 1997. Profitability in customer portfolio planning. In Ford, D. (ed.), *Understanding Business Marketing*. Dryden: London, pp. 305–325.

Turner, J. R. and Müller, R. 2003. On the nature of the project as a temporary organization. *International Journal of Project Management*, 21(1), 1–7.

United States Information Technology Report Q4 2012. Part of BMI's *Industry Report & Forecasts Series*, Business Monitor International, www.businessmonitor.com.

Van De Ven, A., Polley, D., Garud, R. and Venkataraman, S. 1999. *The Innovation Journey*. Oxford University Press: New York, Oxford.

Vavra, T. G. 1994. The database marketing imperative. *Marketing Management*, 1, 47–57.

Venkatesan, R., Kumar, V. and Ravishanker, N. 2007. Multi-channel shopping: Causes and consequences. *Journal of Marketing*, 71(2), 114–132.

Wagner, H. M. 1969. *Principles of Operations Research: With Applications to Managerial Decisions*. Prentice Hall Inc.: Inglewood Cliffs, N. J.

Wahlberg, O., Strandberg, C., Sundberg, H. and Sundberg, K. W. 2009. Trends, topics and under-researched areas in CRM research: A literature review. *International Journal of Public Information Systems*, 3, 191–208.

Wedin, T. 2001. *Networks and Demand: The Use of Electricity in an Industrial Process*. Doctoral Thesis, Uppsala University: Uppsala.

Wernerfelt, B. 1984. A resource-based view of the firm. *Strategic Management Journal*, 5, 171–180.

Whisler, T. L. 1970. *The Impact of Computers on Organizations*. Praeger: New York.

Wilson, D. T. and Vlosky, R. P. 1998. Interorganizational information system technology and buyer-seller relationship disruption. *Journal of Business and International Marketing*, 13, 3.

Wilson, H., Clarke, M. and Smith, B. 2007. Justifying CRM projects in a business-to-business context: The potential of the benefits dependency network. *Industrial Marketing Management*, 36(6), 770–783.

Winer, R. 2001. A framework for customer relationship management. *California Management Review*, 43(4), 89–105.

Wixom, B. H. and Watson, H. J. 2001. An empirical investigation of the factors affecting data warehousing success. *MIS Quarterly*, 25(1), 17–32.

Wynne, B. and Otway, H. J. 1983. Information technology, power and managers. *Office, Technology and People*, 2, 43–56.

Xu, M. and Walton, J. 2005. Gaining customer knowledge through analytical CRM. *Industrial Management & Data Systems*, 105, 955–971.

Xu, Y., Yen, D., Lin, B. and Chou, D. 2002. Adopting customer relationship management technology. *Industrial Management & Data Systems*, 102(8), 442–52.

Yates, J., Orlikowski, W. J. and Okamura, K. 1999. Explicit and implicit structuring of genres in electronic communication: Reinforcement and change of social interaction. *Organization Science*, 10(1), 83–103.

Yin, R. K. 1994. *Case Study Research: Design and Methods*. 2nd Edition. Sage Publications: Thousand Oaks, CA.

Zablah, A., Bellenger, D. and Johnston W. 2004. An evaluation of divergent perspectives on customer relationship management: Towards a common understanding of an emerging phenomenon. *Industrial Marketing Management*, 33(6), 475–489.

Zablah, A. R., Bellenger, D. N., Straub, D. W. and Johnston, W. J. 2012. Performance implications of CRM technology use: A multilevel field study of business customers and their providers in the telecommunications industry. *Information Systems Research*, 23, 418–435.

Zuboff, S. 1988. *In the Age of the Smart Machine*. Basic Books: New York.

Index

Printed and bound by CPI Group (UK) Ltd, Croydon, CR0 4YY